Executive's Guide to COSO Internal Controls

Founded in 1807, John Wiley & Sons is the oldest independent publishing company in the United States. With offices in North America, Europe, Asia, and Australia, Wiley is globally committed to developing and marketing print and electronic products and services for our customers' professional and personal knowledge and understanding.

The Wiley Corporate F&A series provides information, tools, and insights to corporate professionals responsible for issues affecting the profitability of their company, from accounting and finance to internal controls and performance management.

Executive's Guide to COSO Internal Controls

Understanding and Implementing the New Framework

ROBERT R. MOELLER

WILEY

Contents

Preface

NTERNAL CONTROL IS A BASIC management concept that covers all aspects of enterprise operations, from basic accounting processes to production operations to IT systems and more. However, in past years, it was one of those nice-sounding expressions where no one really had a consistent definition about what was meant by *effective internal controls*. Then, after a series of accounting scandals in the early 1990s, a group of professional accounting and finance organizations, including the American Institute of Certified Public Accountants (AICPA), formed what has become the Committee of Sponsoring Organizations (COSO) to develop a consistent framework to define the concept of internal controls.

After a lengthy period of review and comments as a public exposure document, the initial COSO internal control framework was released in 1992. It is not a formal standard or a set of governmental regulations but a framework outlining the characteristics and concepts of an effective system of internal control for enterprises of all types and sizes. It was soon adapted as a requirement for external auditors in their assessments of financial statement internal controls, and it became a key measure for assuring Sarbanes-Oxley Act (SOx) compliance.

Although this framework has remained unchanged and in effect since its 1992 release, that original framework no longer really reflected some of the massive changes in IT and business systems since then, as well as the more collaborative and international nature of business today and growing concerns for improved enterprise governance processes. As a result, COSO has recently revised its internal control framework, with a beginning draft and comment period, and the new revised COSO internal control framework was released in May 2013.

This book provides an executive-level description of the new COSO internal control framework. In the following chapters, we describe the components of the new framework and the elements that are particularly important to enterprise business operations. We have also taken COSO's three-dimensional framework and rotated it around to better explain the importance of all of the internal control framework's elements. Various chapters also look at such supporting guidance materials as COBIT and both ISO internal control and risk management standards, with an emphasis on building and implementing effective enterprise internal controls.

One of this book's objectives is to introduce and explain this revised COSO internal control framework in such a manner that an enterprise executive can use this internal control guidance material to understand and implement effective internal controls processes, as well as to explain the importance of COSO internal controls to board and audit committee members, to other members of the staff, and to IT management, as well as to retain an overall understanding of the importance of COSO internal controls. In addition, we will discuss transition and implementation rules for using this revised COSO framework to achieve Sarbanes-Oxley internal control compliance.

At first glance, the COSO internal control framework looks complex and confusing, but it is an important management tool that should be with us for some years to come. Enterprises may adopt this new framework immediately or may continue to use the old framework until December 15, 2014, at which point the updated framework will supersede the original framework.

CHAPTER ONE

Importance of the COSO Internal Control Framework

I T IS NOT A STANDARD or detailed requirement but only a framework. Some business executives may ask then, "Who or what is COSO?" In our business world of multiple rules and regulations that have been established by numerous governmental and other agencies that often use hard-to-remember acronyms, it is easy to roll our eyes or shrug our shoulders at yet another set of standards. In addition, COSO (Committee of Sponsoring Organizations) internal controls are only a framework model outlining professional practices for establishing preferred business systems and processes that promote efficient and effective internal controls. Also, the "sponsoring organizations" that issue and publish this material are neither governmental nor some other regulatory agencies. Nevertheless, the COSO internal control framework is an important set or model of guidance materials that enterprises should follow when developing their systems and procedures, as well as when establishing Sarbanes-Oxley Act (SOx) compliance.

This COSO internal control framework was originally launched in the United States in 1992, now a long time ago. This was yet another period of notable fraudulent business practices in the United States and elsewhere that identified a well-recognized need for improved internal control processes and procedures to help and guide. The 1992 COSO internal control framework soon became a fundamental element of American Institute of Certified Public Accountants (AICPA) auditing standards in the United States, and eventually became the standard for enterprise external auditors in their reviews, certifying that enterprise internal controls were adequately following the Sarbanes-Oxley Act (SOx) rules. Because of its general nature describing good internal control practices, the COSO framework had never been revised until the present.

Since the release of that original COSO framework, a whole lot has changed for business organizations and particularly for their IT processes during these interim years. For example, mainframe computer systems with lots of batch-processing procedures were common then but have all but gone away, to be replaced by client-server systems. Also, while the World Wide Web was just getting started then, it was not nearly as developed as it is today. Because of the Internet, enterprises' organization structures have become much more fluid, flexible, and international. In addition, things such as social network computing, powerful handheld devices, and cloud computing did not exist back then.

Although some might wonder why it took so long, COSO announced in 2011 that it was revising its internal control framework with a draft version, which was issued in early 2012. That COSO internal control draft was circulated to a wide range of internal and external auditors, academics, and enterprise financial management, and it went through an extensive public comment period. The final revised COSO internal control framework description was released in mid-May 2013.

The following chapters describe the revised COSO internal control framework in some detail and explain why its concepts are very important for enterprise management today. This chapter begins with some background information on the COSO internal control framework from a senior executive management perspective. The COSO internal control framework sets the stage for achieving SOx compliance and will continue to be even more important with its new revised version. This book will conclude with some guidance and rules for implementing the new revised COSO internal control framework.

 ## THE IMPORTANCE OF ENTERPRISE INTERNAL CONTROLS

An effective internal control system is one of the best defenses against business failure. An internal control system is an important driver of business performance, which manages risk and enables the creation and preservation of enterprise value. Internal controls are an integral part of an enterprise's governance system and ability to manage risk, which is understood, effected, and actively monitored by an enterprise governing body, its management, and other personnel to take advantage of the opportunities and to counter the threats to achieving an enterprise's objectives. On a very high-level conceptual manner, Exhibit 1.1 shows the relationship of internal controls as a component of risk-management processes and as a key element of enterprise governance.

Internal controls are a crucial component of an enterprise's governance system and ability to manage risk, and it is fundamental to supporting the achievement of an enterprise's objectives and creating, enhancing, and protecting stakeholder value. High-profile organizational failures typically lead to the imposition of additional rules

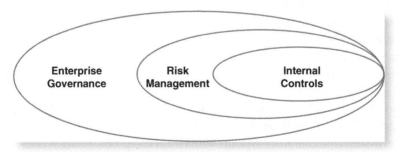

EXHIBIT 1.1 Importance of Enterprise Internal Controls

and requirements, as well as to subsequent time-consuming and costly compliance efforts. However, this obscures the fact that the right kind of internal controls—which enable an enterprise to capitalize on opportunities, while offsetting threats—can actually save time and money and promote the creation and preservation of value. Effective internal controls also create a competitive advantage, because an enterprise with effective controls can take on additional risks.

Internal controls are designed to protect an enterprise and its related business units from the loss or misuse of its assets. Sound internal controls help ensure that transactions are properly authorized, that supporting IT systems are well-managed, and that the information contained in financial reports is reliable. An internal control is a process through which an enterprise and one of its operating units attempts to minimize the likelihood of accounting-related errors, irregularities, and illegal acts. Internal controls help safeguard funds, provide for efficient and effective management of assets, and permit accurate financial accounting. Internal controls cannot eliminate all errors and irregularities, but they can alert management to potential problems.

WHAT ARE ENTERPRISE INTERNAL CONTROLS?

A classic definition states that *internal controls* consist of the plan of organization and all of the coordinate methods adopted within a business to safeguard its assets, check the accuracy and reliability of its accounting data, promote operational efficiency, and encourage adherence to prescribed managerial policies. This definition recognizes that a system of internal controls extends beyond those matters that relate directly just to the functions of the accounting and financial departments. Rather, an internal control is a business practice, policy, or procedure that is established within an enterprise to create value or minimize risk. Although enterprises first thought of internal controls in terms of fair and accurate accounting processes and effective operational management, information technology (IT) controls are also a very important subset of internal controls today. They are designed to ensure that the information within an enterprise operates as intended, that data is reliable, and that the enterprise is in compliance with all applicable laws and regulations.

We should think of internal controls not as just one solitary activity but as a series of related internal system actions. For example, a requirement that all sales receipts must be accurate and assigned to correct accounts may be an important internal control, but processes should also be in place to correct out-of-balance sales receipts and to make related adjustments as necessary. Together, these requirements and processes represent an internal control system. These internal control systems are often complex, and it is not practical or profitable to attempt to independently review every transaction. Instead, management should be alert to conditions that could indicate potential problems.

Enterprise personnel at all levels, and senior executives in particular, should be responsible for understanding internal control concepts and helping to manage and implement effective internal control systems in their enterprises. This is particularly important for senior-level enterprise internal controls, in which different business units and subsidiaries must interact and IT systems must connect through often complex business and international interconnections. In addition, an enterprise must establish overall governance practices and operate in compliance with the numerous laws, regulations, and standards that affect its operations.

In a business operation, finance and accounting personnel have certain internal control responsibilities, a purchasing executive has others, and an IT systems developer has different responsibilities, but a senior executive should have an overall understanding of all aspects of internal controls throughout an enterprise, as well as of the top-level internal control concepts that affect overall enterprise operations and governance processes. The COSO internal control framework ties these all together, and an objective of this book is to help the senior executive understand these internal control concepts and, at a minimum, ask the right questions.

UNDERSTANDING THE COSO INTERNAL CONTROL FRAMEWORK: HOW TO USE THIS BOOK

Internal controls are important enterprise tools and concepts to ensure accurate financial reporting and management. However, in past years, *internal controls* was only a nice-sounding term by which professionals at all levels acknowledged that having effective internal controls was important. That was a long time ago, and matters were very much resolved with the introduction of the COSO internal control framework back in 1992. That best practices guide stood the test of time until it was recently updated.

This book will introduce the revised new COSO internal control framework from the perspective of senior enterprise executives. Chapter 2 will introduce the original framework that has been important for achieving SOx financial reporting compliance. Then, starting with Chapter 3, we will introduce and explain the new revised COSO internal control framework. This approach outlines and explains COSO's complex-looking three-dimensional model for building and establishing enterprise internal controls. The chapters following take COSO's three-dimensional framework and look at it from each of its dimensions to help the enterprise executive understand this internal control framework.

Other chapters cover supplementary standards or frameworks that are closely related to the COSO internal control framework, such as the continuing relationship of this framework to SOx internal control requirements, its relationship with the COBIT framework, and the current status of the related COSO enterprise risk management framework.

This book will conclude with guidance for implementing this revised framework. Although much of the COSO framework describes general practices that are applicable in many dimensions, there are some subtle differences between this new revised framework and the original edition. Following the transition rules outlined in Chapter 20, an enterprise must specify the version of the COSO internal control framework used when releasing its SOx financial reports.

The original COSO framework was with us for many years, and we expect these revisions will also be in place for years into the future. A goal of this book is to provide sufficient summary information about the revised COSO internal control framework such that a senior executive can brief members of the audit committee about the nature of this new revision and can also help members of the enterprise management team understand and implement enterprise internal controls that are consistent with these new revisions.

CHAPTER TWO

How We Got Here: Internal Control Background

ALTHOUGH THE CONCEPT OF BUSINESS and accounting systems internal controls is fairly well understood today by enterprise senior managers, this was not true before the late 1980s. In particular, while we often understood the general concept, there had been no consistent agreement among many interested persons of what was meant by "good internal controls" from either a business process or a financial accounting sense. Those early definitions first came from the American Institute of Certified Public Accountants (AICPA) and were then used by the U.S. Securities and Exchange Commission (SEC) for the Securities Exchange Act of 1934 regulations and provide a good starting point. Although there have been changes over the years, the AICPA's first codified standards, called the Statement on Auditing Standards (SAS No. 1), defined the practice of financial statement external auditing in the United States for many years with the following definition for *internal controls:*

> Comprises the plan of enterprise and all of the coordinate methods and measures adopted within a business to safeguard its assets, check the accuracy and reliability of its accounting data, promote operational efficiency, and encourage adherence to prescribed managerial policies.

That original AICPA SAS No. 1 then was later modified to add administrative and accounting controls to the basic *internal controls* definition. Administrative controls include, but are not limited to, the plan of the enterprise and the procedures and records that are concerned with the decision-making processes that lead to management's authorization of transactions. Such an authorization is a management function directly associated with the responsibility for achieving the objectives of the enterprise and is the starting point for establishing the accounting controls of transactions.

Accounting control comprises the plan of enterprise and the procedures and records that are concerned with the safeguarding of assets and the reliability of financial records and consequently are designed to provide reasonable assurance that

a. Transactions are executed in accordance with management's general or specific authorization.
b. Transactions are recorded as necessary (1) to permit preparation of financial statements in conformity with generally accepted accounting principles or any other criteria applicable to such statement and (2) to maintain accountability for assets.
c. Access to assets is permitted only in accordance with management's authorization.
d. The recorded accountability for assets is compared with the existing assets at reasonable intervals, and appropriate action is taken with respect to any differences.

The overlapping relationships of these two types of internal controls were then further clarified in these pre-1988 AICPA standards:

The foregoing definitions are not necessarily mutually exclusive because some of the procedures and records comprehended in accounting control may also be involved in administrative control. For example, sales and cost records classified by products may be used for accounting control purposes and also in making management decisions concerning unit prices or other aspects of operations. Such multiple uses of procedures or records, however, are not critical for the purposes of this section because it is concerned primarily with clarifying the outer boundary of accounting control. Examples of records used solely for administrative control are those pertaining to customers contacted by salesmen and to defective work by production employees maintained only for evaluation personnel per performance.[1]

Our point here is that the definition of *internal controls*, as originally defined many years ago by the AICPA, has been subject to changes and reinterpretations over the years. However, these earlier AICPA standards stress that the system of internal controls extends beyond just matters relating directly to the accounting and financial statements, including administrative controls but not IT, operations, or governance-related controls. Over this period through the 1970s, there were many definitions *of internal controls* released by the SEC and the AICPA, as well as voluminous interpretations and guidelines developed by the then major external auditing firms.

During the 1970s, in the United States and elsewhere in the world, there were an unusually large number of major corporate accounting fraud and internal control corporate failures. This same set of events was repeated again later in the early years of this century. That first set of events led to the Foreign Corrupt Practices Act in the United States, as well as to an attempt to better understand and define this concept called *internal control*. The result here was the release of the original COSO internal control framework, introduced in this chapter with its new revised version described in the following chapters.

The second set of fraud and internal control corporate failures, with a company called Enron as a major example, resulted in the passage of the Sarbanes-Oxley Act (SOx). Its internal control–related rules were first applicable in the United States and now are important essentially worldwide. This chapter will explain some key components of SOx and why compliance is important for building and implementing effective internal control processes today.

EARLY DEFINITIONS OF INTERNAL CONTROLS: FOREIGN CORRUPT PRACTICES ACT OF 1977

While accounting scandals at the notorious company named Enron and at others brought us SOx in the early years of this century, the United States experienced a similar situation some 30 years earlier. Although it now seems long ago, the period of 1974–1977 was a time of extreme social and political turmoil in the United States. A series of illegal acts was discovered at the time of the 1972 presidential election, including a burglary of the Democratic Party headquarters in a building complex known as Watergate. The events eventually led to the president's resignation, and related investigations found other questionable practices had occurred that were not covered by existing legislation. Similar to how the failure of Enron brought us SOx, the result here was the passage of the 1977 Foreign Corrupt Practices Act (FCPA).

The FCPA prohibited bribes to foreign—non-US—officials and contained provisions requiring the maintenance of accurate books, records, and systems of internal accounting controls. With provisions that apply to virtually all US companies with SEC-registered securities, the FCPA's internal control rules particularly affected enterprise financial management, as well as its internal and external auditors. Using terminology taken directly from the legislation, the FCPA required that SEC-regulated enterprises must

- Make and keep books, records, and accounts, which, in reasonable detail, accurately and fairly reflect the transactions and dispositions of the assets of the issuers,
- Devise and maintain a system of internal accounting controls sufficient to provide reasonable assurances that
  - Transactions are executed in accordance with management's general or specific authorization,
  - Transactions are recorded as necessary both to permit the preparation of financial statements in conformity with generally accepted accounting principles (GAAP) or any other criteria applicable to such statements, and also to maintain accountability for assets,[2]
- Access to assets is permitted only in accordance with management's general or specific authorization, and
- The recorded accountability for assets is compared with the existing assets at reasonable intervals, and appropriate action is taken with respect to any differences.

The FCPA was significant then because, for the first time, management was made responsible for maintaining an adequate system of internal accounting controls. The act required enterprises to "make and keep books, records, and accounts, which, in reasonable detail, accurately and fairly reflect the transactions and dispositions of the assets of the issuer." Similar to and even broader than today's SOx requirements, summarized later in this chapter, the FCPA's record-keeping legislation applied to all public corporations registered with the SEC.

In addition, the FCPA required that enterprises keep records that accurately reflect their transactions "in reasonable detail." Although there was no specific definition here, the intent of the rule was that records should reflect transactions in conformity with accepted methods of recording economic events, preventing off-the-books "slush funds" and payments of bribes. The FCPA also required that companies maintain a system of internal accounting controls, sufficient to provide reasonable assurances that transactions are authorized and recorded to permit preparation of financial statements in conformity with GAAP. Also, FCPA rules stated that accountability is to be maintained for an enterprise's assets, and access to them permitted only as authorized with periodic physical inventories. Passed some 40 years ago, the FCPA was a strong set of corporate governance rules, and because of the FCPA, many boards of directors and their audit committees began to actively review the internal controls in their enterprises.

THE FCPA AND INTERNAL CONTROLS TODAY

When enacted in the United States, the FCPA resulted in significant efforts to assess and document systems of internal controls in major US corporations. Enterprises that had never formally documented their internal control procedures embarked on ambitious documentation efforts, with this FCPA documentation responsibility often given to internal audit departments. Recall that this was in the late 1970s and the very early 1980s, when most IT systems were mainframe batch-oriented processes, and available documentation tools often were little more than plastic flowchart templates and No. 2 pencils. Similar to the first days of SOx, discussed later in this chapter, corporations then went through considerable efforts to achieve FCPA compliance. In their early efforts, many large enterprises developed extensive sets of paper-based systems documentation, with no provisions, once they had been completed, to regularly update them.

Many business professionals back then anticipated a wave of additional regulations following the FCPA's enactment. However, this did not occur. Internal control–related legal actions were essentially nonexistent during FCPA's early days, and thankfully no one came to inspect the files of the assembled documentation that were mandated in the FCPA legislation. Today, the FCPA has dropped off our radar screen of current "hot" management topics, but it is still in force as an actively enforced anticorruption, anti-bribery law. A Web search today will yield few, if any, references to the FCPA's internal control provisions but many regarding foreign trade and bribery actions. The law was amended in the 1990s but only to strengthen and improve its anticorruption provisions.

When enacted in 1977, the FCPA emphasized the importance of effective internal controls, even though there was no consistent definition of *internal controls* at that time. The FCPA was an important early step that encouraged enterprises to think about the need for effective internal controls, even though there were no guidelines or standards over the FCPA's internal control systems documentation requirements. Perhaps if there had been a greater attempt to define the FCPA's internal control compliance documentation requirements then, we might never have had SOx.

EVENTS LEADING UP TO THE TREADWAY COMMISSION

Despite the FCPA requirements for documenting internal controls, it soon became obvious to many that we did not have a clear and consistent understanding of what was meant by "good internal controls." In the late 1970s, external auditors only reported that an enterprise's financial statements were "fairly presented," but there was no mention of the adequacy of the internal control procedures supporting those audited financial statements. The FCPA had put a requirement on the reporting enterprises to document their internal controls but did not ask external auditors to attest to whether an enterprise was in compliance with the FCPA's internal control reporting requirements. The SEC then began a study on internal control adequacy and issued a series of reports during approximately the next 10-year period to better define both the meaning of *internal controls* and the external auditor's responsibility for reporting on those internal controls.

The AICPA also formed a high-level Commission on Auditor's Responsibilities in 1974. This group, also known as the Cohen Commission, recommended in 1978 that a statement on the condition of an enterprise's internal controls should be required as part of its published financial statements. Although these Cohen Commission recommendations took place about the same time as the release of the FCPA, they ran into a torrent of criticism. In particular, the report's recommendations were not precise on what was meant by "reporting on internal controls," and external auditors strongly expressed concerns about their roles in this process. External auditors were concerned about potential liabilities if their reports on internal controls gave inconsistent signals, due to a lack of understanding over the definition of *internal control standards*. Although auditors were accustomed to then attesting to the fairness of financial statements, the Cohen Commission report called for an audit opinion on the fairness of the management control assertions in the proposed financial statement internal control letter. It soon became clear that management did not have a consistent definition of *internal controls*. Various enterprises might use the same terms regarding the quality of their internal controls, with each meaning something a little different. If an enterprise reported that its controls were "adequate" and if its auditors accepted those assertions in that control report, the external auditors could later be criticized or even suffer potential litigation if some significant control problem appeared later.

The Financial Executives International (FEI) professional organization then got involved in this internal control reporting controversy.[3] Just as the AICPA represents public accountants in the United States, the FEI represents enterprise senior financial officers. In the late 1970s, the FEI endorsed the Cohen Commission's internal control recommendations and agreed that corporations should report on the status of their internal accounting controls. As a result, many US corporations began to discuss the adequacy of their internal controls as part of their annual report management letters. These internal control letters were entirely voluntary and did not follow any standard format. They typically included comments stating that management, through its internal auditors, periodically assessed the quality of the enterprise's internal controls, and these reports were phrased as "negative assurance" comments, indicating that nothing was found to indicate that there might be any internal control problem in operations.

This term *negative assurance* will return again in our discussions of internal controls. Because an external auditor cannot detect all problems and faces the risk of potential litigation, pre-SOx external auditor reports were often stated in terms of a negative assurance. That is, rather than saying that they "found no problems" in an area under review, their report would state that they did not find anything that would lead them to believe that there was a problem. This is a subtle but important difference.

Reflecting on what was a controversy many years ago, the SEC then issued proposed rules, based on the Cohen Commission's and the FEI's recommendations, calling for *mandatory* management reports on an entity's internal accounting control system. The SEC stated that information on the effectiveness of an entity's internal control system was necessary to allow investors to better evaluate both management's performance and the integrity of published financial reports. This SEC proposal again raised a storm of controversy, because many chief executive officers (CEOs) and chief financial officers (CFOs) felt that this was too onerous, particularly on top of the then newly released FCPA regulations.

Questions came from many directions regarding the definition of *internal accounting control.* Although corporations might agree to voluntary reporting, they did not want to subject themselves—in those pre-SOx days—to the penalties associated with a violation of SEC regulations. The SEC soon dropped this 1979 proposed separate management report on internal accounting controls as part of the annual report to shareholders but promised to re-release the regulations at a later date.

 ## EARLIER AICPA AUDITING STANDARDS: SAS NOS. 55 AND 78

Prior to SOx, the AICPA was responsible for releasing external auditing standards through Statements on Auditing Standards (SAS). As discussed previously for SAS No. 1, these standards formed the basis of the external auditor's review of the adequacy and fairness of published financial statements. Although there were a few changes to them over the years, the AICPA was frequently criticized in the 1970s and the 1980s that its audit standards did not provide adequate guidance to either external auditors or the users of their reports. This problem was called the "expectations gap," because existing public accounting standards did not meet the expectations of investors.

To answer this criticism, the AICPA released a series of new SAS on internal control audit standards during the period of 1980 to 1985. These included SAS No. 30, *Reporting on Internal Accounting Control,* which provided guidance for the terminology to be used in internal accounting control reports. That SAS did not provide much help, however, on defining the underlying concepts of internal control and was viewed by critics of the public accounting profession as too little too late. SAS No. 55, *Consideration of the Internal*

Control Structure in a Financial Statement Audit, was a subsequent standard that defined *internal controls* in terms of three key elements:

1. Control environment
2. Accounting system
3. Control procedures

SAS No. 55 presented a different approach to understanding internal controls than had been used in the past, and it has provided a foundation for much of our ongoing understanding of internal controls. Prior to SAS No. 55, an enterprise's internal control structure policies and procedures were not directly relevant to the financial statement audit and were often not formally considered by the external auditors. Examples of these internal control processes include policies and procedures concerning the effectiveness, economy, and efficiency of certain management decision-making processes or procedures covering research and development activities. Although certainly important to the enterprise, any related internal control concerns did not ordinarily pertain to the external auditor's financial statement audit.

SAS No. 55 defined *internal controls* in a much broader scope than had been traditionally taken by external auditors, and it provided a basis for the original COSO internal control framework. SAS No. 55 became effective in 1990 and represented a major stride toward providing external auditors with an appropriate definition of *internal controls*. It was superseded by SAS No. 78, which picked up the broad definition of *internal controls* from the COSO report. It went away when SOx rules revoked the AICPA's authority to set auditing standards for public corporations.

 ## THE TREADWAY COMMITTEE REPORT

The late 1970s and the early 1980s were another period with many major US enterprise failures, due then to such factors as high inflation and the resultant high interest rates. There were multiple occurrences in which enterprises reported adequate earnings in their audited financial reports, only to suffer a financial collapse shortly after the release of those favorable audited reports. A few of these failures were caused by outright fraudulent financial reporting, although many others were due to high inflation or other enterprise instability issues. Nevertheless, several members of Congress proposed legislation to "correct" these potential business and audit failures. Bills were drafted, congressional hearings held, but no legislation was passed.

Also in response to these concerns and due to the lack of legislative action, a National Commission on Fraudulent Financial Reporting was formed. It consisted of representatives from five professional organizations: the Institute of Internal Auditors (IIA), the AICPA, and the FEI, all mentioned previously, as well as the American Accounting Association (AAA) and the Institute of Management Accountants (IMA). The AAA is a professional organization for the academic accountants. The IMA is the professional organization for managerial or cost accountants.

The National Commission on Fraudulent Reporting came to be called the Treadway Commission after the name of its chairperson. Its main objectives were to identify the causal factors that allowed fraudulent financial reporting and to make recommendations to reduce their incidence. The Treadway Commission's final report was issued in 1987 and included recommendations to management, boards of directors, the public accounting profession, and others.[4] It again called for management reports on the effectiveness of each company's internal control systems and emphasized key elements in what it felt should be a system of internal controls, including a strong control environment, codes of conduct, a competent and involved audit committee, and a strong internal audit function. The Treadway Commission report again pointed out the lack of a consistent definition of *internal controls*, suggesting further work was needed. The same Committee of Sponsoring Organizations (COSO) that managed the Treadway report subsequently contracted with outside specialists and embarked on a new project to define *internal controls*. Although it issued no standards, the Treadway report was important, because it raised the level of concern and attention in regard to reporting on internal controls.

The internal control–reporting efforts discussed here are presented as if they were a series of sequential events. In reality, many of these internal control–related efforts took place in almost a parallel fashion. This 20-year effort redefined internal control as a basic methodology and outlined a standard terminology for business professionals and auditors. The result has been the original COSO internal control framework, discussed in the following sections and referenced throughout this book.

 ## THE ORIGINAL COSO INTERNAL CONTROL FRAMEWORK

As mentioned, COSO refers to the five professional auditing and accounting organizations that formed a committee to develop this internal control report; its official title is *Integrated Control–Integrated Framework*.[5] Throughout this book, it is referred to as the original COSO internal control framework. These sponsoring organizations contracted with a public accounting firm and used a large number of volunteers to develop a draft report that was released in 1990 for public exposure and comment. More than 40,000 copies of this COSO internal control draft version were sent to corporate officers, internal and external auditors, legislators, academics, and other interested parties with requests for formal comments.

After some adjustments, the previously referenced original COSO internal control report was released in September 1992. Although not a mandatory standard, the report proposed a common framework for the definition of *internal controls*, as well as procedures to evaluate those controls. In a very short number of years, this COSO internal control framework became the recognized standard for understanding and establishing effective internal controls in virtually all business systems. The following paragraphs will provide a more detailed description of the original COSO internal control framework and its use by auditors and business professionals for internal control assessments and evaluations. This framework was unchanged and in place until the revised COSO internal control framework was issued in 2013 and is described in this book.

Virtually every public corporation has a complex control procedures structure. Following the format of a classic organization chart, there may be levels of senior and middle management in multiple operating units or within different activities. In addition, control procedures may be somewhat different at each of these levels and components. For example, one operating unit may operate in a regulated business environment where its control processes are very structured, while another unit may operate almost as an entrepreneurial start-up with a less formal structure. Different levels of management in these enterprises will have different control concern perspectives. The question "How do you describe your system of internal controls?" might receive different answers from persons in different levels or units in each of these enterprise components.

The original COSO internal control framework provided an excellent description of this multidimensional concept of internal controls, defining *internal controls* as follows:

> Internal control is a *process*, affected by an entity's board of directors, management, and other personnel, designed to provide reasonable assurance regarding the achievement of objectives in the following categories:

- Effectiveness and efficiency of operations
- Reliability of financial reporting
- Compliance with applicable laws and regulations[6]

Using this very general definition of *internal controls*, COSO used a three-dimensional model or framework to describe an internal control system in an enterprise. Exhibit 2.1 describes the original COSO internal control framework as a three-dimensional model with five levels on the front-facing side and the three major components of internal controls—effectiveness and efficiency of operations, reliability of financial reporting, and compliance with applicable laws and regulations—taking somewhat equal segments of the model with slices across its top. The right-hand side of the exhibit shows three segments, but there could be multiples of these, depending on the structure of the enterprise. This exhibit shows a concept that has dominated our understanding of internal controls for many years.

Each of the COSO internal control framework's levels, from Monitoring on top down to the internal control environment, will be discussed in the context of the revised new framework in greater detail. The overall COSO framework idea here is that when we look at any internal control activity layer—such as the period ending financial close—we should consider internal controls in terms of a business unit or an entity's multiple divisions from the perspective of the side of the framework where that internal control has been installed. However, in this three-dimensional model, each control is related to all others in the same row, stack, or column.

The concept behind the original COSO internal control framework is that we must always consider each identified internal control element in terms of how it relates to other associated internal controls. Using an example of end of period financial close internal controls that would be in the middle of the framework, an enterprise should have information and communication links attached to the financial close processes,

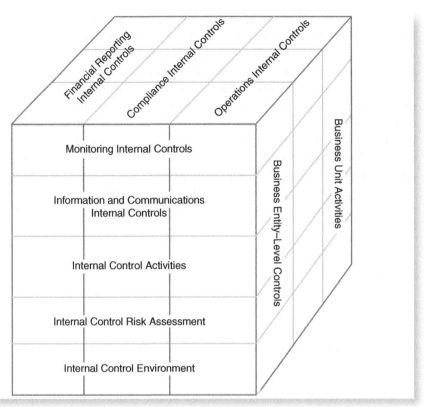

EXHIBIT 2.1   COSO Internal Control Original Framework

and the control should be monitored. Dropping down a level, there should be a risk assessment factor associated with that financial control process, and it should operate in an appropriate internal control environment. Compliance and operations issues may also have factors on the specific controls, which may function at any level in the enterprise organization.

This original COSO internal control framework has provided enterprises worldwide with a definition of, and what we mean when we talk about, effective internal controls. Though powerful, the definition did not initially gain widespread recognition, and over the years it was recognized, first through AICPA auditing standards and then by SOx auditing guidance, as an effective way to evaluate and understand internal controls. Some shortcomings were recognized, such as that the original framework was released in an era when IT systems were not nearly as pervasive as we find them today. Thus, COSO decided to revise and release the new revised internal control framework that will be described in the following chapters.

Our objective in this chapter has been to describe some of the conditions and shortcomings that led business leaders to understand that we needed a consistent framework for building, understanding, and managing internal controls in enterprise business processes. We will build on this framework to describe the revised, new COSO internal control framework that should be an important business tool now and for many years into the future.

THE SARBANES-OXLEY ACT AND INTERNAL ACCOUNTING CONTROLS

As discussed in Chapter 1 and referenced in following sections here, SOx is a US law enacted in 2004 to improve financial reporting audit processes and to correct a series of board of director, public accounting, and other practices. It has had a major impact on businesses processes in the United States and worldwide. Compliance with the law has very much focused our attention on the importance of internal accounting controls.

SOx is a wide-ranging set of requirements that define how we both govern public enterprises and attest that their reported financial results are fairly stated. This section provides a high-level overview of SOx, and a following section will discuss what is known as the SOx Section 404 internal accounting control rules. Every senior manager should have at least a general understanding of SOx rules and its compliance requirements. More information about SOx rules can be found on the Web, as well as in this author's more comprehensive book on SOx.[7]

The official name for this US federal law is the "Public Accounting Reform and Investor Protection Act." It became law in August 2002, with most of the final detailed rules and regulations released by the end of the following year. Its title being a bit long, business professionals refer to it as the Sarbanes-Oxley Act from the names of its principal congressional sponsors. Still too long of a name, most generally refer to it today as SOx, SOX, or Sarbox, among many other variations.

SOx introduced a series of significant new processes for external auditors and gave new governance responsibilities to senior executives and board members. SOx also established the Public Company Accounting Oversight Board (PCAOB), a rule-setting authority introduced in the following section and under the SEC that issues financial auditing standards and monitors external auditor governance. As happens with all comprehensive federal laws, an extensive set of specific regulations and administrative rules has been developed by the SEC, based on the SOx legislation.

US federal laws are organized and issued as separate sections of legislation called Titles, with numbered sections and subsections under each. Much of the SOx legislation contains rules that are not that significant for most business professionals. For example, Section 602 (d) of Title I states that the SEC "shall establish" minimum professional conduct standards or rules for SEC practicing attorneys. While perhaps good to know, this does not have much impact for most business professionals. Exhibit 2.2 summarizes the main sections of SOx, and the sections following describe key SOx Titles. Our intent is not to reproduce the full text of this legislation—it can be found on the Web—but to highlight portions of the law that are more significant to business professionals.[8]

Title I: Public Company Accounting Oversight Board

SOx created new rules for US external auditors. Prior to SOx, the American Institute of Certified Public Accountants (AICPA) provided guidance for all external auditors and their public accounting firms through the administration of the Certified Public Accountant (CPA) examination and the restriction of AICPA membership to CPAs. While State Boards of Accountancy actually licensed CPAs, the AICPA had overall responsibility

EXHIBIT 2.2 Sarbanes-Oxley Act Key Provisions Summary

Section	Subject	Rule or Requirement
101	Establishment of PCAOB	Overall rules for the establishment of the PCAOB, including its membership requirements.
104	Accounting Firm Inspections	Schedule for PCAOB inspections of registered public accounting firms.
108	Auditing Standards	The PCAOB will accept current but will issue its own new auditing standards.
201	Out of Scope Practices	Outlines prohibited accounting firm practices, such as internal audit outsourcing, bookkeeping, and financial systems design.
203	Audit Partner Rotations	The audit partner and the reviewing partner must rotate off an assignment every 5 years.
301	Audit Committee Independence	All audit committee members must be independent directors.
302	Corp. Responsibility for Financial Reports	The CEO and the CFO must personally certify their periodic financial reports.
305	Officer and Director Bars	If compensation is received as part of fraudulent / illegal accounting, the benefiting officer(s) or director is required to personally reimburse funds received.
404	Internal Control Reports	Management is responsible for an annual assessment of internal controls.
407	Financial Expert	One audit committee director must be a designated financial expert.
408	Enhanced Review of Financial Disclosures	The SEC may schedule extended reviews of reported information based on certain specified factors.
409	Real Time Disclosure	Financial reports must be distributed in a rapid and current manner.
1105	Officer or Director Prohibitions	The SEC may prohibit an officer or a director from serving in another public company if guilty of a violation.

for the profession. External audit standards were set by the AICPA's Auditing Standards Board (ASB). Although basic standards—called generally accepted auditing standards (GAAS)—have been in place over the years, newer standards were released as numbered auditing standards called Statements of Auditing Standards, known as SAS. Much of GAAS simply consisted of good auditing practices, such as that accounting transactions must be backed by appropriate documentation, the SAS covered specific areas requiring better definition. SAS No. 79, for example, defined *internal control standards* and SAS No. 99 covered the consideration of fraud in a financial statement audit. The AICPA's code of professional conduct required CPAs to follow and comply with all applicable auditing standards.

The AICPA's GAAS and its numbered SAS standards had been accepted by the SEC, and they defined audit reviews and tests necessary for a certified audited financial statement. However, the accounting scandals that led to the passage of SOx signaled that the process of establishing auditing standards was "broken," and SOx took this audit standards-setting process away from the major public accounting firm-dominated AICPA and created the PCAOB, a nonfederal, nonprofit corporation with the responsibility to oversee all audits of corporations subject to the SEC.

The PCAOB does not replace the AICPA but assumes responsibility for the external auditing practices that were formally managed by AICPA members. The AICPA continues to administer the CPA examination, with its certificates awarded on a state-by-state basis, and sets auditing standards for US private, non-SEC organizations. While SOx Title I defines PCAOB auditing practices for external auditors, other audit process and corporate governance rules have changed how financial managers and their internal auditors coordinate work with external auditors. The PCAOB releases rules to support SOx legislations, and more information on these standards can be found in www.pcaobus.org. The following paragraphs provide some background on SOx Title I external audit process rules.

The PCAOB is administered through a board of five members appointed by the SEC, with three members *required* to be public, non-CPA members. SOx requires that the PCAOB should not be dominated by CPA and public accounting firm interests, and its chairperson must not have been a practicing CPA for at least the previous 5 years. The PCAOB is responsible for overseeing and regulating all public accounting firms that practice before the SEC, including

- Registering the public accounting firms that perform audits of corporations.
- Establishing external auditing standards, including auditing, quality controls, ethics, and auditor independence.
- Inspecting registered public accounting firms, as well as conducting investigations and establishing disciplinary procedures.
- Enforcing SOx compliance.

Information and results on this public accounting firm registration process can be found at www.pcaobus.org. This published registration data may be of particular value for an enterprise that is not using one of the major public accounting firms. There are many medium-size and smaller, yet highly credible, public accounting firms that can provide an enterprise with excellent, high-quality service, but it is always prudent to check these PCAOB registration records.

Title I concludes by affirming that the SEC has authority over the PCAOB, including final approval of the rules, the ability to modify PCAOB actions, and the removal of board members. While the PCAOB is an independent entity responsible for regulating the public accounting industry, the SEC is really the final authority. SOx recognizes the US accounting standards setting body, the FASB, by saying that the SEC may recognize "generally accepted" accounting standards set by "a private entity" that meets certain criteria. The act then goes on to outline the general criteria that the FASB has used for setting accounting standards.

There is and always has been a major difference between accounting and auditing standards. The former define some very precise accounting rules, such as saying a certain type of asset can be written off or depreciated over no more than X years. These are the principles that were called generally accepted accounting principles (GAAP) in the United

States. Auditing standards are much more conceptual, highlighting areas that an auditor *should consider* when evaluating controls in some area. These auditing standards became increasingly loosely interpreted as we went into the 1990s, because management was frequently under pressure to continually report short-term earnings growth, and the external auditors often refused to say "no." The result was the financial scandals of Enron and others, as well as Andersen's audit document destruction when it received news that the SEC was coming. SOx and the PCAOB now oversee public accounting companies.

Title II: Auditor Independence

Internal and external auditors are separate and independent resources, with external auditors being responsible for assessing the fairness of an enterprise's published financial reports, while internal auditors serve management in a wide variety of other areas. In the early 1990s, however, this separation began to change, with external audit firms taking responsibility for some internal audit functions as well. This started when larger enterprises began to "outsource" some of their noncore functions, such as an employee cafeteria or plant janitorial function. The thinking was that employees working in these specialized areas were not really part of core enterprise operations, and all should benefit if people responsible for noncore functions were "outsourced" to another company that specialized in these un-unique areas, such as for janitorial services. The previous in-house janitors would be transferred to a separate janitorial services company, and, in theory, everyone would benefit. The enterprise that initiated the outsourcing would experience lower costs by giving a noncore function, janitorial services, to someone who better understood it. The outsourced janitor, in this example, also might have both better career possibilities and better supervision.

Internal auditor outsourcing started in the late 1980s following this same line of reasoning. External audit firms began offering to "outsource" or take over a client's existing internal audit functions. The idea made sense to senior management and their audit committees because they often did not really understand the distinctions between the two audit functions and were sometimes more comfortable with their external auditors. In addition, senior management and their audit committees were often enticed by the promised lower costs of internal audit outsourcing. Although their prime professional organization, the Institute of Internal Auditors, initially fought against the concept, internal audit outsourcing continued to grow through the 1990s. A few independent firms made efforts as well, but internal auditor outsourcing continued to be the realm of the major public accounting firms.

Internal audit outsourcing became an issue during investigations after the Enron failure. Its internal audit function had been almost totally outsourced to its external audit firm, Arthur Andersen, and the two audit groups worked side by side in Enron's offices. After Enron's fall, after-the-fact questions were raised about how that outsourced internal audit department could have been independent of Andersen. Enron investigators felt it would have been very difficult in that environment for internal audit to raise any concerns to the audit committee about their external auditors. This potential conflict became a reform issue for SOx.

SOx Section 201 forbids a registered public accounting firm from contemporaneously performing both audit and nonaudit services for a client. The prohibition includes internal auditing, many areas of consulting, and senior officer financial planning. For the internal audit professional, it is illegal for a registered public accounting firm to provide internal audit services if it is also doing the firm's audit work. This means that major public accounting firms are out of the internal audit outsourcing business for their audit clients. Other firms, including independent spin-offs from public accounting firms, can still provide internal audit outsourcing, but the era when an internal auditor became an employee of his or her public accounting firm is over.

In addition to the ban on providing outsourced internal audit services, SOx prohibits public accounting firms from providing other services, including

- **Financial information systems design and implementations.** Public accounting firms had been installing financial systems—often of their own design—for clients for many years. They then returned to review the internal controls of the systems they had just installed—a significant conflict of interest. This is no longer allowed.
- **Bookkeeping and financial statement services.** Public accounting firms previously offered accounting services to their clients, in addition to doing the audits. Even for major corporations, it was not unusual for the team responsible for the overall financial statement audit to also do much of the work necessary to build those same consolidated financial statements. Again, a potential conflict of interest that is no longer allowed.
- **Management and human resource functions.** Prior to SOx, external audit firms often helped their own professionals to move to client management positions. As a result, accounting managers in some enterprises often were alumni of their external auditors. This was sometimes frustrating for internal auditors or others who were not from that same public accounting firm, and avenues of promotion seemed limited because of "old boy" network connections with the external audit firm.

Under SOx, external auditors audit the financial statements of their client enterprises, and that is about all. Beyond the above prohibited activities, external auditors can engage in other nonaudit services only if those services are approved in advance by the audit committee. With the increased scrutiny of audit committees under SOx, many are typically wary of approving anything that appears to be at all out of the ordinary.

SOx external audit service prohibitions also have had a major impact on internal audit professionals. Because external audit firms can only be *just the auditors,* internal audit professionals have found increased levels of respect and responsibility for their role in assessing internal controls and promoting good corporate governance practices. Internal audit's relationship with board of directors' audit committees has also been strengthened, because they now seek help for services that were sometimes assumed by their external audit firms.

SOx's Title II specifies that the audit committee must approve all external audit and nonaudit services *in advance.* While most audit committees had been doing this all along, this approval was often little more than a formality prior to SOx. Audit committees in "the old days" often received little more than a brief report from their external auditors and then approved it in a perfunctory manner, similar to how some business meeting minutes are often approved. SOx changed this, and audit committee members can now expose themselves to criminal liabilities or stockholder litigation for allowing a prohibited action to take place. Of course, there are many minor, *de minimus* exception rules, where external auditor activities do not have to go through these formal audit committee approvals in advance.[9]

Title II also covers external audit partner rotation, making it unlawful for a public accounting lead partner to head an engagement for more than five years. The major public accounting firms had already established lead partner rotation, but SOx makes the failure of a firm to rotate a criminal act. Audit partner rotation has sometimes brought challenges to internal auditors who may have been working comfortably with a designated audit partner over extended periods and will need to become accustomed to working with a new external audit team lead from time to time.

Although external auditors have always communicated with their audit committees in the course of the audit engagement, it was discovered in the aftermath of Enron that this communication was sometimes very limited. Management might negotiate a "pass" from their external auditors on some accounting change, but the matter would be reported to the audit committee in only the most general of terms, if at all. External auditors now are required to report on a timely basis all accounting policies and practices used, alternative treatments of financial information discussed with management, the possible alternative treatments, and the approach preferred by the external auditor. If there are disputed accounting treatments, the audit committee should be made well aware of the actions taken.

SOx Title III: Corporate Responsibility

While SOx Title II sets up new rules for external auditor independence, Title III describes a wide range of governance rules covering corporate boards and their audit committees. To begin, *all* registered enterprises must have an audit committee composed only of independent directors. The external audit firm reports directly to that audit committee, which is responsible for its compensation, oversight of the audit work, and the resolution of any audit disagreements. Although most major corporations have had audit committees for some years, these rules have tightened and have very much changed. In addition, while internal audit sometimes had only a nominal reporting relationship to the audit committee, SOx requires a strong, direct-line internal audit reporting relationship to the audit committee. Audit committee communications will be discussed in Chapter 19.

In the many years leading up to SOx, enterprises filed their financial statements with the SEC with the printed names of corporate officers at the footings of those reports. However, the responsible corporate officers who "signed" those reports could argue they were not personally responsible for those reports in the event of any reporting errors, claiming that any errors or problems were the responsibility of their subordinates. With SOx, the bar has now been raised. The CEO, the CFO, or other individuals performing similar functions must personally certify each annual and quarterly report filed that

- ■ The signing officer has reviewed the report.
- ■ Based on that signing officer's knowledge, the financial statements do not contain any materially untrue or misleading information.

- Again based on the signing officer's knowledge, the financial statements fairly represent the financial conditions and results of operations of the enterprise.
- The signing officer:
  - Is responsible for establishing and maintaining internal controls.
  - Has designed these internal controls to ensure that material information about the enterprise and its subsidiaries was made known to the signing officer during the period when the reports were prepared.
  - Has evaluated the enterprise's internal controls within 90 days prior to the release of the report.
  - Has presented in these financial reports the signing officer's evaluation of the effectiveness of these internal controls as of that report date.
- The signing officer has disclosed to the auditors, the audit committee, and other directors:
  - All significant deficiencies in the design and operation of internal controls that could affect the reliability of the reported financial data and has, further, disclosed these material control weaknesses to the enterprise's auditors.
  - Any fraud, whether or not material, that involves management or other employees who have a significant role in the enterprise's internal controls.
- The signing officer has indicated in the report whether there were internal controls or other changes that could significantly affect those controls, including corrective actions, subsequent to the date of the internal control evaluation.

Given that SOx imposes potential criminal penalties of fines or jail time on individual violators of the act, the above signer requirement places a heavy burden on responsible corporate officers. Corporate officers must take all reasonable steps to make certain that they are in compliance.

This personal sign-off requirement should be a major concern for CEOs and CFOs. Strong internal accounting control processes should be in place, and an enterprise needs to set up detailed paper-trail procedures, such that the signing officers are comfortable that effective processes have been used and the calculations to build the reports are all well documented. An enterprise may want to consider using an extended sign-off process whereby staff members submitting the financial reports sign off on what they are submitting. Exhibit 2.3 provides an example of an Officer Disclosure Sign-Off type of statement for senior officers. This exhibit shows a sample company, Global Computer Products, that we will reference in other chapters and is not an official PCAOB form but shows the type of letter an officer might be asked to certify. Under SOx, the CEO or the CFO is asked to personally assert to these types of representations and could be held criminally liable if incorrect. The exhibit references Global Computer Products, an example company that we will reference in other chapters going forward. A senior executive should take every step possible to make certain that these financial reports are correct.

Title III continues with a section labeled "Improper Influence over the Conduct of Audits." Here, SOx makes it unlawful for any officer, director, or related subordinate person to take any action, in contravention of a SEC rule, to "fraudulently, influence, coerce, manipulate, or mislead" any external CPA auditor engaged in the audit for the purpose of rendering the financial statements materially misleading. These are strong

EXHIBIT 2.3   Sarbanes-Oxley Section 302 Officer Certification

Global Computer Products

Sarbanes-Oxley

Officer Certification

I, (*Name of Officer*), certify that:

1. I have reviewed this quarterly report on Form 10-K of Global Computer Products;

2. Based on my knowledge, this quarterly report does not contain any untrue statement of a material fact or omit to state a material fact necessary to make the statements made, in light of the circumstances under which such statements were made, not misleading with respect to the period covered by this quarterly report;

3. Based on my knowledge, the financial statements, and other financial information included in this quarterly report, fairly present in all material respects the financial condition, results of operations and the cash flows of, and for, the periods presented in this quarterly report;

4. The Global Computer Products' other certifying officers and I are responsible for establishing and maintaining disclosure controls and procedures (as defined in Exchange Act Rules 13a-14 and 15d-14) for the corporation and we have:

   a) designed such disclosure controls and procedures to ensure that material information relating to Global Computer Products, including its consolidated subsidiaries, is made known to us by others within those entities, particularly during the period in which this quarterly report is being prepared;

   b) evaluated the effectiveness of Global Computer Products disclosure controls and procedures as of a date within 90 days prior to the filing date of this quarterly report (the "Evaluation Date"); and

   c) presented in this quarterly report our conclusions about the effectiveness of the disclosure controls and procedures based on our evaluation as of the Evaluation Date;

5. The Global Computer Products other certifying officers and I have disclosed, based on our most recent evaluation, to Global Computer Products and the audit committee of our board of directors (or persons performing the equivalent function):

   a) all significant deficiencies in the design or operation of internal controls which could adversely affect Global Computer Products ability to record, process, summarize, and report financial data and have identified for Global Computer Products' auditors any material weaknesses in internal controls; and

   b) any fraud, whether or not material, that involves management or other employees who have a significant role in Global Computer Products' internal controls; and

6. Global Computer Products other certifying officers and I have indicated in this quarterly report whether or not there were significant changes in internal controls or in other factors that could significantly affect internal controls subsequent to the date of our most recent evaluation, including any corrective actions with regard to significant deficiencies and material weaknesses.

words in an environment where there has often been a high level of discussion and compromise between the auditors and senior management when a significant problem was found during the course of an audit.

Prior to SOx, there often were many "friendly" discussions between management and their external auditors regarding a financial interpretation dispute or a proposed adjustment. The result was often some level of compromise. This is not unlike an internal audit team in the field that circulates a draft audit report with local management before departing. After much discussion and sometimes other follow-up work, that draft internal audit report might have been significantly changed before its final issue. The same things often happened in external auditor draft reports covering quarterly or annual preliminary results. SOx rules prohibit such practices. These rules evolved during the congressional hearings leading up to the passage of SOx, in which testimony included tales of strong CEOs essentially demanding that their external auditors "accept" a certain questionable accounting entry or lose the audit business. There can still be friendly disputes and debates, but if an SEC ruling is explicit in some area and if the external auditors propose a financial statement adjustment because of that SEC rule, management *must* accept it without an additional fight.

There can be a fine line between management disagreeing with external auditors over some estimate or interpretation and management trying to improperly influence its auditors. External auditors may have done limited testing in some area and then proposed an adjustment based on the results of that test. This type of scenario could result in management disagreeing with that adjustment and claiming the results of the test were "not representative." However, the external auditors under SOx have the last word in such a dispute.

Title IV: Enhanced Financial Disclosures

This very significant section of SOx mandates a management assessment of internal controls, corrects some financial reporting disclosure problems, tightens up conflict-of-interest rules for corporate officers and directors, and requires senior corporate officer codes of conduct. There is a lot of material here. Many of the unexpected bankruptcies and earnings failures around the time of the Enron collapse were attributed to extremely aggressive, if not questionable, financial reporting. With the approval of their external auditors, some enterprises pushed to the limits and often used what were called pro forma earnings statements to report their results, or others moved the corporate headquarters offshore to minimize taxes. SOx tightened up many rules and made other related tactics difficult or illegal.

A common tactic at that time, for example, pro forma financial reports were frequently used to present an "as if" picture of a firm's financial status by leaving out nonrecurring earnings expenses, such as restructuring charges or merger-related costs. However, because there is no standard definition of, and no consistent format for reporting, pro forma earnings, depending on the assumptions used, it was possible for an operating loss to become a profit under pro forma earnings reporting. SOx rules require that pro forma published financial statements must not contain any materially untrue statements or omit any fact that makes the reports misleading. Furthermore, the pro forma results also must reconcile to the financial conditions and results of operations under GAAP. A common reporting technique prior to SOx, they are not at all common today.

Perhaps the main issue that brought Enron down and led to the passage of SOx was a large number of Enron off–balance sheet transactions that, if consolidated with regular financial reports, would have shown major financial problems. Once they were identified and included with Enron's other financial results, the disclosure pushed that corporation toward bankruptcy. SOx requires that quarterly and annual financial reports must disclose all such off–balance sheet transactions that may have a material effect on the current or future financial reports. These transactions may include contingent obligations, financial relationships with unconsolidated entities, or other items that could have material effects on operations.

The legislative hearings that led to SOx often pictured corporate officers and directors as a rather greedy lot. In arrangements that frequently appeared to be conflicts of interest, large relocation allowances or corporate executive personal loans were granted and then subsequently forgiven by corporate boards. A CEO, for example, might request the board to grant the CFO a large personal "loan" with vague repayment terms and the right to either demand payment or forgive the loan, which certainly created a conflict-of-interest situation. Although exceptions are allowed, SOx makes it unlawful for any corporation to directly or indirectly extend credit, in the form of a personal loan, to any officer or director.

What is the most important component of SOx for many enterprises, Section 404, covers management's assessment of internal controls and requires that all annual 10K reports must contain an internal control report stating management's responsibility for establishing and maintaining an adequate system of internal controls, as well as management's assessment, as of the fiscal year ending date, of the effectiveness of those installed internal control procedures. This is what has been known as the Section 404 rules, and this section of SOx has had as major impact on enterprises and their assessments of internal controls.

Management has had an ongoing responsibility for designing and implementing internal controls over its enterprise's operations, and SOx Section 404 requires the preparation of an annual internal control report as part of an enterprise's SEC-mandated 10K annual report. In addition to the financial statements and other 10K disclosures, Section 404 requirements call for two information elements in each of these 10Ks:

1. A formal management statement acknowledging their responsibility for establishing and maintaining an adequate internal control structure and procedures for financial reporting; and
2. An assessment, as of the end of the most recent fiscal year, of the effectiveness of an enterprise's internal control structure and procedures for financial reporting.

In addition, the external audit firm that issued the supporting audit report is required to review and report on management's assessment of its internal financial controls. Simply put, management is required to report on the quality of its internal controls, and its public accounting firm must audit or attest to the fact that management developed an internal control report, in addition to its normal financial statement audit. Management has always been responsible for preparing its periodic financial reports, and the external auditors then audited those financial numbers and certified that they were fairly stated. With SOx Section 404, management is responsible for documenting and testing its internal financial controls, as well as reporting on their effectiveness. External auditors then review the supporting materials leading up to that internal financial control report to assert that the report is an accurate description of the internal control environment.

To the nonauditor, this might appear to be an obscure or almost trivial requirement. Even some internal auditors who primarily specialize in more operational audits face a challenge grasping the nuances in this process. However, audit reports on the status of internal controls have been an ongoing and simmering issue between the public accounting community, the SEC, and other interested parties going back to at least 1974. Much of the problem then, as we have discussed in previous paragraphs, was that there was no recognized definition for what is meant by internal controls. The release of the COSO internal control framework in 1992 established an accepted standard for understanding internal controls. Under SOx Section 404, management is required to report on the adequacy of their internal controls with their external auditors attesting to the management-developed internal control reports. This internal control reporting followed the original COSO internal control framework and will transition to the new framework, as discussed in Chapter 19.

This process follows a basic internal control on the importance of maintaining a separation of duties, so that the person who develops transactions should not be the person who approves them. Under Section 404 procedures, the enterprise builds and documents its own internal control processes; then an independent party, such as an internal audit function, reviews and tests those internal controls; and finally, the external auditors review and attest to the adequacy of this overall process. Their financial audit procedures should be based on these internal controls.

Another element of SOx's Title IV requires that enterprises adopt a code of ethics for their CEO, CFO, and other senior officers and disclose their compliance with this code as part of their annual financial reporting. While SOx has made this a requirement for senior officers, employee codes of ethics or conduct have been in place in some enterprises for many years. They evolved to more formal ethics functions in larger corporations in the early 1990s but were often established more for employees and supervisors, rather than for corporate officers.

With public concern about the need for strong ethical practices, many enterprises have appointed ethics officers and strengthened their codes of conduct. However, while those codes of conduct received senior officer endorsement, they were often directed at the overall population of employees, not at the senior officers. SOx does not specify the content of enterprise-wide codes of ethics and focuses on the need for standards to apply for senior officers. SOx specifically requires that an enterprise's senior officer code of ethics or conduct must reasonably promote:

▪ Honest and ethical conduct, including the handling of actual or apparent conflicts of interest between personal and professional relationships,
▪ Full, fair, accurate, timely, and understandable disclosure in the enterprise financial reports, and
▪ Compliance with applicable governmental rules and regulations.

The last Title IV Section, 409, mandates that enterprises must disclose "on a rapid and current basis" any additional information containing material financial statement issues. An enterprise can include trend and quantitative reporting approaches, as well as graphics for those disclosures. This is a change from traditional SEC report formats that allowed only text, with the exception of corporate logos. The concept is to get key data to investors as soon as possible, not through slow paper-based reports.

Title V: Analyst Conflicts of Interest

This SOx Title does not directly cover financial reporting, corporate governance, audit committees, or internal control issues and both external and internal audit issues; it was drafted to correct other perceived abuses encountered during the now long ago SOx congressional hearings. Title V was designed to rectify some securities analyst abuses. Investors have relied on the recommendations of securities analysts for years, but these analysts were often tied to large brokerage houses and investment banks, and they were analyzing and recommending securities both to investors and to their financial institution employers. When they looked at securities in which their employer had an interest, there were supposed to be strong separations of responsibility between the people recommending a stock for investment and those selling it to investors. In the frenzy of the late 1990s investment "dot-com" bubble, these traditional analyst controls and ethical practices broke down. In the aftermath of the market downturns during those years, analysts sometimes recommended stocks seemingly only because their investment bank employers were managing the initial public offerings (IPOs). Also, investigators found analysts publicly recommending a stock to investors as a "great growth opportunity," while simultaneously telling their investment banking peers that the stock was a very poor investment or worse.

While Title V attempts to correct those securities analyst abuses, nothing has changed all that much. During the Great Recession years starting around 2008, markets crashed after investors realized that many "Triple A"-rated mortgage bonds were not at all that good. Here the problem was not investment analysts but bond-rating agencies. Investors still were adequately informed.

Titles VI through X: Fraud Accountability and White-Collar Crime

These SOx Titles cover rules to tighten up what had been viewed as regulatory loopholes in the past. Among these, the SEC can ban persons from promoting or trading "penny stocks" because of past SEC misconduct or can bar someone from practicing before the SEC because of improper professional conduct. The latter rule gives the SEC the authority to effectively ban a public accounting firm from acting as an external auditor for corporations.

SOx Titles VIII and IX seem to be very much a reaction to the failure of Enron and the subsequent conviction of the then-major public accounting firm Arthur Andersen for its destruction of Enron's accounting records. At that time, even though Andersen seemed very culpable to outside observers for its massive efforts to shred company accounting records, Andersen initially argued that it was just following its established procedures and had done no wrong. The courts eventually found Andersen innocent of criminal conspiracy, but it is no more. Now, Title VIII of SOx has established specific rules and penalties for the destruction of corporate audit records.

The words in the statute are much broader than just the Andersen matter and apply to all auditors and accountants, including internal auditors. The words here are particularly strong regarding the destruction, alteration, or falsification of records involved in federal investigations or bankruptcies: "Whoever knowingly alters, destroys, mutilates, conceals, covers up, falsifies or makes false entry in any record, document, or tangible object with the intent to impede, obstruct, or influence the investigation . . . shall be fined . . . [or] imprisoned not more than 20 years, or both." Taken directly from the statute, some strong words! This says that any enterprise should have a strong records retention policy. While records can be destroyed in the course of normal business cycles, any hint of a federal investigation or the filing of bankruptcy papers for some affiliated unit should trigger activation of that records retention policy.

A separate portion of this section establishes rules for corporate audit records. Although SOx primarily defines rules for external auditors, it very much applies to internal auditors as well. Work papers and other external or internal audit documentation must be maintained for a period of five years from the end of the fiscal year of the audit. SOx clearly states that these rules apply to "any accountant who conducts an audit" of an SEC-registered corporation. While internal auditors have sometimes argued in the past that they only do operational audits that do not apply to the formal financial audit process, the prudent internal audit group should closely align its work-paper record retention rules to comply with this SOx five-year mandate.

Title XI: Corporate Fraud Accountability

While most sections of SOx focus on the individual responsibilities of the CEO, the CFO, and others, the last Title in the legislation outlines corporate responsibilities for fraudulent financial reporting. For example, the SEC is given authority to impose a temporary freeze on the transfer of corporate funds to officers and others in a corporation that is subject to an SEC investigation. This was done to correct some reported abuses, in which certain corporations were being investigated for financial fraud, while they simultaneously dispensed huge cash payments to individuals. A corporation in trouble should retain some funds until the matter is resolved.

The previous sections in this chapter have provided a general overview of the Sarbanes-Oxley Act. While this discussion did not cover all sections or details of SOx, our intent is to provide an overall understanding of key sections that will have an impact on an enterprise's assessment of its COSO internal accounting controls. Whether a large, "Fortune 100"–size US-based corporation, a smaller company not even traded on NASDAQ, or a private company with a bond issue registered through the SEC, all come under SOx and its public accounting regulatory body, the PCAOB.

SOx compliance requires multiple efforts from enterprises, particularly in the United States but also worldwide. The roles and responsibilities of both external and internal auditors have changed, and enterprises certainly look at the internal controls and business ethics from a much different perspective. A general knowledge of SOx and its procedures for performing Section 404 internal control reviews are important knowledge requirements for all senior managers.

An understanding of SOx and, in particular, its Section 404 internal accounting control rules, as well as how we got to the original COSO internal control framework, is important for understanding and implementing the new COSO internal control framework. The following chapters will reference many aspects of SOx as we introduce and explain the new COSO internal control framework.

 NOTES

1. Statement on Auditing Standards No. 1, Codification of Auditing Standards and Procedures, AICPA, Professional Standards.
2. Generally accepted accounting principles (GAAP) refers to the financial accounting standards that have been used in the United States. for many years. They are being replaced by the worldwide recognized International Financial Reporting Standards (IFRS).
3. Financial Executives International was formally known as the Financial Executives Institute.
4. *Report of the National Commission on Fraudulent Financial Reporting* (National Commission on Fraudulent Financial Reporting, 1987).
5. Internal Control—Integrated Framework, www.coso.org. Note: This reference is for the COSO internal control report that can be ordered through the AICPA at www.cpa2biz .com.
6. AICPA-published COSO internal control standards are described in SAS Nos. 103, 105, 106, 107, 109, 110, and 112.
7. Robert Moeller, *Sarbanes-Oxley Internal Controls – Effective Auditing with AS5, COBIT and ITIL* (Hoboken, NJ: John Wiley & Sons, 2008).
8. As a public document, the text of the law can be found in many Web locations. One source is http://fll.findlaw.com/news.findlaw.com/hdocs/docs/gwbush/sarbanesoxley072302.pdf.
9. A principle of law: Even if a technical violation of a law appears to exist according to the letter of the law, if the effect is too small to be of consequence, the violation of the law will not be considered as a sufficient cause of action, whether in civil or criminal proceedings.

CHAPTER THREE

COSO Internal Controls: The New Revised Framework

THE ORIGINAL 1992 COSO INTERNAL control framework, as well as some of the events that led up its release, was discussed in Chapter 2. As that chapter highlights, prior to the COSO internal control framework, there was no consistent and agreed-on definition of *internal controls*, in business, academic, or government circles, and no agreed-on understanding of the elements and activities needed to establish effective internal controls in an enterprise. This 1992 COSO internal control framework, shown in Exhibit 2.1, really changed our understanding and defined the concepts of internal controls. Starting with what some business professionals and external auditors first viewed as just an "interesting" definition, the COSO framework has become the guiding internal control measure, first in the United States and now worldwide.

During the 20 or so years of its life, the initial COSO internal control framework and concept have not changed, but business and technology have. Although all of these changes will be discussed in the following chapters, the growth of IT systems and technology, our increased emphasis on risk management and corporate governance, and enterprise globalization were all prime examples of the need for a COSO refreshment. When the original COSO internal controls framework was released in 1992, large mainframe-based computer systems were still common, and the Internet was not the enterprise support tool it is today. The revised framework reflects our overall use and reliance on all types of IT systems for establishing effective internal controls today.

This chapter introduces the new revised COSO internal control framework that became effective in May 2013. Some changes and differences in philosophy approaches are highlighted here, while the following chapters discuss components of the new revised framework in greater detail. Enterprises and their senior executives at all levels have a need to understand and apply this new COSO internal control framework as they build and monitor their systems and processes.

UNDERSTANDING INTERNAL CONTROLS

Chapter 2 talked about how what business executives and auditors called internal controls was one of those concepts that everyone agreed was important in business but few could define consistently. Part of the problem then was that many persons looked at internal control following the description of a classic organization chart, with its levels of senior and middle management in its multiple operating units or within different activities. At each level, people looked at internal controls from the perspective of their own line of authority. However, control procedures are often somewhat different at each of these organization levels and components. For example, one enterprise unit may operate in a regulated business environment where control processes are very structured, while another divisional unit of the same core enterprise may be an entrepreneurial start-up operation with a less formal structure. Different levels of management in these enterprises will have different control concern perspectives. The question "How do you describe your system of internal controls?" might receive different answers from persons in different levels or components in each of these enterprise components.

The original COSO internal control framework introduced in Chapter 2 provided an excellent description of this multidimensional concept, defining *internal control* as a process affected by an entity's board of directors, management, and other personnel and covering the achievement of objectives in the following categories:

- ▪ Effectiveness and efficiency of operations.
- ▪ Reliability of financial reporting.
- ▪ Compliance with applicable laws and regulations.

This is the COSO definition of internal control and it *has not changed* with the revised COSO framework. Using this very general definition of *internal controls*, COSO originally used a three-dimensional model to describe an internal control system in an enterprise. Exhibit 3.1 defines the original COSO model of internal controls as a pyramid with five layers or interconnected components comprising the overall internal control system. These are shown with a component called the control environment serving as the foundation for the entire structure. Four of these internal components are described as horizontal layers, with another component of internal control, called communication and information, acting as an interface channel for the other four layers.

Over time, COSO had published some additional guidance materials to support and clarify its internal control framework, but it did not revise its overall internal control framework until now. The overall thrust of this COSO framework has been the design and implementation of systems of internal controls over external financial reporting that support the preparation of financial statements. These include the breadth of public, private, not-for-profit, and governmental entities, all of which have external financial reporting requirements.

An enterprise business operations executive may argue, "What? External financial reporting? I am not a CPA working as an external auditor or even in my accounting department, and why should I be concerned?" This is very much a mistaken assumption.

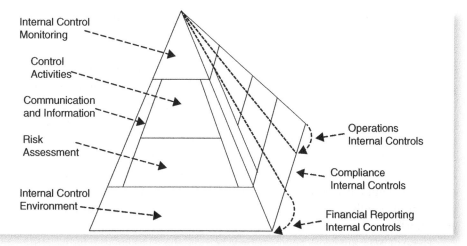

Operations
Internal Controls

Compliance
Internal Controls

Financial Reporting
Internal Controls

Internal Control
Monitoring

Control
Activities

Communication
and Information

Risk
Assessment

Internal Control
Environment

EXHIBIT 3.1   COSO Internal Controls, Pyramid View

The external auditors are reviewing and assessing the internal financial controls that have been installed in enterprise systems, but enterprise management is responsible for designing, installing, and monitoring these internal control processes. The COSO internal control framework is very relevant here, and business executives, as well as their internal auditors, IT specialists, the finance and accounting staffs, and others, should be aware of and understand the COSO internal control framework. All should focus on the five basic principles that support enterprise COSO internal controls:

1. The organization demonstrates a commitment to integrity and ethical values.
2. The board of directors demonstrates independence from management and exercises oversight of the development and performance of internal control.
3. Management establishes, with board oversight, structures, reporting lines, and appropriate authorities and responsibilities in the pursuit of objectives.
4. The organization demonstrates a commitment to attract, develop, and retain competent individuals in alignment with objectives.
5. The organization holds individuals accountable for their internal control responsibilities in the pursuit of objectives.

Each of these principles and concepts was part of the original framework and has continued with the new revised framework described in greater detail in the following sections. We should always remember that there are three major components of internal control—effectiveness and efficiency of operations, reliability of financial reporting, and compliance with applicable laws and regulations—to give three dimensions to this model. Just as the previous pyramid structure showed the internal control structure as the environment for all internal control processes, this view adds equal weight to each of these three components. The revised COSO internal control model and its components for the separate entities and activities in an enterprise will be discussed in more detail in the following sections and other chapters.

REVISED FRAMEWORK BUSINESS AND OPERATING ENVIRONMENT CHANGES

It is important to remember who or what COSO is and the authority of its published guidance materials. As discussed in Chapter 2, COSO, or the Committee of Sponsoring Organizations of the Treadway Commission, is a joint initiative of the five private sector professional organizations. COSO is dedicated to providing thought leadership through the development of frameworks and guidance on enterprise risk management, internal controls, and fraud deterrence. An important point here is that COSO does not have the authority to issue standards such as those found in government rules or professional organization guidance. Rather, this guidance, including COSO internal control framework, outlines only an approach or recommended best practices that others should generally follow.

These COSO framework concepts have become the basis for standards-setting entities in other areas or requirements. For example, SOx requires enterprises to have effective internal control systems in place that are consistent with the COSO internal control framework. Today, however, when an enterprise attests that its internal controls are in compliance with COSO, it may be attesting to the original 1992 COSO framework. As a result, both enterprise management and their external auditors seeking to establish SOx legal compliance have relied on the original COSO framework to assert their legal compliance. Enterprises at all levels have kept this concept in mind when building, implementing, and monitoring their internal control systems and processes. Transition issues to bring us to compliance with the revised COSO framework are discussed in Chapter 20.

In the years after the original COSO internal control framework was first released in 1992, there have been dramatic changes in businesses and their operating environments. In addition, they have become increasingly complex, IT driven systems, and global enterprise arrangements. At the same time, the stakeholders responsible for building and managing business entities have become more engaged in improving the accountability and integrity of their processes. As a result, there had been general feelings within COSO that some level of updates was needed. Our earlier comment on the lack of up-to-date COSO guidance on IT issues is one example here. Although these revised changes are discussed in greater detail in the following chapters, the revised new COSO internal control framework and its supporting guidance materials contain changes in the following areas:

- **Expanded expectations for governance oversight**. Enterprises today have increased regulatory requirements and stakeholder expectations that require boards of directors to boost their emphasis on the adequacy of internal financial controls in their enterprises.
- **Increased globalization of markets and operations**. Enterprises today frequently expand beyond their traditional domestic markets in pursuit of value, often entering into international markets and engaging in cross-border mergers and acquisitions.
- **Changes and greater complexities in the enterprise business operations**. Enterprises change their business models and enter into complex transactions in the

pursuit of growth, greater quality, or productivity, as well as in response to changes in markets or regulatory environments. These changes may involve entering into joint ventures, strategic alliances, or other complex arrangements with external parties, implementing shared services, and engaging with outsourced service providers.

▪ **A greater level of demands and complexities in laws, rules, regulations, and standards**. Governmental authorities often release complex legislation where compliance with these rules is often difficult to achieve and where these rules do not directly follow classic internal control approaches.

▪ **More emphasis on the use of, and reliance on, evolving technologies.** As we highlighted in our introduction to this chapter, the growth of IT systems and related technologies has very much changed our approaches to implementing and managing IT systems and their internal control processes. Today's IT systems are often based on automated internal controls and processes to build, install, and monitor these automated controls.

▪ **A greater need to prevent and detect fraud and corruption**. The US Foreign Corrupt Practices Act (FCPA), introduced many years ago and discussed in Chapter 2, was an earlier example of increased legislative internal control and other legal requirements. Today, an even wider range of anticorruption and antifraud rules and legislation has been put in place, ranging from international to often differing legislation rules in many US states.

Each of these changes requires an enterprise to evaluate these implications on its systems of internal control, with an emphasis on its external financial reporting, and to design and implement appropriate responses so that their systems of internal control adapt and remain effective over time.

As almost a first step toward establishing effective internal controls, an enterprise should communicate to its stakeholders and take necessary actions to implement an overall strategy through a formal published mission statement that signifies its direction to improving its internal control processes. This can take a variety forms or directions. For example, such a mission statement may be to build or market the best or most cost-effective widgets in the Southern California marketplace. Another enterprise may have a documents mission to become a market leader in the sales of some new fast-food product in Spain or many other strategies. In any case, an enterprise's mission should be well thought out, documented, and then approved by its board of directors. Although mission statements can sound impressive, the enterprise should establish objectives to achieve those mission statement goals, as well as develop more specific plans for achieving them.

Objectives should be established covering the total entity or enterprise, but sublevel or detailed objectives can be built by division or operating units or for specific business units or activities. Each should be built to satisfy the COSO framework's financial reporting, operations, and compliance objectives.

External Financial Reporting Objectives

A major component of an effective system of internal control for an enterprise pertains to the preparation of reliable financial and nonfinancial internal and external reports.

External financial reporting objectives should be consistent with generally accepted accounting principles that are suitable and available for an entity and appropriate in the circumstances. External financial reporting objectives address the preparation of financial statements for external purposes and other external financial reporting derived from an enterprise's financial and accounting books and records, including annual and interim financial statements. These statements may, for instance, be publicly filed with a regulator, distributed through annual shareholder meetings, posted to an entity's website, or distributed through other electronic media.

External financial reports may also include financial reports prepared for taxing authorities or regulatory agencies or requirements established through contracts and agreements. Other external financial reporting objectives may include news releases, earnings releases, or financial information posted on enterprise websites.

Although external financial reports are a major area of concern to enterprise management, they are often a small component of overall enterprise reporting requirements. Internal reporting objectives are driven by an enterprise's internal needs to satisfy strategic objectives, operating plans, and performance metric requirements at various levels and units within the enterprise. Although the emphasis of COSO internal controls is on external reporting, enterprise internal reporting should be at least equally important. These internal reports are often consolidated to form the basis for external reports. Our discussions of COSO internal controls will emphasize internal reporting and related management concerns in many of the following sections.

Internal Control Operations Objectives

Operations objectives relate to the achievement of an enterprise's basic mission—the fundamental reasons for its existence. Those objectives vary, based on management's choices relating to structure, industry considerations, and the performance of the enterprise. Operations objectives within an enterprise cascade to related subobjectives for operations within the divisions, subsidiaries, operating units, and functions, with all directed at enhancing the effectiveness and efficiency of moving the enterprise toward its highest-level goals.

Operations objectives may relate to improving overall service delivery of its processes, emphasizing quality, reducing costs, and other innovation improvements. A major area here should be goals to improve customer or employee satisfaction. There are many areas where an enterprise will establish internal control objectives to improve its operations.

Internal Control Compliance Objectives

Enterprises throughout the world face an ever-increasing set of legislative rules and legal requirements. Because these rules are sometimes ill-defined or fuzzy, it may be all but impossible for an enterprise to operate fully in compliance with all of them. Nevertheless, an enterprise needs to establish rules for all of its operating units or functions to operate in compliance with relevant rules and regulations. The roles of effective compliance review and monitoring functions, such as internal audit or quality assurance, are important here for setting these internal control compliance objectives.

In preparing its financial statements and implementing other internal controls, management must exercise judgment in complying with external financial reporting and other related internal control requirements. Management must consider how identified risks to specified financial reporting objectives and subobjectives should be managed. Management's alternatives to respond to risk may be limited, compared to some other categories of objectives. That is, management is less likely to accept a risk than to reduce the risk. For instance, management may decide to mitigate a risk by outsourcing some transaction processing to a third party that is better suited to perform the business process. However, management always retains responsibility for designing, implementing, and conducting its system of internal control, even when outsourcing to a third party. For external financial reporting objectives, risk acceptance or avoidance should occur only when identified risks could not, individually or in aggregate, exceed the risk threshold and result in a material financial reporting misstatement.

Overlapping Internal Control Objectives

Many controls are interrelated and may support multiple objectives. An objective in one category may overlap or support an objective in another. For example, a goal of "closing the financial reporting period within five workdays" may be a goal primarily supporting an operations objective—to support management in reviewing business performance. Yet it also supports a related objective of timely reporting and timely filings with regulatory agencies.

The category in which an objective falls can sometimes vary, depending on its circumstances and connections to other objectives. For instance, controls to prevent the theft of assets—such as maintaining a fence around an outside-stored product inventory, or having a gatekeeper verify proper authorization of requests for movement of these goods—fall under the operations category. These controls may not be relevant to reporting where inventory losses are detected following periodic physical inspection and recording in the financial statements. However, if, for reporting purposes, management relies solely on perpetual inventory records, as may be the case for interim or internal financial reporting, the physical security controls would then also fall within this reporting category. These physical security controls, along with controls over perpetual inventory records, are needed to achieve reporting objectives. A clear understanding is needed of an enterprise's processes and its policies, its procedures, and the respective impact on each category of objectives.

 ## THE REVISED COSO INTERNAL CONTROL FRAMEWORK

In addition to the three internal control objective categories of operations, reporting, and compliance just described, the revised COSO framework defines *internal controls* from two other dimensions or perspectives: separate components of internal control and organization factors. Looking similar but slightly different from the original COSO internal control framework that was introduced in 1992 and described in Chapter 2, Exhibit 3.2 shows the new revised three-dimensional COSO internal control framework.

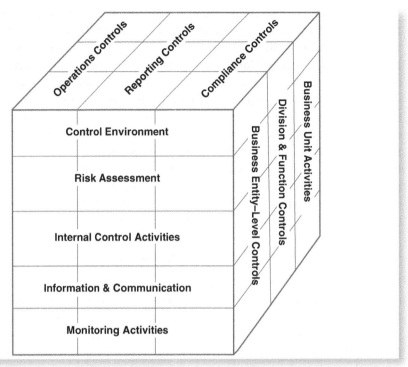

EXHIBIT 3.2 COSO Internal Control Framework

We will be using this internal control cube relationship here and in other chapters going forward. The three categories of internal control objectives—operations, reporting, and compliance—are represented by the columns defined at the top in this diagram. The front-facing side of this COSO cube diagram defines the five key components or levels of internal control:

1. Control environment
2. Risk assessment
3. Control activities
4. Information and communication
5. Monitoring activities

This is the area where there have been the most changes in the new revised COSO internal control framework. Each of these internal control activity levels or key components will be introduced and discussed in the following chapters.

Shown on the right-facing side of the model, an enterprise's organizational structure is the third important dimension of internal control. It represents the internal control–related components of the overall organization structure, including the overall enterprise entity itself, its divisions, subsidiaries, operating units, or functions that encompass key business processes such as sales, purchasing, production, and marketing. As a key point here, we should keep in mind the components of the overall organization entity, starting with the overall enterprise in total and then all business units and component details as well. Some individual control activities may differ from one another in certain operating details, but they all must fit into the control environment for the total entity.

As an example, assume that a European Union–based enterprise has launched a new business product sales venture in Myanmar (Burma), a country that has been closed to the outside world until recently. With limited IT resources and telecommunication connections, we can expect some different control processes in the Myanmar facility than would be found in the entity's headquarters operations. However, additional processes—such as the use of supporting manual control procedures—should be established to achieve internal controls at the overall entity level. These manual processes may have been all but abandoned.

The whole idea of this model is that internal control for today's enterprise is not a single control objective but a multilevel, multifaceted concept, with each unit in the COSO model having a relationship to other components in all three dimensions. Enterprise management should clearly specify its internal control objectives, such as suitable external reporting objectives relating to the preparation of financial statements. Some of these objectives can be very specific, based on some enterprise-planned business activity. Others should define well-understood or assumed objectives. For example, senior management may set an entity-level external financial reporting objective as follows: "Our Company prepares reliable financial statements reflecting activities in accordance with generally accepted accounting principles." This may have been assumed by members of the management team, but there is a value in clearly defining such matters. Management should also specify suitable subobjectives for enterprise divisions, subsidiaries, operating units, and functions with sufficient clarity to support entity-level objectives.

COSO INTERNAL CONTROL PRINCIPLES

As a major change, the revised COSO framework codifies principles that support the five components of internal control. While the 1992 version implicitly reflected some core principles of internal control, the revised version explicitly defines 17 internal control principles representing fundamental concepts associated with the five components of internal control. COSO has decided to make these principles explicit to increase management's understanding as to what constitutes effective internal control. These principles, introduced for the control environment at the beginning of this chapter, are outlined in total in Exhibit 3.3; they are broad, because they are intended to apply to a wide range of enterprises, including for profit and not-for-profit, publicly traded and private, and government bodies and other organizations.

Supporting each of these 17 very important principles are points of focus, representing important characteristics associated with these principles. These points of focus are intended to provide helpful guidance to assist management in designing, implementing, and conducting internal control processes and in assessing whether relevant principles are present and functioning. However, the revised COSO framework does not require separate evaluations of whether they are in place. Management has the latitude to exercise judgment in determining the suitability or relevancy of these points of focus provided in the revised COSO framework and may identify and consider other important characteristics germane to a particular principle based on the enterprise's specific circumstances.

EXHIBIT 3.3   COSO Internal Control Principles

Control Environment

---

   1. Commitment to integrity and ethical values.

   2. Independent board of directors' oversight.

   3. Structures, reporting lines, authorities, and responsibilities.

   4. Attract, develop, and retain competent people.

   5. People held accountable for internal control.

Risk Assessment

---

   6. Clear objectives specified.

   7. Risks identified to achievement of objectives.

   8. Potential for fraud considered.

   9. Significant changes identified and assessed.

Control Activities

---

  10. Control activates selected and developed.

  11. General IT controls selected and developed.

  12. Controls developed through policies and procedures.

Information and Communication

---

  13. Quality information obtained, generated, and used.

  14. Internal control information internally communicated.

  15. Internal information externally communicated.

Control Activities

---

  16. Ongoing and/or separate evaluations conducted.

  17. Internal control deficiencies evaluated and communicated.

     Taken together, these internal control components and principles constitute the criteria, and the points of focus provide guidance that will assist management in assessing whether these components of internal control are present, functioning, and operating together with an enterprise. Each of the points of focus is mapped directly over these 17 principles, and each of those principles is mapped directly to one of the five internal control components. These concepts should become much clearer as we discuss the COSO framework in more detail in the following chapters.

COSO OBJECTIVES AND BUSINESS OPERATIONS

The revised COSO internal control framework emphasizes external financial reporting as its main area of interest. As we discussed in Chapter 2, the original COSO framework had its roots in the Treadway Commission and concerns about inaccurate or even fraudulent external financial reporting. Investors, regulators, and managers at all levels expect that all external financial reports for an enterprise should be correct, accurate, and prepared with strong internal control processes.

The following chapters will discuss the revised COSO internal control framework and the 17 key principles, with COSO's three-dimensional components discussed in greater detail. However, in addition to the COSO internal control framework's primary objectives of external financial reporting, we also introduce two additional internal control objectives or concerns:

▪ **Controls over internal reporting processes.** The typical enterprise, at all levels, devotes considerable resources to developing both financial and nonfinancial reports for internal purposes. While some of these internal reports and supporting processes flow into and support external financial reports, much of the information generated with these internal reports is for regular and normal business activities. These are the types of reports that might support a customer product service function, IT project management activities, or a human resources continuing education program. While many of these types of internal reports are somewhat financial in nature and give some level of support to external financial reports, others may be totally nonfinancial and operational in their nature. It is essential that these internal reports are prepared with the same level and types of internal controls that should be found with external financial reports.

▪ **Internal controls over nonfinancial reports and processes.** Looking at internal and external reporting controls from another dimension, COSO internal control concepts should cover nonfinancial reports and processes, as well as financial. Although many nonfinancial reports may have little direct relationship to financial reporting processes—the employee parking lot automobile registration list would be an example—these reports and their supporting processes should nevertheless be prepared with adequate internal controls. To clarify that last statement, virtually all enterprise reports have some financial implications. In the above-mentioned report covering employee automobile parking lot registrations, report errors might cause the plant security function to spend excessive time—with the associated costs—checking out problems. However, we do not want to reduce things too much.

Our point here is that we should consider the effectiveness of internal controls under the COSO framework in the context of the relationship of internal and external reporting controls, as well as their financial and nonfinancial relationships. Exhibit 3.4 shows some of these types of overlapping internal control categories.

The COSO internal control framework provides guidance that should be useful for all enterprise reports and processes. While many of the chapters going forward will emphasize internal control components in terms of an enterprise's external financial reporting processes, we should think of the COSO internal control framework as a model for improving all enterprise processes and their related reports.

The COSO framework cube looks about the same today, when compared to its original 1992 versions, but the newly defined supporting principles increase the significance and importance of the newly revised COSO internal control framework. The overall assessment of the effectiveness of an enterprise's internal controls is very much tied to its relationship to COSO's five internal control components and the supporting 17 principles. The following chapters will expand on these concepts and requirements.

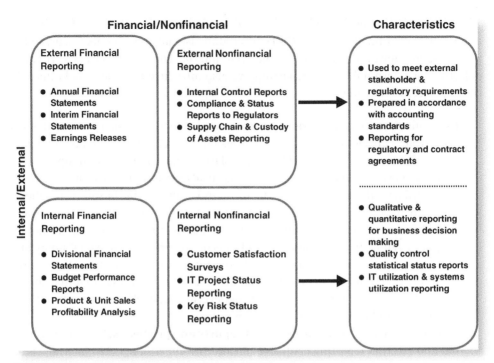

EXHIBIT 3.4   Overlapping Internal Control Categories

 SOURCES FOR MORE INFORMATION

The following chapters describe the revised COSO internal control framework in greater detail. Much of the information here was extracted from its www.coso.org site and has been based on this author's experience with COSO internal controls, going back to directing internal audit functions, participating in developing draft review comments for the original COSO framework, and having been actively involved with multiple levels of internal control activities over the years.

More information can be found by purchasing its more detailed guidance material, from either COSO or the American Institute of Certified Public Accountants. The published material is available in either paperback or e-book format in a collection titled *Internal Control–Integrated Framework* and is published in four volumes titled:

- *Executive Summary*
- *Framework and Appendices*
- *Illustrative Tools for Assessing Effectiveness of a System of Internal Control*
- *Internal Control over External Financial Reporting: A Compendium of Approaches and Examples*

Although there is exhaustive material in this set, we have tried to summarize and explain much of this material from an enterprise executive perspective in the following chapters. Also, while COSO's focus is much more on external financial reporting, a major objective of the COSO internal control framework, our comments cover all important aspects of internal controls, including IT and operational internal control issues.

CHAPTER FOUR

COSO Internal Control Components: Control Environment

THE FRONT-FACING SIDE OF THE revised Exhibit 3.2 framework model shows five levels of internal control categories, the top level of which is called the control environment—the set of standards, processes, and structures that provides a basis or a structure for carrying out effective internal control activities across an enterprise. This chapter reflects on the original 1992 version of this control environment category and introduces the new concepts in the revised framework that make it particularly important.

Control environment internal control concepts should begin with the board of directors and senior management, who establish what has come to be known as management's "tone at the top" for an enterprise; these are the formal senior management–level internal communications regarding the importance of internal controls, including expected standards of conduct. Management should emphasize and reinforce these expectations at the various levels of the enterprise. The control environment comprises the integrity and ethical values of the overall enterprise; the parameters enabling the board of directors to carry out its oversight responsibilities; the organizational structure and assignment of authority and responsibility; the process for attracting, developing, and retaining competent individuals; and the rigor around performance measures, incentives, and rewards to drive accountability for performance. This resulting control environment has a pervasive impact on the overall system of internal controls.

IMPORTANCE OF THE CONTROL ENVIRONMENT

The original version of the COSO internal control framework, in Exhibit 3.1, showed the control environment component as the bottom or, as we have described, the foundation layer of a stack of internal control components. The revised version more appropriately places this component at the top or upper level of the COSO internal control elements. There is really no conceptual change with this rearrangement. Despite its visual location in the diagram, the control environment should be considered the foundation for all other components of internal control, and it has an influence on each of the three objectives and over all unit and entity activities. Its previous placement on the bottom level on the diagram perhaps better characterized this as an internal control foundation, providing support for other components. The new placement at the head of the stack gives the control environment an increased level of importance, just as an enterprise CEO appears at the top of a classic organization chart.

The control environment component of internal controls is influenced by a variety of internal and external factors, including the entity's history and values, its overall market, and the competitive and regulatory landscape. It is defined by the standards, processes, and structures that guide people at various levels in carrying out their responsibilities for internal controls and making decisions in the pursuit of the entity's objectives. An effective control environment creates the discipline that supports the assessment of risks necessary for the achievement of the entity's objectives, performance of control activities, and use of information and communication systems, as well as the conduct of monitoring activities. The revised COSO internal control framework introduces four principles for the risk-assessment component for an organization or an enterprise:

1. The organization specifies objectives with sufficient clarity to enable the identification and assessment of risks relating to objectives.
2. The enterprise identifies risks to the achievement of its objectives across the entity and analyzes risks as a basis for determining how the risks should be managed.
3. The organization considers the potential for fraud in assessing risks to the achievement of objectives.
4. The enterprise identifies and assesses changes that could significantly affect the system of internal controls.

An enterprise that establishes and maintains a strong control environment positions itself to be more resilient in the ever-changing face of internal and external pressures. It does this by demonstrating behaviors of integrity and ethical values, adequate oversight processes and structures, and organizational design that enables the achievement of the entity's objectives with an appropriate assignment of authority and responsibility, a high degree of competence, and a strong sense of accountability for the achievement of objectives. In both the short and the long term, effective control environment processes should position an enterprise and its key elements to be more resilient in the face of external pressures.

An enterprise's control environment can also be seen as synonymous with its internal control culture. Elements of a strong culture, such as integrity and ethical values, oversight, accountability, and performance evaluations, make the control environment strong as well. Culture is part of an enterprise's control environment but also encompasses elements of other components of internal control, such as establishing effective policies and procedures, ease of security controls or access to information, and the responsiveness to the results of monitoring activities. These issues will be discussed further in our review of other elements of the COSO internal control framework. Senior management should recognize that its organization's culture is influenced by the control environment that has been installed and established, as well as by other components of internal controls.

This important internal control objective emphasizes that senior management, the board of directors, or an equivalent oversight body should lead by example in developing values, an enterprise philosophy, and an operating style in the pursuit of the enterprise's objectives. What senior management does and says really sends a message to everyone associated with the enterprise. Effective control environment internal controls can be established through the following five control environment principles.

CONTROL ENVIRONMENT PRINCIPLE 1: INTEGRITY AND ETHICAL VALUES

The first principle of the revised COSO control environment calls for an enterprise to demonstrate a commitment to integrity and ethical values. Enterprise history and culture often play a major role in forming this internal control environment. When an enterprise historically has had a strong management emphasis on producing error-free products, when senior management continues to emphasize the importance of high-quality products, and when this message is communicated to all levels, this becomes a major enterprise control environment factor. The messages from the CEO or other very senior managers are known as the "tone at the top"—management's messages to all stakeholders. The message from the top should be more than just "we will comply with the law" types of statements. They should be far broader and should emphasize that an enterprise is committed to the highest ethical standards in every aspect of its business, including not only compliance but also in its business, sales, legal counseling, and human resource practices, as well as its treatment of employees and customers.

These are the messages and repeated commitments from leadership throughout the enterprise to emphasize the importance of compliance and ethical conduct that should be embraced and integrated into every level of business operations. However, if senior management gains a reputation of "looking the other way" at policy violations and makes other dubious-sounding statements, this same type of negative message will also be similarly communicated to other levels in the enterprise. A positive tone at the top calls for senior management to lead by example on matters of integrity and ethics; positive actions here are a foundation stone for establishing a strong control environment for the enterprise.

While this tone at the top is very important, an effective enterprise-wide code of conduct is equally or even more important in establishing an effective internal control environment. Codes of conduct have been in place at business organizations over the years, but they have traditionally been focused on lower-level staff members and not on the more senior members of management. They should be an important component of an effective system of internal controls for all members of an enterprise, from senior management to the operations staff and other stakeholders.

Establishing an Enterprise Code of Conduct

The effective enterprise today should develop and enforce a code of conduct that covers applicable ethical, business, and legal rules for all enterprise stakeholders, including the financial officers highlighted in SOx, all other employees, or a larger group stakeholders, such as vendors and consultants. The catalyst group to draft or launch such a code of conduct can be a special top management team, internal audit, or perhaps human resources. A select group should be a key participant in both helping to launch and then determining that the enterprise has an effective code of conduct that promotes ethical business practices.

A code of conduct should be a clear, unambiguous set of rules or guidance that outlines rules for what is expected of enterprise stakeholders, whether officers, employees, contractors, vendors, or any others. The code should be based on the values and the legal issues surrounding an enterprise. That is, while all enterprises should expect to have code of conduct prohibitions against sexual and racial discrimination, a defense contractor with many contract-related rules issues might have a somewhat different code of conduct than a fast-food store operation. However, the code should apply to all members of the enterprise, from the most senior level to a part-time clerical employee. For example, a code of conduct rule prohibiting erroneous financial reporting should be the same, whether directed at the CFO for deliberately incorrect quarterly financial reporting or at the part-timer for an incorrect or fraudulent weekly time card. Punishments and remedial measures should be applied to both.

If the enterprise already has a code of conduct, management may want to schedule a review from time to time to revisit that code. All too often, older codes were originally drafted as rules for the lower-level employees, with little attention to the more senior members of the enterprise. SOx and its overall corporate governance guidance was meant for those senior officers but should be delivered in such a manner that it will apply to all enterprise stakeholders. Working with senior members of management and the audit committee, the management function responsible for administering the code of conduct can examine any existing code of conduct to determine if those rules still fit for our post-SOx and improved governance eras of today.

Whether a revision to an existing code of conduct or the development of a new code, a joint team from a cross-section of management, including legal and human resources, should be assembled to develop their code. The team should examine the business issues facing the enterprise and then draft a set of code rules that are applicable to that enterprise, depending on its business and related issues. The code rules must be written in a clear manner, such that the points can be easily understood by all. Exhibit 4.1 lists some examples of code of conduct topics. While this list does not apply to all enterprises, these topics may be appropriate for many enterprises today. The key is that messages delivered in the code must be clear and unambiguous. This author led a project to develop and implement a code of conduct for a large US corporation some years ago. The following is an example of the rules from that code of conduct on a section covering company assets:

> We all have a responsibility to care for all of the company's assets, including inventory, cash, supplies, facilities, and the services of other employees and computer systems resources. If you see or suspect that another employee is stealing, engaging in fraudulent activities, or otherwise not properly protecting company assets, you may report these activities to your manager or to the ethics office.

EXHIBIT 4.1   Example Enterprise Code of Conduct Topics

The following are topic areas found in a typical enterprise stakeholder code of conduct. The actual code should have specific rules in each of these areas.

I. INTRODUCTION

    A. Purpose of This Code of Conduct: A general statement about the background of the code of conduct, emphasizing enterprise traditions.

    B. The Enterprise's Commitment to Strong Ethical Standards: A restatement of the mission statement and a supporting message from the CEO.

    C. Where to Seek Guidance for questions and concerns about the code.

    D. Reporting Noncompliance and Guidance for Whistleblowers.

    E. Stakeholder Responsibility to Acknowledge the Code: A description of the code acknowledgment process for all stakeholders.

II. FAIR DEALING STANDARDS

    A. Enterprise Selling Practices: Guidance for dealing with customers.

    B. Enterprise Buying Practices: Guidance and policies for dealing with vendors.

III. CONDUCT IN THE WORKPLACE

    A. Equal Employment Opportunity Standards: A strong commitment statement.

    B. Workplace and Sexual Harassment Policies: An equally strong commitment statement.

    C. Alcohol and Substance Abuse: A policy statement in this area.

IV. CONFLICTS OF INTEREST

    A. Outside Employment: Limitations on accepting employment from competitors.

    B. Personal Investments: Rules regarding using enterprise data to make personal investment decisions.

    C. Gifts and Other Benefits: Rules regarding receiving bribes and improper gifts.

    D. Former Employees: Rules prohibiting giving favors to ex-employees in business.

    E. Family Members: Rules about giving business to family members, creating potential conflicts of interest, and problematic family member-employee relationships.

V. ENTERPRISE PROPERTY AND RECORDS

    A. Enterprise Assets: A strong statement on the employees' responsibility to protect all assets, including IT resources.

    B. Use of the Enterprise's Name: A rule that the enterprise name should be used only for normal business dealings.

    C. Enterprise Records: A rule regarding employee responsibility for records integrity.

    D. Confidential Information: Rules on the importance of keeping all enterprise information confidential and not disclosing it to outsiders.

    E. Employee Privacy: A strong statement on the importance of keeping employees' personal information confidential from outsiders and even other employees.

    F. Enterprise Benefits: A rule that stakeholders must not take enterprise benefits where they are not entitled.

VI. COMPLYING WITH THE LAW

    A. Inside Information and Insider Trading: A strong rule prohibiting insider trading or otherwise benefiting from inside information.

    B. Political Contributions and Activities: A strong statement on political activity rules.

(Continued)

EXHIBIT 4.1 *(Continued)*

C. Bribery and Kickbacks: A firm rule against using bribes or accepting kickbacks.

D. Foreign Business Dealings: Rules regarding dealing with foreign agents in line with the Foreign Corrupt Practices Act.

E. Workplace Safety: A statement on the enterprise's policy to comply with safety rules.

F. Product Safety: A statement on the enterprise's commitment to product safety.

G. Environmental Protection: A rule regarding the enterprise's commitment to comply with applicable environmental laws.

Affirming Adherence to the Code of Conduct

An enterprise's code of conduct must be a *living document.* It has little value if it has been developed, delivered to all stakeholders with much hullabaloo, and then essentially filed and forgotten after that initial launch. If it is a new code of conduct or even a major revision of the existing code, the enterprise should make a concerted effort to deliver a copy of that code of conduct to all employees and stakeholders. An important step would be to formally present that new code of conduct to the enterprise's top managers, and particularly the financial officers. Codes of conduct in the past sometimes received only token acceptance from the senior officer group, with a feeling that they were really for the staff and not for top-level executives. The reported financial scandals that led up to SOx really highlighted this discrepancy.

Members of the senior management group should be required to formally acknowledge that they have read, understood, and will abide by this code of conduct. With the management team standing behind it, the enterprise should next roll out and then deliver the code of conduct to all enterprise stakeholders. This can be done in multiple phases, with delivery to local or more major facilities first, followed by smaller units, foreign locations, and other stakeholders. Rather than just including a copy of the code with payroll documents, an enterprise should make a formal effort to present the code in a manner that will gain attention.

A new code of conduct can be communicated through a video by the CEO, Webcasts, Webinar training sessions, or other means to communicate the importance and meaning of that code of conduct. Special communication methods might be used for other groups, such as vendors or contractors, but an enterprise objective should be to get all stakeholders to formally acknowledge that they will abide by the enterprise's code of conduct. This can be accomplished by an Internet or telephone response type of system, where every enterprise stakeholder is asked to respond to these three questions:

1. Have you received and read a copy of the Code of Conduct? Answer Yes or No.
2. Do you understand the contents of the Code of Conduct? Answer Yes if you understand this Code of Conduct or No if you have questions.
3. Do you agree to abide by the policies and guidelines in this Code of Conduct? Answer Yes if you agree to abide by the Code and No if you do not.

Every employee and stakeholder should be required to acknowledge acceptance of their enterprise's code of conduct. Responses should be recorded on a database listing the employee name and the date of his or her review and acceptance or nonacceptance. Any questions from number 2, above, can be handled through a whistleblower type of program. The idea is to have everyone—all of the stakeholders—buy into the code of conduct concept and agree to its terms. If someone refuses to accept the code because of questions, supervisors or others should discuss the matter with that person to gain eventual resolution. The final issue here is that the enterprise should expect all employees to agree to accept and abide by the enterprise's code of conduct. Following that code of conduct is just another work rule, and consistent failure to abide by these rules should be grounds for termination.

The whole concept behind this code acknowledgement requirement is to avoid any "I didn't know that was the rule" excuses in the future if any code violations are encountered. It is a good idea to go through the code acceptance process on an annual basis or at least after any revision to the code document. The files documenting these code acknowledgments should be retained in a secure manner.

Code Violations and Corrective Actions

An enterprise-wide code of conduct lays out a set of rules for expected behavior in the enterprise. While SOx requires that financial officers must subscribe to a code containing rules prohibiting fraudulent financial reporting, an enterprise should release a single code of conduct with guidance for all stakeholders—the SOx-designated financial officers, as well as employees at all levels, contractors, vendors, and others. In addition to publishing a code of conduct and obtaining stakeholder acceptance, there also is a need for a mechanism to report code violations and for investigating and handling those violations.

The objective here is that if the enterprise issues a strong code of conduct, along with a message from the CEO about the importance of good ethical practices, all stakeholders are expected to follow those rules. However, we all know that people are people, and there will always be some who violate the rules or run on the edge. An enterprise needs to establish a mechanism to allow employees or even related stakeholders to report potential violations of the code in a secure manner and confidential manner. Much of that reporting mechanism can be handled through the whistleblower facility, as discussed in Chapter 18.

In addition to the whistleblower facility, the enterprise should establish other mechanisms for reporting potential code of conduct violations. An independent facility to anonymously take calls, investigate, and report the concern to appropriate management is often the best solution. A well-publicized post office box address is also sometimes very effective. Stakeholders could be encouraged to write to such a PO box, anonymously or not, to report ethics and other internal control violations. Based on these responses, human resources or some other appropriate function in the enterprise should investigate the matter and take action as necessary.

A code of conduct describes a series of rules for expected actions in the enterprise. When violations are found, the matter should be investigated and actions taken on a consistent basis, no matter the rank of the enterprise stakeholders. If the code of conduct prohibits making copies of corporate software—and it should—the penalties for a staff analyst in a remote sales office or a senior manager in corporate headquarters should be the same. Assuming they both read the prohibition in the code and acknowledged acceptance, penalties for violations should be consistent. Otherwise, there can be an atmosphere where the rules appear to apply only to some.

Most code of conduct violations can be handled through the enterprise's normal human resources procedures, which should have processes where there may be verbal counseling or probation for a first offense and up to termination for reoccurrences. Some matters must be reported to outside authorities. A violation of SOx rules, such as a recently discovered undocumented off-balance sheet arrangement, would be reported to the Securities and Exchange Commission (SEC), or the theft of goods from a warehouse would be reported to a county prosecutor. When these matters are discovered and reported to outside authorities, the matter moves outside of the enterprise's hands. The overall goal here is that the enterprise must have some process in place to encourage all stakeholders to follow good ethical practices, as defined in the code of conduct, and to provide a consistent mechanism for reporting violations and taking disciplinary action when necessary.

CONTROL ENVIRONMENT PRINCIPLE 2: ROLE OF THE BOARD OF DIRECTORS

The control environment is very much influenced by the actions of an enterprise's board of directors and its audit committee with the principle:

> The board of directors demonstrates independence from management and exercises oversight of the development and performance of internal control.

In the years prior to SOx, boards and their audit committees often were dominated by senior management inside directors, often with a limited representation from outside minority board members. This created situations where the boards were not totally independent of management. Enterprise officers sat on the board and were, in effect, managing themselves, often with less concern for the outside investors. SOx changed this and requires audit committees to be truly independent. An active and independent board is an essential component of the COSO control environment. By setting high-level policies and by reviewing overall enterprise conduct, the board and its audit committee have the ultimate responsibility for setting this "tone at the top."

An independent board must have a close relationship with senior management to ensure effective and successful enterprise operations and a strong internal control environment. The board of directors or an equivalent oversight body should identify and understand the expectations of stakeholders, including customers, employees, investors, and the general public, as well as the legal and regulatory requirements. These expectations should help shape the objectives of the enterprise and the oversight responsibilities of the board. The following board of directors' activities may assist management in determining whether this COSO control environment principle is present and functioning.

- **Establish oversight responsibilities**. The board of directors should identify and accept its oversight responsibilities in relation to both established legal requirements and stakeholder, investor, and public expectations.
- **Apply relevant expertise**. The board of directors should define, maintain, and periodically evaluate the skills and expertise needed among its members to enable them to ask probing questions of senior management and take commensurate actions.
- **Operate independently**. The board of directors should have sufficient members who are independent from management and are objective in their evaluations and decision making.
- **Provide oversight for the system of internal controls**. The board of directors retains oversight responsibility for management's development and performance of internal controls.

The board of directors should review and approve policies and practices that support the performance of internal controls across the business in regular meetings between management and the board. The processes and structures particularly relevant to the audit committee of the board are those that provide an oversight for the system of internal control. Through the joint efforts of the board and senior management, the following points of focus may assist in determining whether this control environment principle is present and functioning:

- **Setting the tone at the top**. As we have discussed, the board of directors and management at all levels of the enterprise must demonstrate through their directives, actions, and behaviors the importance of integrity and ethical values to support the functioning of the system of internal controls.
- **Establishing standards of conduct**. The expectations of the board of directors and senior management concerning integrity and ethical values are defined in the entity's standards of conduct and understood at all levels of the enterprise and by outsourced service providers and business partners.
- **Evaluating adherence to standards of conduct**. Processes should be in place to evaluate the performance of individuals and teams against the entities expected standards of conduct.
- **Addressing deviations in a timely manner**. Deviations of the enterprise code of conduct and related standards should be identified and remedied in a timely and consistent manner.

CONTROL ENVIRONMENT PRINCIPLE 3: THE NEED FOR AUTHORITY AND RESPONSIBILITY

Management should establish, with appropriate board oversight, structures, reporting lines, and appropriate authorities and responsibilities in the pursuit of its internal control objectives. Senior management and the board of directors should establish an organizational structure, along with appropriate reporting lines necessary to plan, execute, control, and periodically assess the activities of the overall enterprise. This control environment goal is to provide for clear accountability and information flow within and across the overall enterprise and all of its subunits.

In order to determine that this internal control principle is functioning, management and the board of directors first consider the multiple operating units, legal entities, geographic distribution, and outsourced service providers in the enterprise to support the achievement of these objectives. With today's complex international enterprises having multiple agreements between operating units and outside providers, this can be a complex mix. Management should then design and evaluate lines of reporting for each entity structure to enable execution of authority and responsibilities and flow of information to manage the activities of the entity.

Based on this overall understanding, management and the board of directors should delegate authority, define responsibilities, use appropriate processes and technology to assign responsibilities, and segregate duties as necessary at the following various levels of the enterprise:

- **Board of directors**. There should be a clear understanding that the board retains authority over significant decisions and reviews management's assignments and the limitations of authority and responsibilities.
- **Enterprise officers and senior management**. The senior levels of enterprise management should establish directives, guidance, and controls to enable management and personnel to understand and carry out their internal control responsibilities.
- **Management**. These important members of the enterprise guide and facilitate the execution of senior management directives at the entity and its subunits.
- **All line and staff personnel**. All members of the enterprise should understand and agree to abide by the entity's codes of conduct. In addition, they should have an understanding of assessed risks related to internal control objectives and the related control activities at their respective levels of the entity, the expected information and communication flow, and monitoring activities relevant to their achievement of the objectives.
- **Outsourced service providers**. This group should adhere to management's definition of the scope of authority and responsibility for all nonemployees engaged.

Enterprises are usually structured in multiple dimensions, where legal entity structures are designed to manage business risks, create favorable tax structures, and empower management. In addition, the management operating model may be designed to follow product or service lines to facilitate the development of new products and services; to optimize marketing, production, and customer service; and to reflect appropriate geographic subdivisions. In addition, entities may also enter into a variety of relationships with external parties to support the achievement of objectives, which creates additional structures and reporting lines.

As somewhat of a current trend, we sometimes encounter smaller enterprises where a senior manager does not allow the department or unit heads to publish classic organization charts, feeling that these are too limiting. However, that is an internal control weakness for all but the very smallest of enterprises. Senior management should prepare organizational charts to document, communicate, and enforce accountability for the achievement of the entity's financial reporting objectives. The organizational charts can be used to

- Set forth assignments of authority and responsibility.
- Ensure that duties are appropriately segregated.
- Establish reporting lines and communication channels.
- Define the various reporting dimensions relevant to the organization.
- Identify dependencies for roles and responsibilities involved in financial reporting, as well as for those accountable for external parties.

Each unit or department within the enterprise that is relevant to external financial reporting should align its roles and responsibilities to processes supporting the financial reporting objectives. Senior management and the board of directors should verify that accountability and information flow within each of the various organizational structures, by business segment, geographical location, legal entity, or other, to continually support the achievement of the existing financial reporting objectives.

Many enterprises of all types and sizes today have streamlined their operations and pushed their decision-making authority downward and closer to the front-line personnel. A strong control environment says that front-line employees should have the knowledge and power to make appropriate decisions in their own area of operations, rather than be required to pass the request for a decision up through enterprise channels. The critical challenge that goes with this delegation or empowerment is that although they can delegate some authority in order to achieve objectives, senior management is ultimately responsible for the decisions made by those subordinates. An enterprise can place itself at risk if too many decisions involving higher-level objectives are assigned at inappropriately lower levels without adequate management review. In addition, each person in the enterprise must have a good understanding of the enterprise's overall objectives, as well as how individual actions interrelate to achieve those objectives. Enterprise management should recognize that this control environment component of the COSO framework is greatly influenced by the extent to which individuals recognize they will be held accountable. This holds true for all members of the enterprise, from staff members all the way up to the chief executive, who has ultimate responsibility for all activities within an entity, including the internal control system.

CONTROL ENVIRONMENT PRINCIPLE 4: HUMAN RESOURCE STRENGTHS

The enterprise should demonstrate a commitment to attract, develop, and retain competent individuals in alignment with its objectives. Human resources policies and practices are the high-level guidance and behavior factors that reflect the expectations and requirements of investors, regulators, and other stakeholders. They provide the foundation for defining the competence needed within the enterprise and provide the basis for more detailed procedures for executing and evaluating performance, as well as determining remedial actions as necessary. These human resources factor policies and practices provide

- Requirements and rationales, such as the implications of product safety laws, regulations, and standards, all of which will affect the performance of the enterprise staff and its managers.
- Skills and conduct necessary to support strong internal control practices in the achievement of enterprise objectives. An example here might include the need for some knowledge of the operation of the technology platforms that underpin business processes.
- Defined accountability for the performance of key business functions. An example here might be defining product safety standards and areas of applicability within the entity.
- A defined basis for evaluating shortcomings in operations and defining remedial actions. These might include correcting processes or sharpening the skills of management and other personnel.
- The means to react dynamically to change in such areas as new regulatory requirements, identified new risks, or internal decisions to modify business processes that are reflected in enterprise policies that cascade throughout applicable operating procedures.

Controls and practices here enable a focus on enterprise competence that should permeate the enterprise. Starting with the board of directors' oversight of the CEO, the CEO's responsibility for senior management, and cascading down to various levels in management, the resulting commitment to competence facilitates measuring this achievement of objectives at all levels of the enterprise, as well as outsourced service providers, by demonstrating how processes should be carried out and what skills and behaviors need to be applied.

Commitment to Competence

The COSO internal control element of human resource competencies specifies that policies and measures should be in place to qualify stakeholders to carry out their assigned responsibilities, and this requires relevant skills and expertise, which are gained largely from professional experience, training, and certifications. A commitment to competence is expressed through individuals' attitudes and behaviors in carrying out their responsibilities.

An enterprise human resources function can often help define competence and staffing levels by job role, facilitating training and maintaining completion records and evaluating the relevance and adequacy of individual professional development in relation to the enterprise's needs. COSO goes a bit stronger on individual competence issues than does the typical enterprise human resources function today, which is often more wrapped up in such matters as diversity issues than in concerns with employee skills. This control environment principle calls for enterprises to define their competence requirements as needed to support the achievement of their internal control objectives, with consideration given to

- Knowledge, skills, and experience needs.
- Nature and degree of judgment and limitations of authority to be applied to specific positions.
- Cost-benefit analyses of different levels of skills and experience.
- Trade-offs between the extent of supervision and the requisite competence levels of individual employees.

The above items raise some hard issues that are often not really considered by management when evaluating the firm's employees. The control environment is enhanced when we have only the right people in the right jobs.

This principle goes on to say that the board of directors should evaluate the competence of the CEO, and, in turn, management should evaluate competencies across the enterprise and outsourced service providers in relation to established policies and procedures, as well as act as necessary to address any shortcomings or excesses. The COSO guidance uses the example that a changing risk portfolio may cause an enterprise to shift resources toward areas of the business that require greater attention. Here, as an enterprise brings a new product to market, it may elect to increase staffing in its sales and marketing teams, or as a new applicable regulation is issued, it may focus on those individuals responsible for its implementation. Shortcomings may arise relating to staffing levels, skills, expertise, or a combination of such factors. Management is responsible for acting on such shortcomings in a timely manner.

Attracting, Developing, and Retaining Individual Employees and Stakeholders

COSO's commitment to competence is supported by and embedded in the human resource processes for attracting, developing, evaluating, and training the right fit of management, other personnel, and outsourced service providers. The adequate number of resources should be determined and periodically readjusted with consideration given to the relative importance of risks to be mitigated to support the achievement of the enterprise's objectives. Management at different levels should define policies, procedures, structures, and processes to

- **Attract.** Conduct formal, in-depth employment interviews to describe the enterprise's history, culture, and operating style. In addition, run background and reference checks and conduct procedures to determine whether a particular candidate fits with organizational needs and has the competence for a proposed job role.
- **Train.** Enable individuals to develop competencies appropriate to their assigned roles and responsibilities, reinforce standards of conduct and expected levels of competence for particular assignments, tailor training based on roles and needs, and consider a mix of delivery techniques, including classroom instruction, self-study, and on-the-job training.

- **Mentor.** Provide guidance on individual performance towards expected standards of conduct and competence, align individual personnel skills and experience with the enterprise's objectives, and help personnel adapt to an evolving environment.
- **Evaluate.** Measure the performance of individual personnel in relation to the achievement of objectives and demonstration of expected conduct, and against service level agreements and other standards for recruiting and compensating outsourced service providers.
- **Retain.** Provide incentives to motivate and reinforce expected levels of performance and desired conduct, including training and credentialing as appropriate.

Processes to attract, develop, and retain employees should be regularly reviewed and monitored. Any behavior or activities not consistent with an enterprise's code of conduct, policies, and internal control responsibilities should be identified, assessed, and corrected in a timely manner for all levels of the enterprise. This enables the enterprise to actively address competence to support the achievement of the enterprise's cost-and-benefit objectives.

Planning and Preparing for Personnel Succession

Management should continually identify and assess those performing functions that are considered to be essential to the enterprise's objectives. The importance of these roles is determined by assessing what the impact would be if that role was temporarily or permanently unfilled. For example, the CEO and other members of senior management, strategic suppliers, and channel partners are functions that typically require plans to be in place to make sure those objectives can still be achieved even in the absence of the individuals filling these roles. Senior management and the board should develop contingency plans for assigning these responsibilities that are crucial to internal controls. Succession plans for key managers at all levels should be defined with the identified candidates trained and coached for the assumption of these target roles.

Succession planning also should be undertaken when significant functions are delegated through contractual arrangements to outsourced service providers. When an enterprise places considerable reliance on an external party and has assessed the risk of that provider's processes or systems breaking down as having a direct impact on the enterprise's ability to achieve its objectives, some form of succession plan may be needed. Measures to provide for ongoing knowledge sharing and documentation will ease the succession of a new provider, if necessary.

 CONTROL ENVIRONMENT PRINCIPLE 5: INDIVIDUAL INTERNAL CONTROL RESPONSIBILITIES

An enterprise should hold its stakeholders accountable for their internal control responsibilities in the pursuit of overall enterprise objectives. Management and the board of directors should establish the mechanisms to communicate and hold individuals accountable for performance of internal control responsibilities across the organization and implement corrective action as necessary. As part of this, they should establish performance measures, incentives, and other rewards appropriate for responsibilities at all levels of the entity, reflecting appropriate dimensions of performance and expected standards of conduct and performance.

Accounting for Internal Controls

The board of directors ultimately holds the CEO accountable for internal controls in the enterprise's achievement of objectives. The CEO and other senior management, in turn, are responsible for designing, implementing, conducting, and periodically evaluating whether the defined structures, authorities, and responsibilities establish accountability for internal control at all levels of the enterprise. Accountability here refers to the level of ownership for, and the commitment to, the performance of internal controls in the pursuit of objectives. Management and the board should establish the mechanism to communicate and hold personnel accountable for their performance of internal control responsibilities across the enterprise and should take appropriate corrective actions as necessary.

Accountability for internal controls is interconnected with enterprise leadership and its tone-at-the-top messages. Related management messages throughout the enterprise should be strong, particularly where internal control responsibilities are understood, carried out, and reinforced. Senior management's tone helps establish and enforce accountability through the clarity of these messages, starting with senior management and then cascading throughout the enterprise.

Accountability by the enterprise's tone at the top and supported by the commitment to integrity and ethical values, competence, structure, and other elements of internal controls will collectively influence the control culture of the organization. Corrective action is taken as necessary to reestablish the necessary accountability for internal controls.

Performance Measures, Incentives, and Rewards

Individual performance is greatly enhanced by the extent to which individuals believe they will be held accountable and compensated fairly. Management and the board of directors should establish performance measures, incentives, and other rewards appropriate for responsibilities at all levels of the enterprise, considering the achievement of both short-term and long-term objectives. To support an enterprise's short- and long-term objectives, performance measures should be balanced to reward successes and discipline behaviors, as necessary, in line with the range of objectives. For example, an enterprise seeking to win customer loyalty with quality products should seek to reduce its production defect rate and align its performance measures, incentives, and rewards with both the operating unit's production goals and its expectations to comply with product safety standards.

Management and the board should regularly evaluate the performance of individuals and teams in relation to defined performance measures, which include business performance factors, as well as adherence to and support for standards of conduct and demonstrated competence. In general, effective human resource policies and procedures are a critical component in the overall control environment. Messages from the top of strong enterprise structures will accomplish little if the enterprise does not have strong human resource policies and procedures in place. The internal audit should always consider this element of the control environment when performing reviews of other elements of the internal control framework.

COSO CONTROL ENVIRONMENT IN PERSPECTIVE

Many senior business managers today often do not appropriately consider these control environment factors when looking at internal control systems. However, control environment factors are an important first step for establishing effective internal control processes. If management is setting the right example and employees know and respect management values, ethics and integrity, that attitude will be passed down to all employees, and the business will have a strong foundation.

The strength of any system is in its underlying foundation. No matter how complex the structure, if it doesn't have a solid foundation, its integrity will be unreliable. The foundation of a control system is the philosophy of the business and the people controlling the business. Before designing the controls, one must consider the foundation—its environment. The COSO control environment framework asks enterprise management to consider the following questions:

- Does management take undue business risks to achieve objectives?
- Does it encourage risk taking or an "achieve at all costs" attitude?
- Does management attempt to manipulate performance measures so that they appear more favorable?
- Does it bend the truth?
- Does management pressure employees to achieve results, regardless of the methods, or with little concern for those methods?
- Does management believe that the financial ends justify the means?
- Is management open and honest with employees about performance and results?

Enterprises are led from the top by senior management and the board of directors, and their business ethics and philosophies will be passed down from senior management to all levels of employees and stakeholders. The more ethical and responsible the management style, the more likely that employees will respond to that style and behave in an ethical and responsible manner. Alternately, if management shows little concern for honest and ethical behavior, the employees will tend to follow that lead.

The COSO framework control environment and its supporting principles are key and very important elements for establishing effective internal controls in an enterprise. COSO describes the importance of setting the tone of an enterprise and influencing the control consciousness of its people. An effective control environment supports and strengthens the other control elements, whereas a weak control environment undermines these elements, rendering them useless. In an effective control environment, personnel and all stakeholders know that doing the right thing is expected and will be supported by upper-level management, even if it hurts the bottom line. In a weak environment, control procedures can be frequently overridden or ignored, providing an opportunity for fraud.

This control environment and its five supporting principles are perhaps the most important component in the new revised COSO internal control framework. Its emphasis on the "tone at the top" provides guidance on how enterprise management should incorporate risk awareness and control activities into its daily work routines in the various managers' areas of responsibility. By maintaining a positive attitude toward internal controls and compliance with established enterprise policies, as well as with various legal requirements, management sets the tone for the entire area. Control environment also encompasses the culture, ethical values, teamwork, morale, and development of administrative employees.

This chapter has provided an overview of the COSO control environment as it is described in the new revised version of the COSO internal controls. We have extracted some of the more significant sections from the published control COSO document, but many others can be found in the actual COSO source materials at www.coso.org that provide, in total, some other general management guidance.

CHAPTER FIVE

COSO Internal Control Components: Risk Assessment

E VERY ENTERPRISE FACES A VARIETY of risks from both internal and external sources. Risk here is defined as the possibility that an event may occur that adversely affects the achievement of enterprise objectives. Risk assessment is an interactive process for identifying and assessing those risks that may limit the achievement of enterprise objectives. Risks to achieve these objectives are considered relative to risk tolerances established by the enterprise.

Risks are defined in the COSO internal control framework as the possibility that an event may occur that will adversely affect the achievement of some enterprise objectives. As part of the process of identifying and assessing risks, an enterprise may also identify opportunities when the occurrence of a risk-related event may positively affect the achievement of enterprise objectives. These opportunities are important to capture and to channel back to the enterprise strategy and/or objective-setting processes. However, the identification and assessment of potential risk-related opportunities are often not directly part of enterprise internal controls but are sometimes dependent on external factors.

Risks affect an enterprise's ability to succeed, compete within its industry, maintain its financial strength and positive reputation, and maintain the overall quality of its products, services, and people. There is no practical way to reduce risk to zero, because all business activities involve some amount of risk. Management, however, must determine how much risk is to be prudently accepted and must strive to maintain risk within these limits, understanding how much tolerance it has for exceeding its target risk levels.

This chapter introduces and summarizes the very important risk assessment component of the newly revised COSO internal control framework. This component has caused some confusion among professionals in the past because several years after the original 1992 internal control framework was issued, COSO released its enterprise risk management framework—COSO ERM—which looked very similar to, but was different from, COSO internal controls. COSO ERM and the risk assessment component here are separate but related concepts. Chapter 16 introduces and discusses COSO ERM, as well as the principles and the important elements of risk assessment as part of effective internal control processes.

RISK ASSESSMENT COMPONENT PRINCIPLES

A very fundamental risk management definition that supports this COSO element is:

> Risk management is a central part of any organization's strategic management. It is the process whereby organizations methodically address the risks attaching to their activities with the goal of achieving sustained benefit within each activity and across the portfolio of all activities.[1]

Risk assessment forms the basis for determining how all levels of risks will be managed, and a precondition to risk assessment is the establishment of risk-related objectives, linked at different levels of the enterprise. However, because of the types and nature of the risks an enterprise will encounter, management should identify and specify its risk objectives within operations, reporting, and compliance categories with sufficient clarity to be able to identify and analyze the risks to those objectives. Management should also consider the suitability of the objectives for the entity. In addition, risk assessment requires management to consider the impact of possible changes in the external environment and within its own business model that may render its internal controls ineffective.

Although the original and current revised frameworks look very similar, there have been major changes in COSO's published internal control guidance.[2] In this chapter and all others following, we have summarized many key points from this guidance material, but the interested manager should acquire a personal copy from www.coso.org for a complete description. This document is available for purchase either in a hard copy or a downloaded version. The COSO internal guidance materials outline a series of risk assessment principles, including the following four key concepts:

1. The organization specifies objectives with sufficient clarity to enable the identification and assessment of risks relating to its objectives,
2. The organization identifies risks to the achievement of its objectives across the entity and analyzes those risks as a basis for determining how the risks should be managed,
3. The enterprise considers the potential for fraud in assessing risks to the achievement of objectives,
4. The organization identifies and assesses changes that could significantly affect the performance of its of internal controls.

The first and a key internal control principle here calls for an enterprise to specify its risk objectives with sufficient clarity to enable the identification and assessment of risks relating to those objectives. The senior manager may recognize that this sounds good but may wonder about what COSO means by a "risk objective." Some examples may help. Consider a for-profit retail merchandiser who may establish business and environmental risk objectives that include

- Providing customers with a broad range of merchandise at prices consistently lower than its competitors,
- Increasing the enterprise-wide inventory turnover ratio to 12 times per year,
- Lowering enterprise packaging and shipping department CO_2 emissions and reducing and recycling 40 percent of all packaging materials,
- Broadening the number of supply vendors to speed up time to market and reduce exposures to loss of supply from any one vendor.

A clear set of objectives for these operations risks provide a clear focus on which ones the enterprise will commit the often substantial resources needed to achieve desired performance goals. This is often an area where things can break down. It is easy for any senior manager, from the CEO on down, to state that he or she wants to accomplish some warm and fuzzy-sounding goal in some future period, but these words are of little value unless they are backed up by firm objective performance goals or numbers. These include goals relating to financial performance, which pertain to all types of enterprises. A for-profit entity may focus on revenue, profitability, or some other measures, while a not-for-profit or governmental unit may have less financial emphasis overall but still pursue goals relating to revenue, liquidity, and spending. If an enterprise's risk objectives are not clear or well-conceived, its resources may be misdirected.

As an important element of defining and developing risk objectives, an enterprise should identify risks that may hamper the achievement of these risk objectives across the overall entity and analyze them as a basis for determining how they should be managed. In particular, the enterprise should identify and assess changes that could significantly affect the system of internal controls. In addition, consideration should be given to both the potential for fraud in assessing risks to the achievement of objectives and the relative materiality of the matter. That is, if the risk leads to a potentially fraudulent situation, much more attention should be given to establishing protections to cover that risk.

Materiality is a financial reporting concept, in which an enterprise or its external auditors can say that when a potential error or loss is not large enough to affect enterprise earnings in a significant way, it will not be considered material and therefore can be all but ignored. Prior to the enactment of SOx in 2002, public accounting firms frequently ignored what seemed to be large errors or losses because they viewed them as "not material," reasoning that the amount of the loss would not affect a measure such as financial earnings per share. With SOx, financial rules for materiality have tightened, but management should establish clear and reasonable risk management rules based on the size and scope of the risks it encounters. The COSO internal control guidance for the revised framework emphasizes the importance of materiality with regard to enterprise risks.

Risks to the achievement of these objectives from across the enterprise also should be considered relative to established risk tolerances. Thus, risk assessment forms the basis for determining how risks will be managed. A precondition to risk assessment is the establishment of objectives linked at different levels of the enterprise. Management specifies objectives within categories relating to operations, reporting, and compliance with sufficient clarity to be able to identify and analyze risks to those objectives. Management should also consider the suitability of the objectives for the entity. In addition, risk assessment requires management to consider the impact of possible changes in the external environment and within its own business model that may render internal controls ineffective.

 ## RISK IDENTIFICATION AND ANALYSIS

Enterprise management at all levels should endeavor to identify all possible risks that may affect the success of an enterprise, ranging from the larger or more significant risks to the overall business down to the less major risks associated with individual projects or smaller business units. The risk identification process requires a studied, deliberate approach to looking at potential risks in each area of operations and then identifying the more significant risk areas that may affect each operation in a reasonable time period. The idea is not to simply list every possible risk but to identify those that might affect operations, with some level of probability, within a reasonable time period. This can be a difficult exercise because we usually do not know the probability of some risk occurring or the nature of the consequences if the enterprise has to face the risk.

While COSO's focus is on external financial reporting, the risk identification process should occur at multiple levels in an enterprise. A risk that affects an individual business unit or project may not have that great of an impact on the entire enterprise or beyond. Conversely, a major risk that affects the entire economy will flow down to the individual enterprise and the separate business units. Some major risks are so infrequent but still can be so cataclysmic that it is difficult to identify them as possible future events.

Identifying and analyzing risks should be an ongoing iterative process conducted to enhance an enterprise's ability to achieve its objectives. Although an enterprise may not explicitly state all of its risk-related objectives, this does not mean that an implied objective is without either internal or external risk, and the enterprise should consider all risks that may occur.

A good way to start the risk identification process is to begin with a high-level enterprise chart the lists corporate-level, as well as operating, units. Each of those units may have facilities in multiple global locations and also may consist of multiple and different types of operations. Each separate facility will then have its own departments or functions. Some of these separate facilities may be closely connected to one another, while others represent little more than corporate investments. A difficult and sometimes complicated task, an enterprise-wide initiative should be launched to identify all risks in various individual areas. This type of exercise can gain interesting and/or troubling results. For example, a corporate level may be aware of some almost trivial product liability risks, but a front-line supervisor in an operating unit may look at the same risks with an entirely different and more severe perspective.

Various members of the enterprise at different organization levels will look at some of the same risks from varying viewpoints. A marketing manager may be concerned about competitor pricing strategies or the risk of pricing activities that would put the enterprise in violation of restraint-of-trade laws. An IT manager may be concerned about the risk of a computer virus denial of service attack on application systems but will have little knowledge of those same pricing-issue risks. More senior management typically will be aware of a different level and set of risks than would be on the minds of the operations-oriented staff members. Still, all of these risks should at least be identified and considered on an operating unit-by-unit basis and over the entire enterprise.

To be effective, an enterprise risk identification process should be supported by a variety of activities, techniques, and mechanisms, each relevant to the overall risk assessment. Management should consider these risks at all levels and take necessary steps to manage them. The risk assessment should consider factors that influence the severity, velocity, and persistence of the risk, its likelihood of the loss of assets, and the related impact on operations, reporting, and compliance activities. In addition, the enterprise needs to understand its tolerance for accepting risks and its ability to operate within those risk levels. While certainly not all inclusive, Exhibit 5.1 lists some example major risk areas that may affect the enterprise, including strategic, operations, and finance risks. This is the type of high-level list that a chief executive officer might use to jot down in response to a stockholder meeting question, "What worries you at the end of the day?" Certainly not listing all risks facing the enterprise, this is the type of first-pass list that an enterprise can use to get started on a detailed identification of risks. The people responsible for risk management in the enterprise—often, an enterprise risk management team—can meet with senior management and ask some of these "What worries you . . ." types of questions to identify such high-level risks.

Once the enterprise has performed this preliminary risk identification, it should consider all significant risk-related interactions—including goods, services, and information—internal to the enterprise and between it and relevant external parties. Those external parties can include potential and existing suppliers, investors, creditors, shareholders, and other stakeholders, as well as customers, intermediaries, and competitors. In addition, the enterprise should consider such external issues as new laws and regulations, environmental issues, and potential natural events, among many others.

Risk identification is an iterative process and is often integrated with other major business processes, such as planning. The COSO guidance here states that it may be useful to take a fresh look at the identified risks and not merely default to taking an inventory of risks that may have been identified in a previous review. The focus here should be on identifying all risks that potentially affect the achievement of objectives, as well as emerging risks—those risks that are increasingly important to the enterprise and may be addressed by analyzing all relevant risk factors, as remote as they may seem.

The risk identification process should consider all risks within an enterprise, including its subunits and operational functions, such as finance, human resources, marketing, production, purchasing, and IT management. In addition, this process should consider risks originating from outsourced service providers, key suppliers, and channel partners that directly or indirectly affect an enterprise's achievement of objectives. COSO suggests that management should consider risks in relation to internal and external factors.

In conducting these risk assessments, management should consider the rate of change in determining the frequency of the risk assessment process. Although risk assessment is a dynamic process, enterprises should use a combination of ongoing and periodic risk assessments. While it may not be feasible to continuously consider all risks due to their rate

EXHIBIT 5.1 Types of Enterprise Business Risks

Strategic Risk		
External Factors Risks	**Internal Factors Risks**	
• Industry Risk • Economy Risk • Competitor Risk • Legal and Regulatory Change Risk • Customer Needs and Wants Risk	• Reputation Risk • Strategic Focus Risk • Parent Company Support Risk • Patent / Trademark Protection Risk	

Operations Risks		
Process Risks	**Compliance Risks**	**People Risks**
• Supply Chain Risk • Customer Satisfaction Risk • Cycle Time Risk • Process Execution Risk	• Environmental Risk • Regulatory Risk • Policy and Procedures Risk • Litigation Risk	• Human Resources Risk • Employee Turnover Risk • Performance Incentive Risk • Training Risk

Finance Risks		
Treasury Risks	**Credit Risks**	**Trading Risks**
• Interest Rate Risk • Foreign Exchange Risk • Capital Availability Risk	• Capacity Risk • Collateral Risk • Concentration Risk • Default Risk • Settlement Risk	• Commodity Price Risk • Duration Risk • Measurement Risk

Information Risks		
Financial Risks	**Operational Risks**	**Technology Risks**
• Accounting Standards Risk • Budgeting Risk • Financial Reporting Risk • Taxation Risk • Regulatory Reporting Risk	• Pricing Risk • Performance Measurement Risk • Employee Safety Risk	• Information Access Risk • Business Continuity Risk • Availability Risk • Infrastructure Risk

of change, other operational priorities, or other cost considerations, it is useful to accelerate the frequency of assessing the related risks or assess the risks on a real-time basis.

Examples of external risk factors:

▪ Economic changes that can affect financing, capital availability, and barriers to competitive entry.
▪ Natural or human-caused catastrophes or ongoing climate changes that can lead to changes in operations, reduced availability of raw materials, or loss of information systems, highlighting the need for contingency planning.
▪ A new financial reporting standard that can require different or additional reporting policies and strategies.

- A new antitrust law or regulation that can affect product development, production processes, customer service, pricing, or warranties.
- Technological developments that can affect the availability and use of data, infrastructure costs, and the demand for technology-based services.

Some internal risk factors may include:

- Decisions on the use of capital resources that can affect operations and the ongoing availability of infrastructure resources.
- A change in management responsibilities that can affect the way certain internal controls are effected.
- The quality of personnel hired and methods for training and motivation that can influence the level of control consciousness within the enterprise.
- The nature of the enterprise's activities and employee accessibility to assets that can contribute to misappropriation of resources.
- The expiration of labor agreements that can affect the availability of staff.
- A disruption of IT systems processing that can adversely affect an enterprise's overall operations.

The identification of these internal and external risk factors is critical for an enterprise. Once major factors have been identified, management can then consider their relevance and significance and, where possible, link these to specific factors and activities. Where these factors are noted, management should also consider—in conjunction with the COSO Information and Communication principles discussed in Chapter 7—whether some form of internal and/or external communications is needed.

After risks have been identified at both an entity level and the transaction level, a risk analysis needs to be performed. This methodology can vary, largely because many risks are difficult to quantify. However, this process includes assessing the likelihood of the risk occurring and estimating its impact. In addition, the process could consider other criteria to the extent that management considers necessary. While the COSO internal control descriptive materials includes no formal guidance, enterprise management should develop a formal or even informal risk assessment process that it can use on a consistent basis.

Exhibit 5.2 is an example of a risk assessment process based on a sample company, Global Computer Products, that we are first introducing in this chapter and will encounter in other chapters going forward. The exhibit outlines the process of determining the significance or impact and the likelihood of identified risks for determining the higher-risk items that require risk response plans.

"Likelihood" indicates the possibility—such as high, medium, or low—that a risk will even occur, and "impact" represents its effect. Although these two terms are commonly used, other expressions, such as *severity*, *probability*, or *seriousness*, are appropriate as well.

Another term, *risk velocity*, refers to the pace with which the enterprise is expected to experience the impact of the risk. For example, our sample company, Global Computer Products, a manufacturer of consumer electronics, may be concerned about changing

- Establish a scoring system for impacts and probabilities.
- List threats to urgent processes that were determined by a management analysis.
- Estimate the impact on the enterprise-identified threats using the scoring system.
- Determine the likelihood or probability of each threat and weigh them per an established scoring system.
- Calculate a relative risk for each identified item and weigh them according to a numerical scoring system.
- Calculate relative risks for each item by combining the scores for impact and probability for each threat using an agreed-on formula.
- Prioritize calculated risks using an approach that includes measures to controls these threats.
- Obtain management approval for these risk priorities.
- Review any earlier risk management control strategies with an objective to bring all assessments in concurrence with current risk management approaches for the threats.
- Consider the use of other appropriate risk management strategies, such as:
  - Transferring risks through increased insurance.
  - Formally accepting risks where impacts or probabilities are low.
  - Reducing risks through the introduction of other controls.
  - Avoiding risks through such tactics as removing the source or the cause of a threat.
- Ensure that planned risk measures do not increase other risks, such as outsourcing an activity that may decrease some risks but increase others.
- Obtain senior management and audit committee approval for these proposed risk management controls.

EXHIBIT 5.2 Risk Assessment Process Steps

---

customer preferences and compliance with radio frequency energy limits. Failing to manage either of these risks may result in significant erosion in enterprise value, even to the point of being put out of business. In this instance, changes in regulatory requirements develop much more slowly, and have a low velocity, while consumer preference changes are a high-velocity risk.

Inherent risk and *residual risk* are two other important terms in risk analysis; COSO guidance calls for management to consider both inherent and residual risk in its risk management activities. In financial auditing, inherent risk refers to the risk of a material misstatement of facts prior to (or excluding the possible effects of) any internal controls. Inherent risk is a risk that is impossible to manage or transfer away. The bottom line here is that we will always have some inherent risk in all levels of operations and processes.

Residual risk is the risk that remains after management's risk responses have been developed. No matter how strong a risk assessment and correction program is, there will always be some residual risk. There are no zero-risk situations.

 ## RISK RESPONSE STRATEGIES

Enterprises should develop risk management strategies as part of their risk management processes. Risk management strategies address how an enterprise intends to assess risk, respond to, and monitor risk—making explicit and transparent the risk perceptions that an enterprise routinely uses in making both investment and operational decisions. Risk response strategies are a key part of enterprise risk management strategies.

As a key component of COSO internal controls, response strategies are essential. Once the potential significance of risks has been assessed, management should consider how these risks should be managed. This often involves judgments based on assumptions about the risk and a reasonable analysis of the costs associated with reducing the levels of risk. The risk response process need not necessarily result in the least amount of residual risk. However, where a risk response would result in residual risk exceeding levels acceptable to management and the board, management should revisit and revise this risk response or, in certain instances, reconsider the established risk tolerance.

The COSO revised internal control guidance materials identify four basic risk response strategy approaches:

1. **Avoidance**. This is a strategy of walking away from the risk—such as selling a business unit that gives rise to the risk, exiting from a geographic area of concern, or dropping a product line. The difficulty here is that enterprises often do not drop a product line or walk away until after the risk event has occurred, with its associated costs. Unless an enterprise has a very low appetite for risk, it is difficult to walk away from a business area or a product line only on the basis of a potential future risk, if all is going well in the present with other respects. Avoidance can be a potentially costly strategy, if investments were made to get into an area with a subsequent pull-out to avoid the risk.

   A collective "lessons learned" understanding of past activities can often help with this strategy. If the enterprise had been involved in some area in the past with unfavorable consequences, this may be a good way to avoid the risk once again. With the tendency of constant organizational changes and short employment tenures, this collective history is often lost and forgotten. An enterprise's well-understood and communicated appetite for risk is perhaps the most important consideration when deciding whether a risk avoidance strategy is appropriate.

2. **Reduction**. Many business decisions may be able to reduce certain risks. For example, product line diversification may reduce the risk of too strong of a reliance on one key product line. Splitting an IT operations center into two geographically separate locations will reduce the risk of some catastrophic failure. There are a wide range of often effective strategies to reduce risks at all levels that go down to the mundane but operationally important step of cross-training employees.

3. **Sharing**. Virtually all enterprises regularly reduce some of their risks by purchasing insurance to hedge or share their risks. Many other risk-sharing techniques are available here as well. For financial transactions, an enterprise can engage in hedging operations to protect itself from possible price fluctuations. A common example of hedging is the investor's use of put or call options to cover strong price movements. An enterprise can also share potential business risks and rewards through joint venture agreements. The idea is to arrange to have another party accept some of a potential risk, with the recognition that there will be costs associated with that activity.

4. **Acceptance**. This is the strategy of no action. An enterprise can "self-insure" itself, rather than purchase an insurance policy. Essentially, an enterprise should look at a risk's likelihood and impact in light of its established risk tolerance and then decide

whether to accept that risk. For the many and varied risks that an enterprise might encounter, acceptance is often the appropriate strategy for some risks.

Management must develop a general response strategy for each of its risks, using an approach built around one of these four general strategies. In doing so, it should consider the costs versus benefits of each potential risk response to best align them with the enterprise's overall risk appetite. For example, an enterprise's recognition that the impact of a given risk is relatively low would be balanced against a low risk tolerance that suggests that insurance should be purchased to provide a potential risk response. For many risks, appropriate responses are obvious and almost universally understood. An IT operation, for example, spends the time and resources to back up its key data files and implement a business continuity plan. There should be no question regarding this basic approach, but various levels of management may question the frequency of backup processes or how often the continuity plan needs to be tested.

An enterprise, at this point, should go back to the several risk objectives that have been established, as well as the tolerance ranges for those objectives. Then it should readdress both the likelihood and the impact associated with each of the identified risks within those risk objectives to develop an assessment of both of the risk categories, as well as an overall assessment of the planned risk responses and how those risks will align with overall enterprise risk tolerances.

The basic message here is that an enterprise needs an overall risk response plan in order to be compliant with the COSO internal control framework. The original framework looked about the same at a top level, but back in 1992, risk management was considered to be little more than an insurance department function in many large enterprises. Since then, COSO ERM has changed our appreciation and understanding of risk management concepts, and our movement to a global, interconnected world has made risk management even more significant.

Although each type of response can have an associated strategy, there should be an overall strategy for selecting from among the basic response types. This overall risk response strategy and a strategy for each type of response are discussed later. In addition, specific risk mitigation strategies are presented, including a description of how such strategies can be implemented within organizations. Risk response strategies specify:

- Individuals or organizational subcomponents that are responsible for the selected risk response measures and specifications of effectiveness criteria (i.e., articulation of indicators and thresholds against which the effectiveness of risk response measures can be judged).
- Dependencies of the selected risk response measures on other risk response measures.
- Dependencies of selected risk response measures on other factors (e.g., implementation of other planned information technology measures).
- Implementation time line for risk responses.
- Plans for monitoring the effectiveness of the risk response measures.
- Identification of risk monitoring triggers.
- Interim risk response measures selected for implementation, if appropriate.

Risk response implementation strategies may include interim measures that organizations choose to implement. An overall risk response strategy provides an organizational approach to selecting between the basic risk responses for a given risk situation. A decision to accept risk must be consistent with the stated organizational tolerance for risk. Yet there is still a need for a well-defined, established organizational path for selecting one or a combination of the risk responses of avoidance, reduction, sharing, and acceptance. Enterprises are often placed in situations where there is greater risk than the designated senior leaders and executives desire to accept. Some risk acceptance will likely be necessary. It might be possible to avoid risk or to share or transfer risk, and some risk mitigation is probably feasible. Avoiding risk may require the selective reengineering of organizational mission/business processes and forgoing some of the benefits being accrued by the use of information technology organization-wide, perhaps even what organizations perceive as necessary benefits. Mitigating risk requires the expenditure of limited resources and may quickly become cost-ineffective, due to the pragmatic realities of the degree of mitigation that can actually be achieved. Finally, risk sharing and transfers have ramifications as well, some of which, if not unacceptable, may be undesirable. The risk response strategies of organizations empower senior leaders and executives to make risk-based decisions compliant with the goals, objectives, and broader organizational perspectives.

 ## FRAUD RISK ANALYSIS

When the original COSO internal control framework was released in the early 1990s, fraud assessment and detection were really not much of an issue or concern for most internal or external auditors. Both sides essentially argued that it was not their job to investigate and detect fraud. Their excuse was that auditors did not have proper fraud investigation and detection skills. That was the responsibility of legal authorities, and the auditors were only there to assess internal controls. How things have changed in 20-plus years. At about the same time that SOx became a law, the AICPA released its SAS 99 auditing standards for considering fraud when performing financial statement audits, and both the IIA and the ISACA have since released fraud-detection internal audit guidance in the same period.

Although various levels and types of financial fraud activities have perhaps always been with us, it was usually considered to be a *criminal* activity and beyond the activities of professional internal or external auditors. However, concerns about fraudulent financial activity reached a crescendo level about the time SOx became a law, around 2002. The financial failures at that time were replete with questionable financial activities that seemed barely legal, if not totally fraudulent. In the course of their reviews, auditors today now have a professional responsibility to assess and test for fraudulent activities.

There are no direct fraud-related changes to the revised COSO internal control framework. However, the supporting guidance material contains a principle calling for considering the potential for fraud risks that could limit the achievement of objectives. Thus, risk assessment includes management's assessment of the risks related to safeguarding the enterprise's assets and fraudulent reporting. In addition, management should consider possible acts of corruption, by both in-house and external parties, which can directly affect an enterprise's ability to achieve its objectives.

Fraudulent reporting can occur when an enterprise's financial reports are willfully prepared with misstatements or omissions. These events may occur through unauthorized receipts or expenditures, financial misconduct, or other disclosure irregularities. As part of its risk assessment process, an enterprise should identify the various ways that fraudulent reporting can occur, considering:

- The degree of estimates and judgments in external reporting,
- Fraud schemes or scenarios common to the industry or markets where the enterprise operates,
- History or logistics issues in the geographic regions where the enterprise does business,
- Incentives of all types that may motivate fraudulent behavior,
- Automation and system-related issues, including weak security and integrity controls,
- Vulnerability of management override and potential schemes to circumvent existing internal control activities.

There may be instances where the enterprise is not able to directly manage the information captured for financial reporting, yet is expected to have internal controls that identify, analyze, and respond to the particular risk. From these considerations, management should make an informed assessment of specific areas where fraud might exist and the likelihood of its occurrence and potential impact. Fraud detection and management have become a very important element of the revised COSO internal control framework.

 ## COSO RISK ASSESSMENT AND THE REVISED INTERNAL CONTROL FRAMEWORK

As we stated in our introductory comments, the basic concepts in the Risk Assessments component of the COSO internal control framework have not changed that much since the original framework, but the supporting internal control guidance very much has. Management should build and tailor its risk management processes following the four principles listed at the beginning of this chapter and discussed throughout.

Enterprise risk assessments should cover (1) operations, and (2) compliance activities, as well as (3) reporting needs.

With regard to COSO risk assessment operations objectives, a main area of concern for many enterprises is the need to consider tolerances for risk. Another risk management term that sounds impressive but is often difficult to define, *risk tolerance* can be defined through two basic questions:

1. How much can the enterprise afford to invest to achieve its goals?
2. How much is the enterprise prepared to lose?

Those two critical questions are best addressed by the board, and only after the executive management and the board have an understanding and an agreement about the enterprise's risk attitude or risk philosophy.

Risk assessment operations objectives should reflect management's choices about structure, industry consideration, and enterprise performance. Consideration should be given to financial and performance goals for the enterprise within these operations objectives. Management should use these operations objectives as a basis for allocating resources needed to attain desired operations and financial performance.

While our focus here is more on operational risks, similar levels of attention should be given to compliance and a combination of internal, external financial, and external nonfinancial reporting risks. Our overall area of emphasis here is that the newly revised COSO internal control risk assessment element is an important component. When building effective internal control processes, following the COSO framework, an enterprise needs to build effective risk management and assessment processes.

 NOTES

1. The Institute of Risk Management, 2002.
2. *Internal Control—Integrated Framework*, May 2013.

6

COSO Internal Control Components: Control Activities

ERHAPS THE CORE ELEMENT IN the overall COSO internal control framework, control activities are actions—established through enterprise policies and procedures—that help ensure that management's directives to mitigate risks to the achievement of objectives are carried out. Control activities are performed at all levels of an enterprise, at various stages within business units and processes, and over the technology environment. These control activities may be preventive or detective in nature and may encompass a range of manual and automated activities, such as authorizations and approvals, verifications, reconciliations, and business performance reviews. A basic or fundamental internal control, segregation of duties, is typically built into the selection and development of COSO control activities. Where internal controls are not effective or even practical for the segregation of duties, management must select and develop alternative control activities.

Control activities are an area where, on one hand, basic internal control activity concepts have not changed all that much from the original COSO internal control framework. For example, segregation of duties is a basic internal control concept that really has not changed all that much. The person or the automated function that initiates a financial transaction should not be the same person or process that approves it. On the other hand, there have been massive changes in many aspects of control activities guidance since the original COSO framework. The guidance behind that original framework goes back to the many past years of mainframe computer systems, with lots of batch-processing procedures.

This chapter discusses the new revised control activities component of the COSO internal control framework, with an emphasis on key control activities principles. A key concept here is that an enterprise should select and develop control activities that contribute to the mitigation of risks to the achievement of enterprise internal control objectives at acceptable levels.

COSO CONTROL ACTIVITY PRINCIPLES

The COSO control activities component is built around the three principles for defining how key controls should be identified and documented:

1. The organization selects and develops control activities that contribute to the migration of risks to the achievement of its objectives at acceptable levels,
2. The organization selects and develops general control activities over technology to support the achievement of objectives,
3. The enterprise deploys control activities through policies that establish what is expected and in procedures that put policies in action.

Although COSO's guidance is focused only on the internal control financial reporting network, the enterprise manager should think of the importance of these controls throughout most enterprise processes and activities. Although we need effective internal controls for external financial reporting, they are a key to all business operations.

The goals of these COSO control activity principles are to allow for the importance of establishing key internal controls at various layers and levels within an enterprise in order to reduce risks for the achievement of effective internal control and financial reporting objectives. The following sections will discuss each of the three control activity principles within this COSO component. Also, when the revised framework was first released in draft form, there was a fourth control activity principle covering IT principles. This was dropped from the draft version but has been incorporated into the other three principles. Effective IT processes are an important part of COSO control activities and are particularly important in today's environment of ever-changing technologies and constantly increasing reliance on IT systems and processes.

Control Activity Principles: Integration with Risk Assessment

This important COSO control activity principle states that as part of its overall internal control environment, an enterprise should select and develop control activities that contribute to the mitigation of internal control risks to the achievement of its objectives at acceptable levels. As we discussed in Chapter 5 on COSO's risk assessment component, the revised COSO internal control framework here again places an increased high emphasis on the importance of risk management for establishing effective internal controls. This principle focuses on the importance of integrating an enterprise's control activities with risk assessments, understanding and improving business process control activities, and establishing an effective segregation of duties controls.

Control activities support all of COSO's internal control components, but this COSO element should be particularly aligned with the COSO risk assessment component, as was introduced in Chapter 5. Along with assessing risks, management should identify and put into effect actions that are needed when an enterprise chooses to either accept or avoid a specific risk and chooses to develop control activities to avoid that risk. This action to reduce or share some risk serves as a focal point for developing and selecting control activities for that risk element. The nature and extent of the risk response and associated control activities will depend, at least in part, on the desired level of risk mitigation acceptable to enterprise management. By mitigation, we mean some management action that reduces either exposure to the identified risk or the likelihood of its occurrence.

Control activities include actions that ensure that responses to assessed risks, as well as other management directives—such as establishing an enterprise code of conduct—are carried out properly and in a timely manner. For example, a member of senior management may establish an operations objective "to meet or exceed operating unit sales targets for the ensuring reporting period," but senior staff management may subsequently identify a risk that its key personnel have insufficient knowledge about current and potential customer needs to easily meet this objective. Management responses to this identified risk may include reviews of sales histories from existing customers and developing market research initiatives to better attract potential customers. Control activities here might include tracking the progress of customer buying histories against established timetables, as well as taking steps to improve the quality of the reported marketing data.

When determining what actions to take to mitigate risk, management should consider all aspects of the enterprise's system of internal controls, as well as its relevant business processes, IT systems, and other locations where control activities are needed. This may include considering control activities outside the operating unit, such as shared service, data centers, or processes performed by outsourced service providers. For example, an enterprise may need to establish control activities to address the integrity of information sent to and received from an outsourced service provider.

Enterprise-Specific Control Activity Factors

Because every enterprise has its own set of objectives and implementation approaches, there will always be differences in each enterprise's objectives, risks, responses, and related control activities. Every enterprise is managed by different people with different skills, who use their individual techniques in effecting internal controls. In addition, controls reflect the environment and the industry in which the enterprise operates, as well the complexity of its organization, history, culture, and scope of operations.

Enterprise-specific factors can affect the control activities needed to support an enterprise's system of internal controls, including

- The enterprise's environment and complexity, as well as the nature and scope of its operations, both physically and logically, can all affect enterprise control activities,
- Highly regulated enterprises generally have more complex risk responses and control activities than do less regulated entities,
- The scope and nature of risk responses and control activities for multinational enterprises with diverse operations generally address a more complex internal control structure than do those of a domestic enterprise with less varied activities,

- An enterprise with a fairly sophisticated resource planning system, as discussed further in the following sections, will have different control activities than one using less sophisticated IT systems.
- Decentralized operations and an emphasis on local autonomy and innovation presents a different control environment than for another whose operations are constant and highly centralized.

The previous points were chosen from the supporting COSO internal control guidance materials. They highlight an obvious issue regarding the COSO internal control framework. When establishing internal control processes, an enterprise always needs to think of the relative size and complexity of the enterprise. One size does not fit all, and management must consider the relative size of the enterprise and should make internal control accommodations based on these relative size and other operating environment considerations.

Business Process Control Activities

Business processes are established across an enterprise to enable it to achieve its objectives. These processes may be common to all business activities—such as purchasing, payables, or sales processing—or may be unique to a particular industry. Each of these processes transforms input into output through a series of related transactions or activities. Control activities that directly support actions to mitigate transaction-processing risks in an enterprise are usually called "application controls" or "transaction controls."

Transaction controls are often the most fundamental control activities in an enterprise, because they directly address the risk responses to business processes in place to meet management's objectives. Transaction controls should be selected and developed wherever the business process may reside, ranging from centralized enterprise financial consolidation processes to customer support processes at local operating units.

A typical business process will cover many objectives and subobjectives, each with its own set of risks and risk responses. A common way to consolidate these business process risks into a manageable form is to group them according to the business process objectives of completeness, accuracy, and availability. If the objectives are achieved for each of the transactions within a particular business process, then the business process subobjectives will likely be achieved.

The control activities element of the revised COSO internal control framework uses the following information processing objectives:

- **Completeness.** Transactions that occur should be recorded. For example, an enterprise can mitigate the risk of not processing all transactions with vendors by selecting actions and transaction controls that support the idea that all such invoice transactions are processed within appropriate business processes.
- **Accuracy.** Transactions should be recorded in a correct amount in the right account and on a timely basis. For example, transaction controls over such key system elements, such as an item price or vendor master database of descriptive elements,

can address the accuracy of processing a purchasing transaction. Accuracy in the context of an operational process can be defined to cover the broader concepts of quality, including the accuracy and precision of the recorded part.
■ **Validity.** Recorded transactions represent an economic event that actually occurred and then were executed according to prescribed procedures. Validity is generally achieved through control activities that include the authorization of transactions as specified by enterprise policies and procedures.

The risk of untimely transaction processing may be considered a separate risk or included as part of the completeness or accuracy of overall information-processing objectives. Restricted access should generally also be considered an IT processing objective because without appropriately restricting access over transactions in a business process, the control activities in that business process can be overridden, and segregation of duties controls may not be achieved.

While IT objectives are most often associated with financial processes and transactions, the concept can be applied to any enterprise activity. For example, IT processing objectives and related control activities apply to management's decision-making processes over critical judgments and estimates. In this environment, management should consider the completeness of the identification of significant factors that affect estimates for which it must develop and support these assumptions. Similarly, management should consider the validity and reasonableness of those assumptions and the accuracy of its estimation models.

This does not mean that if management considers and pays close attention to these established objectives, the enterprise will never make a faulty judgment or estimate, because these are all subject to human error. However, when appropriate control activities are in place and when management uses good and well thought-out judgments, the likelihood of better decision making is improved.

Types of Transaction Control Activities

Sometimes basic internal control concepts that have been with us many years are almost forgotten or dropped from our everyday dialogue regarding the designing and building of effective internal controls. The revised COSO internal control guidance material does a good job of reminding business executives of important control activities. For example, the COSO internal control framework guidance material highlights the following types of transaction control activities:

■ **Verifications.** This is a transaction type of control that compares two or more items with one another or compares an item with policy rules, and performs a follow-up action when the items compared do not match or are considered inconsistent with policy. Examples here include IT applications with programs that have matching or programmed reasonableness tests. Verifications generally address the completeness, accuracy, or validity of processing transactions.
■ **Reconciliations.** This transaction process compares two or more data elements, and, if references are identified, actions are taken to bring the data into agreement. Reconciliations generally address the completeness and/or accuracy of processing transactions.

- **Authorizations and approvals.** An authorization process affirms that a transaction is valid, particularly those representing an actual economic event. An authorization typically takes the form of an approval by a higher level of management or of a system-generated verification and determination that a transaction is valid.
- **Physical controls.** Equipment inventories, securities, cash, and other assets are typically secured physically in locked or guarded storage areas. These physical control transactions here should be periodically counted and compared with supporting control records.
- **Controls over standing data.** A term first introduced some years ago by one of the major public accounting firms, *standing data* are the data elements developed from outside the enterprise (often from a standards organizations) that support the processing of transactions within that enterprise. Control activities over the processes to populate, update, and maintain the accuracy and completeness, as well as the validity of this standing data, should be established by the enterprise.
- **Supervisory controls.** These transaction control processes assess whether other transaction control activities, such as verifications, approvals, controls over standing data, or physical control activities, are being performed completely, accurately, and according to enterprise policy and procedures. Management normally should judgmentally select and develop supervisory controls over higher-risk transactions, including high-level reviews to see if any reconciling items have been either followed up and corrected or an appropriate explanation provided.

These comments about control activity transactions say much about the supporting guidance provided as part of the revised COSO internal control framework. Many of the words about common transaction types will be common sense to many enterprise senior managers, but the new COSO guidance emphasizes that they are all necessary for effective internal controls.

Control Activity Principles: Selection and Development of General IT Controls

An enterprise should select and develop general control activities over technology to support its achievement of objectives. The concept of general IT controls has been with us for many years, but many senior managers, with experiences from older IT mainframe days, sometimes still think of an IT general control as such matters as the importance of locks on the computer room door—a general control dating back to the long ago IT mainframe system days. IT general controls are much more than computer room door locks, and Exhibit 6.1 summarizes some of today's IT general control concepts.

The revised COSO control activities principle really highlights a major difference between the original framework and today's internal controls environment. Now, the COSO guidance material emphasizes that the reliability of technology within business process, including automated controls, depends on the presence and proper functioning of general control activities over the broader area of what COSO calls *technology general controls.* These might include such things as the automated matching and edit checking

IT general controls apply to all IT- and systems-related components, processes, and data for a given enterprise and its IT environment. The objectives of IT general controls are to ensure the proper development and implementation of applications, as well as the integrity of programs, data files, and computer operations. That is, no matter what the IT application and associated business process, IT general control procedures should apply to all of them.

The most common IT general controls include:

▪ **Logical access controls over infrastructure, applications, and data.** Although there are many different general control procedures here, an example would be password controls over access to files and data.
▪ **System development life cycle controls.** An enterprise should have standard processes in place for building, implementing, and revising or retiring, as appropriate, new IT systems and applications.
▪ **Change management procedures.** Controls should be designed to ensure that changes to systems and processes meet business requirements and are authorized.
▪ **Data center physical security controls.** Physical and logical controls should be in place over IT equipment, including network control resources and all other facilities and supplies.
▪ **System and data backup and recovery controls.** IT continuity plans should be in place, and all IT transactions and data files should be regularly, and in some cases continuously, backed up, such that operations can continue in the event of an unexpected IT service disruption.
▪ **Computer operations controls.** Error control procedures and other management measures, including regular hardware and software upgrades, should be in place to ensure error-free IT system operations following established schedules.

EXHIBIT 6.1   IT General Controls Definitions

---

of data entered online, over the Internet, or through a wireless connection. If something does not match or is in the wrong format, immediate feedback should be provided so that corrections can be made. Error messages should indicate what is wrong with the data, and exception reports should allow for subsequent follow-up.

Technology general controls must be implemented and operating for these automated controls to work properly when first developed and implemented. Technology general controls also help IT systems continue to function properly after they are initially developed and implemented. An automated technology matching transaction control, for example, will work properly only if technology general controls are designed, implemented, and operating so that the right files are being used in the matching process and the files are complete and accurate. We once thought of these as specific application controls, where each enterprise application had different and often unique error checking routings, ranging from some being very good to poor on others. An enterprise IT function should install similar technology general controls for virtually all of its applications.

As with other enterprise functions, processes should be put in place to select, develop, operate, and maintain an enterprise's technology resources. These processes may also be limited to a few activities over the use of standard technology purchased from external parties or expanded to support both in-house and externally developed technologies. Control activities should be selected and developed that will contribute to the mitigation of specific risks surrounding the use of technology processes.

Control Activity Technology General Controls

Technology general controls include control activities over the technology infrastructure, IT and other security management resources, as well as enterprise technology acquisition, development, and maintenance processes. They apply to all enterprise IT technologies, ranging from IT applications on client-server, portable computers and mobile devices to such operational facilities as physical plant control systems or manufacturing robotics. The extent and rigor of these technology general control activities will vary for each of these technologies, depending on various factors, such as the complexity of the technology and risks associated with the underlying business processes being supported. Similar to business transaction controls, technology general controls may include both manual and automated control activities.

Technology resources and processes define the infrastructure in which an enterprise operates, ranging from communication networks for linking technologies to the computing network resources for their applications to operate, down to the electricity to power these technologies. For many enterprises, the technology infrastructure can be complex. It may be shared by different business units within an enterprise or outsourced to third-party service organizations that provide such services as cloud computing resources. The infrastructure complexities often present risks that need to be understood and addressed. Given the broad range of possible changes in the use of technology that are likely to continue into the future, an enterprise also needs to track technology changes and assess and respond to any evolving new risks.

Control activities support the completeness, accuracy, and availability of technology processing. Whether the enterprise's technology ranges from the once-prevalent IT mainframe batch processing to today's mobile wireless or another more sophisticated communications environments, the technology should be actively checked for problems, with corrective actions taken when needed. Maintaining technology almost always includes backup and recovery procedures, as well as disaster recovery plans, depending on the risks and consequences of a full or partial outage.

Although senior management, as well as its internal and external auditors, has always been concerned about the importance of strong IT general controls, the original COSO internal control framework did not give it much specific emphasis. Today, however, the guidance supporting the revised COSO internal control framework really highlights the importance of all types of IT general controls. Senior executives should work with their chief audit executive (CAE) and internal auditors to assure that enterprise IT general controls have been appropriately assessed and tested to assure that they are operating properly. The adequacy of these IT general controls also can be important in a SOx Section 404 internal control assessment.

Security Management Processes

Security management includes subprocesses and control activities over who and what has access to an enterprise's IT technology. They generally cover access rights to the data, operating systems, software, the network, all applications, and physical layers. Security controls over the access to an enterprise's IT technology protect it from inappropriate access and unauthorized use of the system, as do strong technology controls in an enterprise's security management systems.

Security threats can come from both internal and external sources. External threats are particularly important today for the many enterprises that now depend on telecommunications or wireless networks and Internet business processes. Technology users, customers, and malicious party threats may be located halfway around the world. The many potential uses of technology and points of entry underscore the importance of security management. External threats have become prevalent in today's highly interconnected business environments, and continued efforts are required to address these risks.

User access to enterprise IT technology should be generally controlled through authentication control activities, where a unique user identification or token is authenticated against an approved list. These control activities generally employ a policy where authorized users are restricted to the applications or functions commensurate with their job responsibilities and support an appropriate segregation of duties.

Control activities are used to check requests for access against approved lists. Other control activities should be in place to allow reviews of access rights against established policy rules or to check whether access remains appropriate. Access also needs to be controlled when different technology elements are connected to one another.

These comments summarize some basic IT security management processes outlined in the COSO guidance materials. They are only highlights of what can be a wide range of complex control issues. When implementing the COSO internal control framework, the senior executive should use the basic but high-level comments here and work with enterprise IT security resources to establish and implement appropriate security-related IT internal controls.

Technology Acquisition, Development, and Maintenance Processes

Technology general controls support the acquisition, development, and maintenance of an enterprise's technology resources. For example, many IT functions historically have used a systems development methodology called a systems development life cycle (SDLC) approach to provide a structure for their systems' design and implementation, outlining specific phases, documentation requirements, approvals, and checkpoints to control the acquisition, development, and maintenance of new applications and other technologies. Illustrated in Exhibit 6.2, this type of methodology provides appropriate controls over reviewing, changes, approvals, and testing results, as well as implementing protocols to determine whether changes are being made properly.

The SDLC concept was developed by IBM back in the 1970s—days of mainframe systems. Many outside providers subsequently developed paper-intensive SDLC

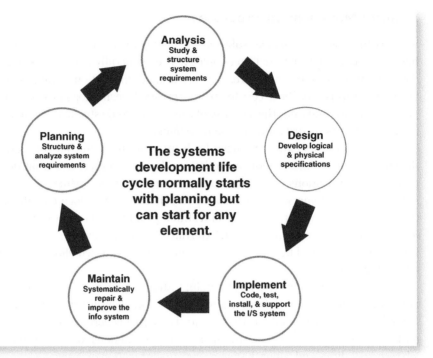

EXHIBIT 6.2 Systems Development Life Cycle Process

approaches back in the earlier days of IT systems development, when we often designed, programmed, and implemented our own application systems. Properly installed, these SDLC approaches assured that new application developments were well managed and documented. However, they typically had weak revision controls and change management processes and often required heavy amounts of paper-based documentation. With our move to purchased software, cloud computing and rapid application development approaches in use today, the SDLC has fallen into disuse for many IT functions. However, the revised COSO internal control framework suggests we should still consider using an SDLC approach for developing technology general controls.

Some enterprises have used their SDLC approaches on a continuum, from large development projects to smaller changes. In others, there is a distinct process and methodology for developing new technology and a separate process for change management. In either case, a change management process should be in place to track changes from initiation to final disposition. Changes may arise as a result of a problem in technology that needs to be fixed or a request from the user community.

The technology general controls included in an SDLC methodology will vary depending on the risks associated with new technology initiatives. A large or complex development initiative will generally have a greater risk than a small or simpler effort. The extent and rigor of the controls should be sized accordingly. The COSO guidance goes on to address technology general controls for development efforts using packaged software, as well as outsourced services. The overall message here is that no matter how big or small an in-house IT development is or whether it is being launched through packaged software or an outside service provider, an enterprise should always ensure that there are adequate IT general controls in place.

Control Activity Principles: Policies and Procedures

An enterprise should deploy control activities through policies that specify and establish what is expected and procedures that put those policies into action. Although an enterprise will normally have many policies and procedures in place to achieve its objectives, control activities should be initiated that specifically relate to those policies and procedures that contribute to the mitigation of risks to the achievement of objectives at acceptable levels. An enterprise security dealer's policy, for example, might call for a regular review of customer trading activities by a retail branch manager. This procedure is the review itself, performed in a timely manner and with attention given to factors outlined in that policy, such as the nature and volume of the securities traded and their relation to customer net worth and age.

A policy should be more than just the CEO saying he or she generally wants to do something or take some action, without any more specific details. Going through a formal review-and-approval process, procedures should be published statements outlining management's intention to implement some policy or take some action. Often published on a customer service database, enterprise published policies should have the following elements:

- **Policy purpose**. There should be a high-level statement outlining the intent or high-level objectives of the policy.
- **Location and applicability**. The scope should be defined including whether the policy applies only to some units or is worldwide.
- **Roles and responsibilities**. Descriptions should describe everyone involved in the policy.

Although there are many styles and formats of enterprise policy statements, Exhibit 6.3 shows a sample IT governance policy covering a sample organization's governance, risk, and compliance (GRC) policy. A high-level document, the policy outlines an overall corporate set of planned objectives, and it is based on our sample company, Global Computer Products, which we will encounter in other chapters.

In some cases, policies and procedures may be communicated orally. Unwritten policies can be effective where communications channels involve limited management layers and close interactions with the supervision of personnel. But whether or not they are written, policies must establish clear individual responsibility and accountability and must be deployed diligently and consistently by competent personnel. A procedure will not be useful if performed in a rote manner, without a sharp, continuing focus on the risks to which the policy is directed.

It is essential that questionable matters identified as a result of potential procedure discrepancies be investigated and, if appropriate, corrective actions be taken in a timely manner. For example, suppose an accounting supervisor performs a reconciliation of cash accounts and detects a discrepancy in one of its accounts. The supervisor should

EXHIBIT 6.3   Management GRC Philosophy Procedure Example

Management Philosophy

Global Computer Products

Our Governance, Risk, and Compliance Policy

Governance, Risk, and Compliance (GRC) management is not just a process or procedure. It is a fundamental component of Global Computer Products' business. Our company is dedicated to keeping GRC management issues as key components of all of our business dealings.

We believe that overall GRC management is first and foremost the responsibility of all associates, including management up to the most senior level. Just as a successful business must manage its costs, it must manage its risks. This includes hazard risk, financial risk, and credit risk.

The management of governance, risks, and compliance with rules must be incorporated into the fiber of our organization. All associates must understand established rules and procedures; comply with rules, laws, and regulations; and consider potential risks as they make all decisions, whether in sales, product development, or other areas of operations.

follow up with the person in charge of recording cash and determine whether a cash receipt was not recorded properly. The receipt should be reapplied, and the correction should be reflected in a subsequent reconciliation.

The message in the control activities principle is that an enterprise should deploy policies that define what is expected and initiate relevant procedures to reflect these policies. This control activities principle calls for the following action steps:

- **Establish policies and procedures to support the deployment of management's directives**. Management should establish control activities that are built into business processes and employees' day-to-day activities through policies establishing what is expected and relevant procedures specifying these actions.
- **Establish responsibility and accountability for executing policies and procedures**. Management should establish responsibility and accountability for all relevant control activities of the business.
- **Perform using competent personnel**. Selection and training processes should be in place such that competent personnel are assigned to perform control activities with diligence and focus.
- **Perform in a timely manner**. Responsible personnel should perform control activities in a timely manner, as defined by enterprise policies and procedures.
- **Take corrective actions when appropriate**. Responsible personnel should investigate and act on matters identified as a result of executing control activities.
- **Reassess policies and procedures**. Management should periodically review control activities to determine their continued relevance and should refresh them when necessary.

COSO CONTROL ACTIVITIES TODAY

Effective control activities are a key component in the overall COSO internal control framework. In a physical or visual sense, they reside in the front and center middle of the COSO internal control cube. They occupied that same position in the original COSO internal control framework as well, but the original supporting guidance materials did not give them the level of importance that they certainly should have today. For example, this author was part of a team that developed and submitted potential revision comments regarding the first 1992 draft of COSO internal controls. Perhaps because IT operations were much more separate from business operations than they are now, we did not think of many of the important aspects of the control activities, as outlined in the revised internal control framework.

The new control activities element published guidance provides direction for one of the key areas that was missing in the original COSO document—an emphasis on the importance of having and implementing effective IT controls in order to establish effective internal control objectives. An enterprise today must establish internal controls over its IT applications, as well as good general controls, covering all aspects of the IT environment from systems security principles to controls of a computers system's electrical power. Enterprise management at all levels should understand the importance of a wide range of effective general and application controls, covering all aspects of business and IT operations.

The control activities guidance material highlights another important change from the original COSO framework and a key consideration for installing effective internal control processes. We are referring to COSO's emphasis on giving consideration to the size and extent of the enterprise. That is, one size does not fit all, and management and its internal auditors should keep the size and extent of the enterprise in mind when installing and implementing internal controls. Auditors—both internal and external—have sometimes been unreasonable here, in the minds of many senior managers, when recommending internal control improvements. The revised COSO internal control framework guidance recognizes that we should consider risks and enterprise objectives when installing effective control activities.

Although we have historically focused more on elements of the COSO control environment when developing standards and systems following the original COSO internal control framework, that original framework was perhaps deficient on outlining IT-related internal control considerations, and this control activities COSO element is particularly better for helping people understand and implement effective internal controls in today's IT-centric world.

CHAPTER SEVEN

COSO Internal Control Components: Information and Communication

NFORMATION IS NECESSARY FOR AN enterprise to carry out its internal control responsibilities to support the achievement of its objectives. Management obtains or generates and then uses relevant and quality information from both internal and external sources to support the functioning of all components of its internal controls. Communication, as defined here by COSO, is the continual, iterative process of providing, sharing, and obtaining necessary information. Internal communication is the means by which information is disseminated throughout an enterprise, flowing up, down, and across the entity. It enables personnel to receive clear messages from senior management that control responsibilities must be taken seriously. External communication also enables inbound communications of relevant external information and provides this information to external parties in response to requirements and expectations.

Although its principles have not changed very much since the original COSO internal control framework, the revised COSO information and communications guidelines are structured differently and look a bit different in this revised COSO internal control framework. In addition, information and communication concepts have changed in today's world of using such practices as outsourced service providers in our Internet-driven global economy. In this chapter, we will explore COSO's visually very different-looking information and communications element and will discuss why this is a key component in developing and implementing effective internal control processes.

INFORMATION AND COMMUNICATIONS: WHAT HAS CHANGED?

When it was first released in 1992, the COSO internal control framework was not described as a cube but often as a pyramid structure, as was shown in Exhibit 3.1. The relative placement and order of the COSO elements or components were also different. For example, the control environment component, now at the top of the stack, as discussed in Chapter 4, was really described as the base or foundation component of the COSO internal control elements. This author, for example, has described the importance of this foundation element in several of his other books on internal auditing and risk management.[1] COSO's information and communication element was described as a component on the edge of the pyramid, covering multiple other elements. The idea was that information and communication processes should be thought of as important to a series of other related COSO components. That characterization of information and communication as an element somewhat on the edge of other framework elements was perhaps difficult to describe, and over the years, public accounting firms and others began to describe information and communication as an element of COSO's internal control cubical framework.

The overall concept supporting this original COSO internal controls information and communication element or component is that an enterprise needs to develop and deliver many forms and types of competent information, from and to management. This concept is more than the information flow described on a classic IT flow chart and calls for the delivery of effective messages, understood by all parties and with effective internal controls. The key high-level elements here are that processes should be in place to identify, capture, process, and distribute all types of information and then communicate relevant elements of this information to appropriate parties.

The COSO information and communication system control objective describes the types of information stored by an enterprise and how it is communicated to various parties. The element's information system portion records, processes, stores, and reports data. The communication system dictates how information is reported, who gets it, and how it is used in fraud control. This entire information and communication process should

- Record transactions as they occur, breaking them into their component parts (dates, amounts, names, accounts, authorizations, etc.).
- Process, summarize, and report that information for management purposes and pure accounting purposes.
- Store captured and processed data in formats that can be summarized, audited, reviewed, and reported quickly and easily.
- Report that information in a format that can be used for management analysis and internal control purposes.

The information and communications component of the COSO framework primarily supports the functioning of other internal control components, including objectives relevant to internal and external reporting. COSO internal control framework users should differentiate their reporting objectives from the somewhat separate information and communication components of this internal control element in establishing their systems of internal controls.

Terminology changes over time, but today we too often think of the term *information* as just an IT issue. However, the COSO internal control framework defines it in a broader sense, stating that information encompasses *all* of the data that is combined and summarized based on its relevance to enterprise requirements. These information requirements are determined by the ongoing functioning of other internal control components, taking into consideration the expectations of all users, both internal and external. Information systems, as defined by COSO, support decision making by improving the processing of relevant, timely, and quality information from internal and external sources.

The communication element of this COSO component enables an enterprise to share relevant and quality information, internally and externally. Management communicates information internally to enable its personnel to better understand the enterprise's objectives and the importance of their control responsibilities. Internal communication facilitates the functioning of other components of internal controls by sharing information up, down, and across the enterprise. External communication enables management to obtain and share information between the enterprise and external parties about risk, regulatory matters, and changes in circumstances, customer satisfaction, and other information relevant to the functioning of various internal control components.

The revised COSO information and communication internal control objective is supported by three principles that call for the enterprise to emphasize and use relevant information and to employ effective and internal communications:

1. The enterprise obtains or generates and uses relevant quality information to support the functioning of internal controls.
2. The enterprise internally communicates information, including objectives and responsibilities for internal controls, necessary to support the functioning of internal controls.
3. The enterprise communicates with external parties regarding matters affecting the functioning of internal controls.

This is an important internal control component with guidance helping an enterprise to better understand and rationalize its links with other internal and external sources.

 ## INFORMATION AND COMMUNICATION PRINCIPLE 1: USE OF RELEVANT INFORMATION

An enterprise should obtain or generate and use relevant quality information to support the functioning of its other components of internal controls. Information is necessary for an enterprise to carry out its internal control responsibilities in support of the achievement of objectives. Information about an enterprise's objectives should be gathered from the board of directors and senior management activities and summarized in a way that line management and others can understand these objectives and their role in their achievements. For example, in a not uncommon situation, senior managers may find that their key line managers do not have a solid understanding of the main objectives of the enterprise. Supporting business plans here are sometimes far too broad and vague or may have been too detailed or difficult to concisely communicate. In either case, senior management should summarize these important objectives in a clear narrative document that strongly outlines and emphasizes these objectives.

This communication problem is often a "Management 101" type of basic issue, in which we should always remember that this relevant information is a pivotal component of effective internal controls. Sometime it requires the services of an outside consultant to remind senior management of this lack of a relevant information problem. However, members of senior management, in addition to working together as a team, should be able to survey past operational and financial management results, as well as input staff surveys, to identify and define better and more relevant information requirements.

Obtaining relevant information, as defined in the supporting COSO guidance materials, requires management to identify and define information requirements at a strong level of detail and specificity. Identifying information requirements is an iterative and ongoing process that occurs throughout the performance of an effective internal control system. Exhibit 7.1 is an example showing how information in

EXHIBIT 7.1　Information Requirements Examples for COSO Components

Internal Control Component	Examples of Using Relevant COSO Information
Control Environment	Management performs an annual enterprise-wide survey of its employees to gather information about their personal conduct and an understanding of the enterprise's code of conduct. The survey should be part of a process that produces information to support the COSO control environment component and may also provide input into the selection, development, implementation, and maintenance of control activities.
Risk Assessment	As a result of changes in customer demands, an enterprise changes its product mix and delivery mechanisms. Expanded online sales have caused credit card transactions to increase significantly. To assess the risk of noncompliance with security and privacy regulations associated with credit card information, management gathers information about the number of transactions, the overall value, and the nature of the data retained for the last fiscal year and reevaluates its significance in conducting its risk analysis.
Control Activities	Certain equipment used in a high-volume production environment deteriorates if it is operated longer than a specified time period. To maximize equipment life spans, management obtains and reviews established daily up-time logs and compares them to ranges set by senior management. The up-time information supports control activities that address mitigation procedures required when maximum up-time levels are exceeded.
Monitoring Activities	A large utility company gathers, processes, and reports accident and injury records related to the power-generating operating unit. Comparing this information with trends in worker's compensation health insurance claims identifies variations from established expectations. This may indicate that control activities over the identification, processing, reporting, investigation, and resolution of incident and injury events may not be functioning as intended.

support of the functioning of other COSO internal control components is identified and defined.

Information requirements are established through activities performed in support of the other internal control elements or components. These requirements facilitate and direct management and other personnel to identify relevant and reliable sources of information and underlying data. The amount of information and underlying data available to management may often be more than is needed because of increased sources of information and advances in data collection, processing, and storage. In other cases, data may be difficult to obtain at the relevant level or requisite specificity. Therefore, a clear understanding of the COSO-defined information requirements directs management and other personnel to identify relevant and reliable sources of information and data.

Information from Relevant Sources

With our growing use of video and voice communications over the Internet, and wireless sources, in addition to traditional printed reports, internal and external information is received from a variety of sources and in a variety of forms and formats. Exhibit 7.2 shows some examples of types of information that enterprise management encounters on a regular basis.

In managing its information from external sources, management should consider them in terms of a comprehensive scope of potential events, activities, and data sources available internally and from reliable sources, and select those that are most relevant and useful to the current organizational structure, business model, or objectives. As changes to an enterprise occur, its information requirements also change. For example, an enterprise operating in a highly dynamic business or economic environment may experience continual changes, often caused by the activities of highly innovative and quick-moving competitors who shift customer expectations. In addition, this type of enterprise may face evolving regulatory issues, globalization issues, and the challenges from technology innovations. Thus, management must regularly reevaluate its information requirements and adjust to the nature, extent, and sources of information and underlying data to meet its ongoing needs.

Processing Data through Information Systems

COSO uses the phrase "information system" in a rather broad sense, meaning both information technology (IT) based systems and other overall manual processes for capturing, analyzing, storing, and distributing all types of business information. Enterprises develop information systems to source, capture, and process large volumes of data from internal and external sources into meaningful, actionable information to meet defined information requirements. Information systems encompass a combination of people, processes, and technology that support a business's basic or fundamental processes managed internally, as well as those supported through relationships with outsourced service providers and other external parties.

EXHIBIT 7.2 Information from Relevant Sources Example

Information Source	Example of Relevant Information	Data Example
Internal	E-mail communications	Organization changes
Internal	Inspection reports from production floor.	Online and quality production information
Internal	Minutes or notes from operations committee meeting	Actions in response to reported metrics
Internal	Personnel time reporting system	Hours incurred on time-based projects
Internal	Reports from manufacturing systems	Production results—number of units shipped
Internal	Responses to customer surveys	Factors affecting customer repeat purchases
Internal	Whistleblower hotline	Complaints on management behavior
External	Data from outsourced service provider	Products shipped from contract manufacturer
External	Industry research reports	Competitor product information
External	Peer company earning releases	Market and industry metrics
External	Regulatory bodies	New or expanded requirements
External	Social media, blogs, or other posts	Opinions about the enterprise
External	Trade shows	Evolving customer interests and preferences
External	Whistleblower hotline	Claims of fraud, bribery, etc.

Information can be obtained through a variety of forms, including manual input or compilation or through the use of IT processes, such as the use of electronic data interchange (EDI) or applications programming interfaces (API) automated links. Conversations with customers, suppliers, regulators, and employees are also sources of critical data and information needed to identify and assess both risks and opportunities. In some instances, information and underlying data captured require specificity. In other cases, information may be obtained directly from an internal or external source.

The volume of information accessible to an enterprise presents both opportunities and risks. Greater access to information will generally enhance internal controls. The increased volume of information and underlying data, however, may create additional risks, such as operational risks caused by inefficiency due to data overloads or compliance risks associated with the laws and regulations around data protection, retention, and privacy and security issues arising from the nature of data stored by or on behalf of the enterprise.

The nature and extent of information requirements, the complexity and volume of this information, and the dependence on external parties affects the range of sophistication of information systems, including the extent of the technology deployed.

Regardless of the level of sophistication adopted, all types of information systems support the end-to-end processing of transactions and data that enable the enterprise to collect, store, and summarize quality and consistent information across relevant processes, whether manual, automated, or a combination of both.

Information systems developed with integrated, technology-enabled processes provide opportunities for an enterprise to enhance the efficiency, speed, and accessibility of information to users. In addition, such information systems may enhance internal controls over security and privacy risks associated with the information obtained and generated by the enterprise. Information systems should be designed and implemented to restrict the access to information only to those who need it and to reduce the number of access points to enhance the effectiveness of migrating risks associated with the security and privacy of information.

Enterprise resource planning (ERP) and related management systems, corporate private networks, collaboration tools, interactive social media processes, data warehouses, business intelligence systems, factory and other operational systems, and other technology solutions present opportunities for management to leverage technology in developing and implementing effective and efficient information systems.

Achieving the right balance between the benefits and the costs to obtain and manage information and the supporting information systems is a key consideration in establishing an information system that meets an enterprise's needs. The guidance for the revised COSO internal controls very much elevates the importance of all enterprise information systems—both IT and other processes—in establishing effective internal controls. Enterprise management should think of the importance of the information systems not only in terms of processes managed by an IT function or department, but also in terms of overall enterprise information flow as a vehicle for improving enterprise internal controls.

Importance of Information Quality

Maintaining the quality of information is necessary for establishing an effective internal control system, particularly with the volume of data and an enterprise's dependence on sophisticated automated IT systems. The ability to generate quality information systems begins with the quality of data gathered through information systems. Inaccurate or incomplete data and information derived from such data could result in potentially erroneous judgments, estimates, or other management decisions.

Quality is one of those terms and concepts frequently found on the manufacturing production floor but not that often in financial or even IT operations. However, to achieve effective internal controls, COSO emphasizes that an enterprise should focus on the quality of its information systems. That information system quality depends on whether enterprise information systems are

- ▪ **Sufficient.** There should be enough information at the right level of detail that is relevant to information requirements. To enhance information system quality, extraneous data should be eliminated to avoid inefficiency, misuse, or misinterpretation.

- **Timely.** Information should be available from information systems when needed. Timely information helps with the early identification of events, trends, and issues.
- **Current.** The data gathered should be from current sources and gathered with the timing and frequency needed.
- **Correct.** The underlying data should be accurate and complete. Information systems include validation checks that address accuracy and completeness, including necessary exception resolution procedures.
- **Accessible.** System information should be easy to obtain by those who need it. Users should know what information is available and where it is accessible within the overall enterprise information system.
- **Protected.** Access to sensitive information should be restricted to authorized personnel. Data should be categorized by such classifications as confidential and top secret to support information protection.
- **Verifiable.** Information should be supported by evidence from its source, a process well understood by internal and external auditors.
- **Retained.** Information should be available over an extended period of time to support inquiries and inspections by appropriate external parties.

Senior management should establish information policies with a clear responsibility and accountability for the quality of its information. For example, senior management in a decentralized, geographically dispersed enterprise may identify risks specific to achieving their operational objectives that are associated with the quality of operational data collected from these multiple field units. Management, in this example, should develop a set of specified data requirements and a reporting format for use by all field units. Senior management here should perform regular reviews of key metrics received from the data across all units. Those field units, with the best and the poorest performance, could be required to explain the source of all data to the internal audit for follow-up and collaborative reviews and answer questions about the unit's understanding of the data on these reports.

Although not mentioned in the COSO framework, these principles point to a need for internal control quality reviews. Quality review and improvement processes are common in manufacturing and formal production process organizations, but they are less common in financial, IT, or sales and marketing groups. However, basic quality improvement principles can also be very applicable for making internal control processes more effective.

Most quality review and improvement processes are based on the principles first established by Frederick Deming in Japan in the years following World War II. Deming worked as a US consultant in postwar Japan, with an objective to help repair and rebuild its shattered manufacturing resources. Deming introduced many quality management techniques that were initially ignored by US manufacturers, such as General Motors, but those same techniques led to very high-quality and innovative Japanese products, such as the offerings of Toyota or Sony in the 1970s and the 1980s.

Although it is very simple in thought, a basic concept in Deming's work and a component of quality review and implementation activities is what was called his Plan/Do/Check/Act (PDCA) cycle. Illustrated in Exhibit 7.3, this is a continuous improvement

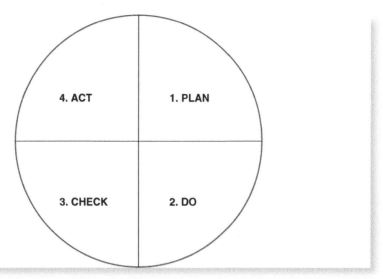

EXHIBIT 7.3 The DEMING PDCA Quality Cycle

cycle, in which a team of quality specialists would work to improve processes. They would use the PDCA cycle to review a process by the following steps:

1. **Plan:** What are the objectives of a quality improvement process? What changes are desirable to improve processes, and what data is needed? What types of tests are needed? How will operations be observed?
2. **Do:** Implement the quality improvement process changes and then execute the planned assessment tests.
3. **Check:** Observe the results of tests to develop preliminary conclusions.
4. **Act:** Study all test results to assess what was learned and what can be predicted from the exercise. Based on these results, determine areas for process improvements.
5. **Repeat** this four-step cycle as necessary: Repeat the quality improvement steps, while gaining more knowledge.

This is a simple process for process quality improvement, and it is quite different from the traditional internal audit steps of a review and then finding only exceptions and recommended corrective actions. Quality review is a key element leading to process improvement. Quality specialists do not simply review an area and then report results, such as in a formal internal audit report. Rather, they will look at some area, evaluate their findings, and seek to return and improve the process.

Internal control and other process quality audits are often much more extensive than traditional internal audits. Quality review specialists are interested in compliance with all types of applicable standards with these objectives:

- To verify that the implemented system is working.
- To verify that supporting training programs are cost effective.

- To identify people or groups that are not following procedures.
- To provide evidence to management and others that processes are working as documented.

Management should consider using quality improvement processes to enhance its internal controls. The interested executive can find out more about quality review and improvement processes through the American Society for Quality at www.asq.org.

 ## INFORMATION AND COMMUNICATION PRINCIPLE 2: INTERNAL COMMUNICATIONS

An enterprise should internally communicate information, including its objectives and responsibilities that are necessary to support the functioning of other components of internal controls. This communication of information that should be initiated and endorsed by senior management and conveyed to all elements across an enterprise organization should include

- The importance, relevance, and benefits of effective internal controls.
- The roles and responsibilities of management and other personnel in performing those internal control processes.
- The expectations of the enterprise to communicate up, down, and across any matters of significance relating to internal controls, including instances of weakness, deterioration, or nonadherence.

An enterprise should establish and implement policies and procedures that facilitate effective internal communication. This includes specific and directed communication that addresses individual authorities, responsibilities, and standards of conduct across the enterprise. Senior management should communicate the enterprise's objectives clearly throughout so that other management and personnel, including such nonemployees as contractors, understand their individual roles in the organization. Such communication occurs regardless of where personnel are located, their level of authority, or their functional responsibility.

Internal Control Communication

Internal communication, as defined by COSO, begins with the communication of management objectives. As management cascades communication of enterprise-specific objectives throughout an enterprise, it is important that related subobjectives or specific requirements are communicated to appropriate personnel in a manner that allows them to understand how their roles and responsibilities affect the achievement of an enterprise's objectives.

All personnel should also receive a clear message from senior management that their internal control responsibilities must be taken seriously. Through the communication of objectives and subobjectives, personnel should understand how their roles, responsibilities, and actions relate to the work of others in the enterprise, their responsibilities for internal controls, and what is deemed acceptable and nonacceptable behavior. As discussed in Chapter 4 on the control environment, by establishing appropriate control structures, authorities, and responsibilities, communication to personnel on their expectations for internal controls is affected. However, communication about internal control responsibilities may not on its own be sufficient to ensure that management and other personnel embrace their accountability responsibilities and respond as intended. Often, management must take timely action that is consistent with such communication to enforce the messages conveyed.

In addition, information that is shared through internal communications helps management and other personnel recognize any actual or potential problems, determine their cause, and take corrective action. For example, the internal audit department conducts an audit over commissions paid to distributors in one international location. The audit, in this example, reveals instances of the fraudulent reporting of sales through certain distributors. Further investigation exposes payments by the distributor to the sale representative responsible for the related distributors. This information would be published by the internal audit department in a report addressed to the board and senior management. Once the internal audit findings have been confirmed, the control weakness should be shared with members of sales management in other locations, enabling them to analyze information more critically to determine whether the issue is more pervasive and to take any necessary actions.

Communications between management and the board of directors provide needed information to exercise oversight responsibility for internal control. Information relating to internal controls that is communicated to the board generally should include significant matters about adherence to, changes in, or issues arising from the system of internal controls. The frequency and level of detail of the communication management and the board of directors must be sufficient to enable the board members to understand the results of management's separate and ongoing assessments and the impact of those results on the achievement of objectives. In addition, the frequency and level of detail must be sufficient to enable the board of directors to respond to indications of ineffective internal controls on a timely basis.

SOx rules and their relationship with the revised COSO internal control framework are discussed in Chapter 15. SOx rules have changed and very much broadened communications between internal audit and an enterprise's board of directors. For example, internal audit departments report directly to the board, and internal audit is required to provide the board with detailed reports of its findings regarding the status of enterprise internal controls. In addition, the board is mandated to accept and receive whistleblower communications from all enterprise stakeholders and to take appropriate actions on them as necessary.

In addition to the board's SOx whistleblower responsibilities, the revised COSO internal control guidance encourages direct communication between board members and other personnel. Members of the board of directors should have direct access to employees without reference to management. This is the type of guidance that sounds good in theory but is not that effective in practice. With the exception of open forum sessions at annual meetings, most employees and other stakeholders of all but the very smallest of corporations do not have that much opportunity to directly interact with their board members. Management-led open forum sessions may change this relationship, but communication barriers will continue to exist, despite COSO's good intentions.

Communication beyond Normal Channels

For information to flow up, down, and across the enterprise, there must be open channels of communication and a clear-cut willingness to report and listen. Management and other personnel must believe that their supervisors truly want to know about internal control-related problems and that they will deal with them as necessary. In most cases, normal established reporting lines, such as a traditional organization chart in an enterprise, are the appropriate channels of communication. However, personnel are usually quick to pick up signals if management does not have the time or interest to deal with problems they have uncovered. Compounding the problem is that an unreceptive manager is usually the last to know that the normal communication channel is inoperative or ineffective.

In some circumstances, separate lines of communication are needed to establish a fail-safe mechanism for anonymous or confidential communications when normal channels are inoperative or ineffective. Some smaller enterprises have provided, and made their employees aware of, a channel for such communications to be received by a member of the board or a member of the audit committee. Many other enterprises, and typically very large ones, have established an ethics function and some type of a hotline function where personnel at all levels can call in their concerns, on a 24/7 basis, and report them, ask questions, or even act as whistleblowers to report on some issue. This author played a major role in launching an ethics function and in establishing an ethics hotline function for a then major US corporation several years ago, and some of these basic concepts are described in his book on SOx internal controls.[2]

Enterprise employees and stakeholders should fully understand how these communication channels operate and how they will be confidentially protected for their use. Policies and procedures should be in place requiring that all communication through these channels be assessed, prioritized, and investigated. Escalation procedures should be in place to ensure that necessary communications will be made to a designated board member, the head of internal audit, or the chief ethics officer, if such a function exists, who would be responsible for ensuring that timely and proper assessments and investigations and appropriate actions are performed. These separate mechanisms encourage employees and affiliated stakeholders to report suspected violations of an enterprise's code of conduct without fear of reprisal and send a clear message that senior management is committed to open communication channels and will act based on the information that is reported to them.

Methods of Communication

Both the clarity of the information and the effectiveness with which it is communicated are important to ensuring that messages are received as intended. Active forms of communication, such as face-to-face meetings, are often more effective than passive forms, such as broadcast e-mails or Intranet postings. Periodic evaluation of the effectiveness of enterprise communication practices helps ensure these methods are working. This can be done through a variety of existing processes, such as employee performance evaluations, annual management reviews, and feedback programs.

Management should select appropriate methods of communication, taking into account the audience, the nature of the communication, the timeliness, the cost, and any legal or regulatory requirements. Exhibit 7.4 shows an example of various COSO internal control-related communication formats. No one of these is necessarily better than another, as long as the method selected appropriately communicates desired messages to the intended recipients.

When choosing a method or a format for communication, management should consider the environment where these messages are transmitted. For example, cutural, ethnic, and generational differences can affect how messages are received, and the method of communication should be adjusted, based on those factors. Regardless of the method of communication used, management should consider its requirements to deliver communications to internal parties and to retain communications to those external parties, particularly those that relate to compliance with laws and regulations. Given the potential volume of, and ability to store and retrieve, such information, these communication requirements may be challenging when management relies on real-time, technology-enabled communications. Control activities over the retention of internal control information should consider the challenges of advances in technology, including communication and collaboration technologies that are used to support internal controls.

Communication of information related to internal control responsibilities alone may not be sufficient to ensure that management and other personnel receive it and respond as intended. Consistent and timely actions taken by management regarding such communications reinforce the messages conveyed. With ever-changing technologies, management today has many options in its choice of delivering effective messages to all involved personnel regarding internal controls. However, management should consider the environment and the intended recipients of these messages and use what it considers the more effective methods.

EXHIBIT 7.4   Methods of Communication

Dashboards	Policies and Procedures
E-mail Messages	Presentations
Live or Online Training	Social Media Postings
Memoranda	Text Messages
One-on-One Discussions	Webcasts and Video
Performance Evaluations	Website Postings

INFORMATION AND COMMUNICATION PRINCIPLE 3: EXTERNAL COMMUNICATIONS

An enterprise should use internal channels to communicate information, including objectives and responsibilities, that are necessary to support the functioning of other components of its internal control processes. Communication occurs not only within an enterprise, but with those outside as well. With open two-way external communication channels, important information concerning an enterprise's objectives may be obtained from and provided to shareholders, business partners, owners, customers, regulators, and other external parties.

An enterprise should establish and implement policies and procedures that facilitate effective external communication. This includes mechanisms to obtain or receive information from external parties and to share that information internally, allowing management and other personnel to identify trends, events, or circumstances that may affect their achievement of internal control objectives.

Communication to external parties allows those external parties to readily understand events, activities, and other circumstances that may affect how they should interact with an enterprise. Management's communication to external parties should send a message about the importance of internal controls in the enterprise by demonstrating these open lines of communication. Communication to external suppliers and customers is critical for establishing an appropriate control environment. Suppliers and customers need to fully understand an enterprise's values and culture. They should be informed of such things as an enterprise's code of conduct and should recognize their responsibilities in helping to ensure compliance with this and other values. For example, management may distribute its policies and practices for business dealings with vendors on the approval of a new vendor and may require the vendor to acknowledge its adherence prior to the approval of an initial purchase order with the vendor.

Inbound Communications

Communications from external parties may also provide important information on the functioning of an enterprise's internal control system. These may include

- Independent assessments of internal controls at an outsourced service provider related to the enterprise's objectives.
- An external auditor's assessment of internal controls over the non-financial reporting at the enterprise.
- Customer service feedback related to such matters as product quality, improper charges, and missing or erroneous receipts.
- New or changed laws, regulations, standards, and other requirements from a standard or other rule-making body.
- Results from regulatory compliance reviews of examinations such as banking, securities, or taxing authorities.
- Vendor questions related to timely or missing payments for goods sold.

Information resulting from external assessments about the enterprise's activities that relate to internal control issues should be evaluated by management and, where appropriate, communicated to the board of directors. For example, management may have entered into an arrangement that allows the enterprise to periodically use externally managed technology services to perform transaction processing in lieu of hiring personnel and purchasing, as well as implementing, additional hardware and software internally. Also assume that this example organization uses sensitive customer data in certain processes. To maintain compliance with the enterprise's policies and external laws, regulations, and standards, an assessment of internal controls over the security and privacy of this externally transmitted data might be performed by a third party. The results of such an assessment could potentially reveal weaknesses in internal controls that could affect the security and privacy of data. Management assesses the significance for the weaknesses and reports the information necessary to enable the board of directors to carry out its oversight responsibilities.

The interdependence of business processes between the enterprise and its outsourced service providers can blur the lines of responsibility between an enterprise's internal control system and those of outsourced service providers. This creates a need for more rigorous communication between these parties. For example, supply chain management in a global retail company occurs through the dynamic, interactive exchange of activities between the company and its vendors, logistics providers, and contract manufacturers. Internal control over end-to-end processes becomes a shared responsibility, but there may be uncertainty about which entity is responsible at a particular stage of the process. Communicating with external parties that are responsible for activities supporting an enterprise's objectives may facilitate the need for a risk-assessment process. There is a need here for the oversight of business activities, decision making, and the identification of responsibility for internal controls throughout the process, regardless where the activities occur.

Communications beyond Normal Channels

Business relationship complexity issues between the enterprise and its external reviewers may arise through service providers and other outsourcing arrangements, joint ventures, alliances, and other transactions that create mutual dependencies between these parties. Such complexity may create concerns over how business is being conducted between the parties. In this case, an enterprise should consider making separate communication channels available to external service providers to allow them to communicate directly with management and other personnel. For example, a customer of products developed through a joint venture may learn that one of the joint venture partners sold products in a country that was not agreed to under the joint venture arrangements. Such a breach may affect the customer's ability to use or resell the products, affecting that customer's business. The enterprise should facilitate channels in which it can communicate concerns to others in the enterprise without disrupting ongoing operations.

Similar to internal communications, the means by which management should communicate externally affects its ability to obtain the information needed, as well as to ensure that key messages about the enterprise are received and understood. Management should consider the many forms and methods of communications used, taking into account the audience, the nature of the communication, its timeliness, and any legal or regulatory requirements.

This is an area that was not even considered with the original COSO framework. Today, enterprises are making numerous and varied agreements with outside service providers to provide a wide range of facilities and resources. It is to the credit of the new version of COSO internal controls that these arrangements are recognized and their concerns addressed.

 ## THE IMPORTANCE OF COSO INFORMATION AND COMMUNICATION

As we mentioned in our introduction to this chapter, the information and communication objective of the original COSO 1992 framework was a little difficult for many to understand when that first framework was issued. The element was visually pictured along the edge of an otherwise integrated framework, and because COSO guidance dictated that all of its internal control elements were integrated, it was difficult to explain how these elements fit into the rest of the model. Things have now changed significantly in our understanding of the new revised information control elements of internal control information and communication. With the updated COSO internal control framework, this element better integrates with other key COSO internal control objectives.

As we have discussed, the concept of information processes as an element of internal control is much more than the IT systems supporting an enterprise. With our worldwide ties to the Internet and with the vast amount of data and information available about various other organizations, industries, and national economies, an enterprise needs to develop processes to capture, act on when appropriate, and use this internal and external information as tools to improve its internal control processes. Key elements introduced here are that an enterprise needs to develop processes to maintain the quality of its information systems and to consider their costs and benefits.

There have also been major changes in enterprise structures since the time of the original COSO internal control framework. Although things were changing even then, enterprise organization structures were typically simpler, with much less reliance on today's frequently outsourced service providers and resources. In addition, enterprises often operated primarily within their own national domestic borders for many major business transactions. How we have changed and are continuing to change!

The typical enterprise uses a wide variety of outsourced serviced providers and other affiliated organizations to provide many of the resources needed to accomplish overall goals and to complete internal control objectives. Strong communication practices and processes are needed here to provide and receive information for and from internal and external parties. The revised COSO internal control framework provides good guidance for establishing effective communication processes here as well as effective information distribution techniques with an overall goal of better achieving internal control objectives.

NOTES

1. Robert Moeller, *Brink's Modern Internal Auditing*, 7th ed. (Hoboken, NJ: John Wiley & Sons, 2009), p. 39, provides a description of the original COSO 1992 internal control framework
2. Robert R. Moeller, *Sarbanes-Oxley Internal Controls, Effective Auditing with AS5, COBIT and ITIL* (Hoboken, NJ: John Wiley & Sons, 2008).

NOTES

CHAPTER EIGHT

COSO Internal Control Components: Monitoring Activities

O NGOING EVALUATIONS OR A COMBINATION of separate evaluations should be used to ascertain whether each of the components of internal controls discussed in the preceding chapters is present and functioning. Enterprise management should monitor these control activities and also consider the information and communication procedures needed to make those internal controls operate effectively. Well-planned and well-designed internal control systems and processes may work as planned, but people may forget or bypass these established system internal controls, and if so, they need to be monitored with corrective actions applied to adjusting these exceptions as needed. Monitoring is a key objective in the revised COSO internal control and framework. In the original version of the COSO internal controls, as shown in Exhibit 3.1, it appeared at the top level or peak of the COSO pyramid. The revised framework, as shown in Exhibit 3.2, now places monitoring solidly at the base, beneath the other components.

Despite its position in the COSO internal control diagram, monitoring is a key element in the COSO internal control framework, and senior management needs to recognize that unmonitored controls tend to deteriorate over time. Monitoring, as defined in the COSO framework, is implemented to help ensure that internal control processes continue to operate effectively. When monitoring is designed and implemented appropriately, an enterprise will benefit from these monitoring processes because it is more likely to

- Identify and correct internal control problems on a timely basis.
- Produce more accurate and reliable information for use in decision making.
- Prepare accurate and timely financial statements.
- Be in a position to provide periodic certifications or assertions on the effectiveness of internal controls.

This chapter introduces the monitoring activities objective or element of the revised COSO internal control framework. Under the original COSO framework, we tended to think of internal control monitoring as primarily an internal audit or high-level management review of installed internal controls. With today's typical enterprise internal control environment, with the frequent use of outsourced service providers, shared technologies, and often complex organization structures, effective monitoring processes are often more difficult and complex to install. Nevertheless, an enterprise needs these effective internal control monitoring processes in place, coupled with the related reporting of monitoring activities to management and the board of directors.

IMPORTANCE OF COSO MONITORING INTERNAL CONTROL ACTIVITIES

Monitoring activities assess whether each of the five objectives or components of internal controls, including the control environment, risk assessment, and others, is present and functioning. An enterprise should use ongoing and separate evaluation processes to ascertain whether established internal control principles, across both the enterprise and its subunits, are in effect, present, and functioning. Monitoring, here, is a key input into the organization's assessment of the effectiveness of internal controls. The revised COSO internal controls framework identifies two principles for the monitoring activities internal control component:

1. The organization selects, develops, and performs ongoing and/or separate evaluations to ascertain whether the components of internal controls are present and functioning.
2. The enterprise evaluates and communicates internal control deficiencies in a timely manner to those parties responsible for taking corrective action, including senior management and the board of directors, as appropriate.

An enterprise's system of internal controls will often change over time, and the entity's objectives and its components of internal controls may also change as well. Also, procedures may become less effective or obsolete, may no longer be in place and functioning, or may be deemed insufficient to support the achievement of new or updated internal control objectives. Monitoring activities should be selected, developed, and performed to ascertain whether each control component or principle from the five internal control components is present and functioning and whether some forms of internal control deficiencies exist. Management also needs to determine whether their systems of internal controls continue to be relevant and able to address new risks.

Where appropriate, monitoring activities identify and examine expectation gaps relating to internal control anomalies and abnormalities, which may indicate that either one or more components of internal controls, including controls to affect principles across the enterprise and its subunits, are not present and functioning. Monitoring activities will generally identify root causes of such breakdowns and may operate within various business processes across the enterprise and its subunits. These words are taken from the supporting COSO internal control guidance materials and say that appropriate monitoring processes help to dig out and identify potential problems that have been all but ignored. This author's background in directing and managing a relatively large internal audit functions found that scheduled audits frequently pointed to this role. In this internal audit role at a then-large U.S. corporation, we frequently found such internal control anomalies as part of scheduled reviews.

Enterprises need to consider underlying details in determining whether an activity is a control activity, as was discussed in Chapter 6, versus a monitoring activity, especially when the activity involves some level of supervisory review. Review activities are not automatically classified as monitoring activities. For example, the intent of a monthly completeness control activity would be to detect and correct errors, where a corresponding monitoring activity would only be to ask why there were errors in the first place and then to task management with fixing the process to prevent future errors. In simple terms, a control activity responds to a specific risk, whereas a monitoring activity assesses whether controls within each of the five components of internal controls are operating as intended, among other things. Exhibit 8.1 shows an example of the relationship of control activities and monitoring activities, using an accounts payable reconciliation process as an example. As always, when we consider any aspect of COSO internal controls, we should take into account the three-dimensional nature of the COSO framework and control relationships: up, down, and across.

The COSO revised framework monitoring activities guidance materials principles emphasize that an enterprise should conduct ongoing evaluations to support its monitoring activities and that an enterprise should identify and communicate any

EXHIBIT 8.1   Monitoring Activities for an Accounts Payable Reconciliation

Control Activities	Monitoring Activities
The accounts payable at one enterprise unit, Division A, reconciles the Division A payable subledger on a periodic basis. Reconciling items are investigated and resolved on a timely basis.	Management should be independent of those involved in the performance of the control activity: • Inspects documentation that the reconciliations were performed across all divisions and subsidiaries. • Examines for identifiable trends in the volume and/or nature of the reconciling items noted. • Management should evaluate whether the sources and quality of information used for the payable reconciliation are appropriate. • Management should evaluate whether new risks relating to changes in internal and external factors were identified, assessed, and responded to in the payables reconciliation.
The accounts payable supervisor periodically reviews and approves the payables subledger to general ledger account reconciliation.	Management should periodically evaluate whether the supervisors performing the review and approval processes are properly trained and knowledgeable.

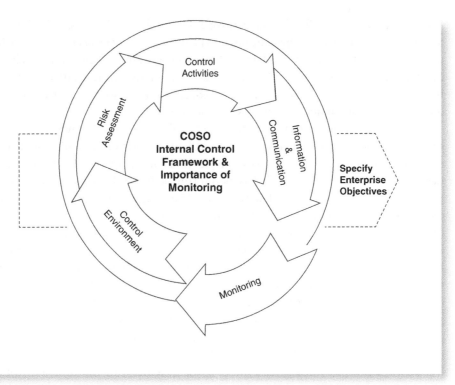

EXHIBIT 8.2 COSO Monitoring Process

known internal control deficiencies as part of its monitoring activities. Installation of appropriate monitoring activities brings to completion a full circle of internal control processes, as illustrated in Exhibit 8.2. The idea behind this exhibit is that when an enterprise develops and implements enterprise objectives, that action should go through each of the COSO control components. In a circular fashion, moving from establishing or building an appropriate control environment, this cycle moves to monitoring activities, and those monitoring activities act as a review factor over all other internal control components.

 ## COSO MONITORING PRINCIPLE 1: CONDUCT ONGOING AND SEPARATE EVALUATIONS

An enterprise should select, develop, and perform ongoing and/or separate evaluations to monitor or ascertain whether the components of internal controls are present and functioning. Monitoring can be done through some combination of separate evaluations or continuous monitoring processes. A separate onetime internal audit over some area of operations or internal controls is an example of a separate monitoring activity. Internal audit may schedule a single review of an area, based on its risk assessment, and then may return to review that same area again, based on any internal control deficiencies found in the first review or just part of its regular internal audit scheduling.

However, there would be no internal audit reviews or monitoring from one audit to the next, unless management makes a special request for an additional audit. Separate evaluations should be conducted periodically by management, internal audit, or external parties, among others. The scope and frequency of separate evaluations are a matter of management judgment.

Continuous monitoring processes are similar to the continuous internal audit processes that some internal audit functions are adopting today. They also are like an oil pressure light in an automobile that flashes a warning only if the pressure is out of bounds. Ongoing evaluations are generally defined as routine operations that are built into business processes, performed on a real-time basis, and that react to changed conditions. Where ongoing evaluations are built into business processes, their internal controls components are usually structured to monitor themselves on an ongoing basis.

Unmonitored controls tend to deteriorate over time. The COSO framework defines monitoring as processes to help ensure that internal controls continue to operate effectively. When monitoring is designed and implemented appropriately, an enterprise should benefit because it is more likely to

- Identify and correct internal control problems on a timely basis.
- Produce more accurate and reliable information for use in decision making.
- Prepare accurate and timely financial statements.
- Be in a position to provide periodic certifications or assertions on the effectiveness of internal control.

Over time, effective monitoring can lead to organizational efficiencies and reduced costs associated with public reporting on internal controls because problems are identified and addressed in a proactive, rather than a reactive, manner.

Ongoing Evaluation Processes

Both manual and automated ongoing evaluation processes can be powerful tools to monitor the presence and functioning of the components of internal controls in the ordinary course of managing the business. Ongoing evaluations are generally performed by line operating or functional managers, who are competent in the area of review and have sufficient knowledge to understand what is being evaluated, giving thoughtful consideration to the implications of the information they receive. By focusing on relationships, inconsistencies, or other relevant implications, they can raise issues to follow up with other personnel as necessary to determine whether corrective or other actions are needed.

The nice words in the COSO internal control guidance notwithstanding, what is COSO ongoing monitoring? It is nothing really unique or special as a COSO process. From our interpretation, much of the COSO ongoing evaluation monitoring process is really a call for enterprise direct supervision. Today, this is almost an old-fashioned concept with work today often performed by remote employees through Internet sites, team structures in performing work duties, and often very short tenure and limited experience managers. It was the old-line direct supervisor who worked directly with a work crew, helped them with some problems and fixed others, checked attendance and approved limited overtime hours, and reported problems and performance data to the next level up of management. These kinds of people and roles often really do not exist today, but these processes and concepts are a way to implement ongoing monitoring evaluations.

While senior management should always review summary reports and take corrective actions, the first level of supervision and the related enterprise structure often play an even more significant role in monitoring. Direct supervision of clerical activities, for example, should routinely review and correct lower-level errors and assure improved clerical employee performance. This is also an area in which the importance of an adequate separation of duties is emphasized by COSO. Dividing duties between employees allows them to serve as a monitoring check on one another.

Of course, an enterprise will frequently use technology to support control activities and to monitor its components of internal control. Technology offers an opportunity to use IT automated monitoring, which has a high standard of objectivity—once properly programmed and tested—and it allows for efficient reviews of large volumes of data at low cost. Automated monitoring activities can be very effective and efficient, but they should be well documented, with strong audit trails covering these monitoring actions.

Separate Monitoring Evaluations

Separate monitoring evaluations are typically not integrated into business operations but are independent, external processes for taking a fresh look to assess whether each of the five components of internal controls is present and functioning. These evaluations include observations, inquiries, reviews, and other examinations, as appropriate, to ascertain whether internal controls to affect principles across the enterprise and its subunits are present and functioning. Internal audit reviews are good examples of these types of separate monitoring evaluations.

Separate evaluations of internal control components may vary in their scope and frequency, depending on the significance of the risks, risk responses, results of ongoing evaluations, and expected impacts on internal control components in managing them. Higher-priority risks and their responses should often be evaluated in greater depth and frequency than lower-priority risks. While higher-priority risks can be evaluated using both ongoing and separate evaluation processes, these evaluations may provide feedback on the results of ongoing evaluations, and the number of separate evaluations can be increased as necessary. A separate evaluation of the overall internal control system or its specific components may be appropriate for a number of reasons, including changes due to corporate acquisitions or dispositions, changes in economic or political conditions, or changes in operations or methods of processing information. The evaluation scope here is determined by whether COSO's three objectives categories—operations, reporting, or compliance—are being addressed.

The enterprise's internal audit function typically takes the lead role in performing separate business unit monitoring evaluations. While an internal audit function is not a *requirement* for establishing COSO internal controls, SOx rules call for it in a publicly traded company, and such a function is almost necessary to enhance the scope, frequency, and objectivity of COSO monitoring separate evaluation reviews.

Monitoring has long been the main responsibility of internal auditors, who perform separate evaluation reviews to assess compliance with established procedures; however, COSO takes a broader view of monitoring as well. The revised COSO internal control framework recognizes that control procedures and other systems change over time. What appeared to be effective when it was first installed may not be that effective in the future, due to changing conditions, new procedures, or other factors.

Because separate evaluations can be conducted periodically by independent managers, employees, or external parties, this is particularly an important role for internal audit. They are evaluators who are knowledgeable about an enterprise's activities and how its monitoring activities function. Along with internal audit, COSO internal controls separate evaluation reviews include

- **Internal audit evaluations.** Supported by strong professional standards, internal auditors, whether in-house or outsourced, are objective and competent resources who perform separate evaluations as part of their regular duties or at the specific request of senior management and the board of directors. As part of its activities, an internal audit function will typically develop an annual plan of areas selected for review, built on risk-based approaches aligned with an enterprise's objectives and stakeholder priorities. Reports of internal audit's reviews are distributed to senior management, the audit committee, and other parties positioned to take action on the recommendations outlined in these reports.
- **A strong, effective internal audit department**. This is a major requirement for building effective enterprise internal controls. For the executive interested in building a strong internal audit function, we would recommend our book on *Modern Internal Auditing*, in which we outline common body of knowledge areas for internal auditors, what they should understand and perform in their internal audits.[1] This is a good source to help people understand some of the areas where internal audit can perform reviews to help enhance enterprise internal controls.
- **Other objective evaluations.** Some entities, such as a not-for-profit organization, may lack a formal internal audit function. Others may have a quality function or a controls compliance group that performs internal audit-like activities that management may use for other internal or external objective evaluation reviews. These evaluators might include compliance officers, production operations specialists, IT security specialists, consultants, and others involved in considering the presence and functioning of an enterprise's internal control components. For example, an IT security specialist might periodically evaluate an enterprise's compliance with security standards, such as the ISO internal control and risk management standards, discussed in Chapter 18.
- **Cross-operating unit or functional evaluations.** An enterprise may use personnel from different operating units or functional areas to evaluate the components of their internal controls. For example, quality audit personnel from one operating unit may periodically evaluate the internal controls of a different operating unit. Adding personnel from different operating units or functional areas on these evaluations also may improve communications between operating units or functional areas.
- **Benchmarking and peer evaluations.** Some enterprises compare or benchmark components of their internal controls against those of other entities. Such comparisons

might be done directly through formal arrangements with another company, often through personnel professional contacts or under the auspice of trade or industry associations. Other enterprises may be able to provide comparative information. Benchmarking studies, however, may not be the best way to monitor one's own internal controls. There may be reluctance for another entity to disclose fully accurate information, and there will always be differences that exist in objectives, facts, and circumstances.

- **Self-assessments.** Separate evaluations may take the form of self-assessments, where those responsible for a particular unit or function may assess the presence or functioning of designated internal controls relating to their direct activities within their operating unit. Self-assessments have less objectivity than other separate evaluation approaches. When a manager is asked to evaluate some internal control area that is part of that same manager's day-to-day area of responsibility, there is a tendency to look at things with rose-colored glasses and not provide a truly objective evaluation. When using this monitoring evaluation information, one should consider the weight and value to be placed on the results.

Many enterprises today use outsourced service providers in such areas as third-party warehousing, Internet hosting, health-care claims processing, retirement plan administration, or loan services. There is a need to understand the activities and controls associated with those designated services and how the outsourced service provider's internal control system affects an enterprise's own system of internal controls.

The types of information available to assess these service providers' internal controls may vary and often can be difficult to collect. An enterprise should try to determine whether an outsourced service provider has its own internal audit or other monitoring processes in place and should take actions to obtain appropriate information about that service provider's control processes. Also, the enterprise using these outsourced services should add a right-to-audit clause in its contracts with these outsourced providers.

Relevant information concerning internal controls at an outsourced service provider may be attained by reviewing an independent audit or examination report, known as a service organization control (SOC) report, typically provided by an external audit firm. A relatively new type of third-party internal control report, SOC reports are introduced in Chapter 20.

When considering circumstances such as the nature and scope of information transferred between parties and the nature of the processing and reporting that the outsourced service provider performs, an enterprise should determine that there is sufficient internal control processing provided by the outsourced service provider without the need for requesting additional documentation.

 ## COSO MONITORING PRINCIPLE 2: EVALUATE AND COMMUNICATE DEFICIENCIES

An enterprise should evaluate and communicate its internal control deficiencies in a timely manner to those parties responsible for taking corrective actions, including senior management and the board of directors, as appropriate. In conducting these monitoring activities, the enterprise should identify monitoring-related matters worthy of attention. Those that represent a potential or real shortcoming in some aspect of the enterprise's system of internal control and that have the potential to adversely affect the ability of the enterprise to achieve its objectives should be referred to as internal control deficiencies. In addition, the enterprise may identify opportunities to improve the efficiency of its internal controls or areas where changes to the current system of internal control may provide a greater likelihood that the enterprise's objectives will be achieved. Although the identifying and the assessing of potential opportunities are not part of the system of internal controls, an enterprise will typically want to capture any opportunities identified and communicate those to the strategy- and objective-setting processes.

Deficiencies in an enterprise's components of internal controls and its underlying principles may also surface from a variety of sources, including

- Reported results from ongoing monitoring evaluations of an enterprise, including managerial activities and the everyday supervision of employees, generate insights from those who are directly involved in the enterprise's activities. These insights are obtained in a real-time manner and can quickly identify deficiencies.
- Separate monitoring evaluations performed by management, internal auditors, functional managers, and other personnel can highlight areas that need to be improved.
- Other components of internal controls provide input relative to the operation of that component.
- External parties, such as customers, vendors, external auditors, and regulators, frequently provide important management information about an entity's components of internal controls.

Communication of Monitoring Findings

The results of ongoing and separate monitoring evaluations should be assessed against management's criteria to determine whom to report to and what is to be reported. All identified internal control deficiencies that can affect an enterprise's ability to develop and achieve its objectives should be communicated to those members of the enterprise's management who are in positions to take timely corrective actions. The scope and approach of these monitoring results, as well as any identified deficiencies, may need to be reported to those enterprise managers conducting the overall assessment of the effectiveness of an enterprise's internal controls.

The nature of the monitoring findings to be communicated will vary, depending on how the deficiency is evaluated against management's criteria, the enterprise individuals' authority to deal with circumstances that arise, and the oversight activities of senior managers. After any identified deficiencies are evaluated, management should determine that remediation efforts are conducted on a timely basis.

Internal control deficiencies are usually reported both to the parties responsible for taking corrective actions and to at least one level of management above that person. This higher level of management provides needed support or oversight for taking corrective actions. Where findings cut across organizational boundaries, the deficiencies should be reported to all relevant parties and to a sufficiently high level to drive appropriate action. That is, deficiencies should be reported as prescribed by established reporting protocols to the full board, the chair of the board, and appropriate board reporting committees.

In considering what needs to be communicated, it is necessary to look at the implications of deficiency findings. It is essential not only that a particular transaction or event be reported, but also that related faulty procedures be reevaluated. Alternative communication channels should also exist for reporting sensitive information, such as illegal or improper acts.

Reporting to Senior Management and the Board of Directors

Providing information on internal control deficiencies to the right parties in the enterprise is critical. Deficiencies that are categorized as material weaknesses, significant deficiencies, minor nonconformities, and major internal control deficiencies should be reported to senior management and the board of directors, as appropriate and in accordance with reporting directives that the enterprise has established. For example, the board of directors may ask senior management or its internal or external auditors to communicate material weaknesses, significant deficiencies, major nonconformities, and other deficiencies or nonconformities that have been encountered in monitoring reviews.

This issue of what or how much to report to senior management and the board of directors, and its audit committee, has been an internal control issue over the years. Prior to SOx in the years before about 2003 or 2004, public accounting firms developed what it called materiality guidelines that effectively said that unless an internal or external audit–reported deficiency affected corporate earnings per share by more than some designated amount, it did not have to be reported to the board and its audit committee as a deficiency. In the years that this author directed an internal audit function and severely questioned this issue with external auditors, one understood why so many deficiencies were never reported to the board.

The financial scandals that led to the passage of SOx revealed that too many internal control deficiencies were ignored by external auditors as nonmaterial and not necessary to report to the board and senior management. The revised audit guidelines issued directly after the passage of SOx threw out materiality rules and said that an error is an error, despite its size. In the years around 2005 and following SOx compliance rules, many board audit committees were faced with material error efficiencies such as the failure to obtain duplicate approving signatures on office supply requisitions.

This whole "what to report" issue was better resolved through the SOx-related Auditing Standard No.5 (AS No.5), and auditors now must take risk into account in their decisions to report a deficiency matter to senior management and the board. The relationship of COSO internal control monitoring and reporting and SOx rules will be discussed further in Chapter 15.

COSO INTERNAL CONTROL MONITORING IN PERSPECTIVE

Effective COSO monitoring processes are a key component to assure that an enterprise has effective internal controls. Management needs to design, develop, and launch internal control processes, but there needs to be some form of monitoring process in place to provide assurances to senior management and others, such as internal auditors, that those internal controls are in place.

Management can launch these monitoring processes by encouraging enterprise staff members with control system responsibility to understand COSO's internal controls framework and its monitoring guidance and then to consider how best to implement monitoring processes or whether they have already been incorporated into certain areas. Furthermore, personnel with appropriate skills, authority, and resources should be charged by management with addressing these four fundamental questions:

1. Have established monitoring processes identified the meaningful risks to enterprise objectives—for example, the risks related to producing accurate, timely, and complete financial statements?
2. Which are the "key controls" that will best support effective monitoring processes regarding the efficacy of internal controls in those risk areas?
3. What information collected from monitoring processes will be persuasive in telling management and the board of directors whether these controls are continuing to operate effectively?
4. Are we presently performing effective monitoring that is not well utilized in the evaluation of internal controls, resulting in unnecessary and costly further testing?

Senior management and the board of directors should understand these concepts of effective monitoring and how they can serve their respective enterprise interests. Chapter 19 talks more about the role of the board in managing and implementing COSO internal controls, but an important board role is to ask management in relation to any area of meaningful risk, "How do you know the internal control system is working? Are the installed monitoring processes providing that guidance?"

COSO's internal control monitoring objective should help enterprises answer these and other questions within the context of their own unique circumstances—circumstances that will change over time. As they progress in achieving effectiveness in monitoring, enterprises likely will have the opportunity to further improve the process through the use of such tools as continuous monitoring or auditing tools, as discussed in Chapter 13, and exception reports tailored to their processes. Over time, effective COSO monitoring processes should lead to organizational efficiencies and reduced costs associated with public reporting on internal control, because internal control problems can be identified and addressed in a proactive, rather than a reactive, manner.

 ## NOTE

1. Robert Moeller, *Brink's Modern Internal Auditing: A Common Body of Knowledge*, 7th ed. (Hoboken, NJ: John Wiley & Sons, 2009).

CHAPTER NINE

COSO Internal Control GRC Operations Controls

G OING BACK TO ITS ORIGINAL 1992 release, the COSO internal control framework was always meant to be viewed as a three-dimensional model or framework, where each cell component in any one dimension was meant to have a relationship with corresponding cells in the other two dimensions. For example, when we consider the internal control activities depicted in Exhibit 3.2, we should evaluate them in terms of the operations, reporting, and compliance controls described in the cells above them, as well as the business unit cells described on the side of the COSO framework. All too often, descriptions of the original COSO internal controls have all but ignored the other two dimensions of the COSO internal control framework and have focused on front-facing components, ranging from the control environment to monitoring activities.

In this chapter and the three chapters following, we will rotate or flip the COSO internal control framework and look at internal control components from COSO's other two dimensions. Here, we will look at the top level of the framework and its operations, reporting, and compliance controls. All three of these components highlight the governance, risk, and compliance (GRC) concepts that have become increasingly important to enterprises today. This perspective is usually ignored in other COSO internal control materials, but we feel it makes it easier to understand and use this three-dimensional internal control model.

 ## COSO OPERATIONS OBJECTIVES

Exhibit 9.1 shows our familiar COSO internal control framework, but here it is flipped over 90 degrees, with the panels for operations, reporting, and compliance controls front facing. These internal control components are very important for establishing effective

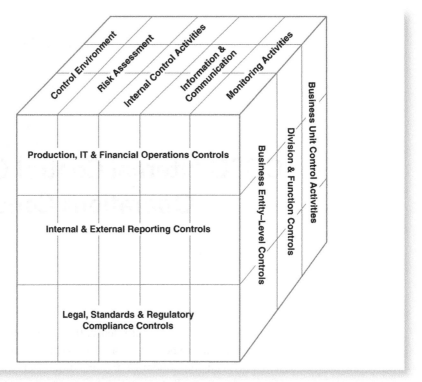

EXHIBIT 9.1 COSO Internal Controls, GRC Perspective

enterprise GRC processes, and this chapter will focus on important operations controls and how they relate to the other components and dimensions of the COSO internal control framework.

In this section, we will start with just one of these COSO framework elements—operations controls or operations objectives. Operational objectives are typically a series of short-term or limited goals that are structured to move an enterprise closer to the realization of its long-term goals. Also known as tactical objectives, each operational objective should address some aspect of the business operation and implement some types of changes that improve the position of the enterprise in a direct or indirect manner. It is not unusual for several operational objectives to be pursued concurrently, with various objectives focusing on the function of different areas of the enterprise.

Operational objectives are important for the overall process of enterprise-wide operational planning. By identifying specific tasks that incrementally move the enterprise closer to its longer-term goals, management can measure progress as those tasks are performed. For example, if a sales department has a long-term goal of achieving a specific amount in sales within a three-year period, the department may implement tasks that allow the sales team to generate new sales collateral for use with prospective customers. At the same time, other objectives may focus on creating a new database that makes tracking prospects and their progress toward becoming customers with greater ease and enhancing the way that leads are generated by and for the team. As each of these operational objectives is identified and implemented, sales are expected to increase and thus move the department closer to that three-year goal.

The basic idea here is that an enterprise needs to establish some operational goals and plans at all levels. At its very simplest level, these goals and plans can be viewed as the budgets established within an enterprise, whether they be the high-level annual performance budgets, developed by senior management and approved by the board, or the individual expense budgets developed by individual departmental units to plan for such matters as clerical labor costs and miscellaneous expenses. Planning processes are needed here, and then these approved budgets effectively become operations controls for various levels of the operation.

Going beyond just planning and budgeting, operations controls should be developed and established at several levels in the enterprise. While a full discussion of them would almost result in a treatise on management techniques, this chapter will briefly discuss IT systems operational controls and operations procedures operational controls, in addition to planning budgeting operational controls. We will link each of these with the other two dimensions of the COSO internal control framework.

 ## PLANNING AND BUDGETING OPERATIONS CONTROLS

Effective budgeting systems are an important operations control and help both organizational units and their responsible managers perform major internal control functions. Budgets are prepared at various levels of an enterprise and can be defined as management's quantitative expression of plans for a forthcoming period. While we generally think of budgets as an overall financial plan for a current or future period, almost every enterprise resource can be subjected to budget controls, whether the usage of IT resources, the land available for an agricultural project, the time required for new customer sales calls, or other matters. Each of these eventually can be translated into some measurable unit of monetary terminology; we can build effective budgetary controls using other units, such as the number of clicks needed on a computer mouse device.

Budgeting, when done properly, can serve as a planning and operational control. An enterprise's goals and performance objectives should be documented in financial or otherwise measurable unit terms. Once formulated, these plans are used throughout a typical year period, with monthly performance reports to compare budgeted results with actual results. To control operations, management can examine the performance reports and take any necessary corrective actions.

The role that effective budgeting plays in the development of effective operations controls is best understood when it is related to the fundamentals of management. The many existing definitions of management can be expressed in terms of the five major business management functions of planning, organizing, staffing, directing, and controlling. Management must first plan, and that plan is executed by organizing, staffing, and directing operations. To control operations, management must institute appropriate techniques of observation and reporting to determine how actual results compare to plans. Budgeting is concerned primarily with the planning and controlling functions of management.

Budget planning is a future-oriented process that specifies in some form what management wants to do. Management has certain operations control variables, including financial resources, plant and equipment, products, production methods, and human resources. Planning also involves making forecasts and assumptions about the enterprise's external environment, which is uncontrollable. Examples of uncontrollable factors in the external environment are government actions, consumer spending, interest rates, and actions of competitors. Because management cannot manipulate external environmental variables, it must confine its plans to controllable factors. Thus, a plan consists of what management is going to do with the variables it can control.

Operations Goals

The management of enterprise operations controls processes begins with the establishment of management goals for these processes, stated in terms of profit, return on investment, product leadership, market share, product diversification, or simply survival. These goals can be general in their nature or very specific. General goals, which are directional in nature, usually are set first. Examples of general goals are growth of the enterprise, quality leadership, being the lowest-cost producer, and maintenance of the current level of service to customers.

Larger enterprises usually develop a hierarchy of goals. Corporate goals should be set by senior management, with the degree of participation in this process varying by company. Goals can then be set at successively lower levels in the enterprise, with subgoals being set in harmony with upper-level goals to help lower-level managers visualize how their efforts contribute to the accomplishment of corporate goals.

The success or failure of this goal-setting and planning is determined by the policies adopted by the top executives, including the CEO and the board of directors. Company goals should be established in a number of important areas, such as the following:

- Product mix goals to change from a wide range of product lines to a core of fewer units that reflect the enterprise's core competencies.
- Production goals to change the character of operations by redesigning methods and activities.
- Marketing goals to change the share of market desired, such as identifying new market areas or changing distribution methods.
- Advertising goals to determine what media will be used and what resources will be allocated to each.
- Research and development goals regarding new or improved products.

The preceding is hardly a list of the types or the hierarchy of goals that an enterprise might establish. A next step here is for management at multiple levels to use strategic planning to translate these goals into short- and long-range plans.

Strategic planning is the process of actively planning the future direction of an enterprise by adopting realistic goals and programs for the enterprise and its key business units in relation to its environment. It typically involves short-, intermediate-, and long-range questions, and strategic actions taken today will affect the enterprise's competitive position in the future. An enterprise, however, does not need a strategic plan to have a long-range plan.

Enterprise goals and both long-range and strategic plans are important elements of COSO operations controls. They are needed at all levels, from the overall enterprise to individual business units. They should also be part of other COSO internal control elements, from the control environment through internal control activities and monitoring.

Budgeting and Budget Performance Monitoring

Effective budgeting and budget-monitoring processes are important operations control processes needed to translate planning and goal setting objectives into measurable processes. A budget can be defined as management's quantitative expression of plans for a forthcoming period. Budgets should be prepared at various levels of an enterprise, but with a master budget reflecting enterprise goals and objectives that becomes the overall financial plan for a period. The budgeting process includes operating and financial budgets.

Operating budgets show an enterprise's planned sales and operating expenses, while financial budgets reflect financing plans, such as borrowing, leasing, and cash management. Budgeting, when done properly, can serve as an important set of planning and controlling processes as part of system operations controls. These established and authorized budgets will usually represent an enterprise's goals and performance objectives documented in financial terms. Once formulated, these plans can then be used throughout the year, as well as in monthly performance reports to compare budgeted results with actual results.

Exhibit 9.2 shows the interactions of various levels of budgets in a larger enterprise. We start with a top-level, long-range, or strategic forecast that drives both a sales forecast and a capital expenditures budget. In other words, what do we expect to sell or produce and what types of assets do we need to acquire? These forecasts flow into a series of supporting budgets, product costs, inventory, administrative costs, and others. This budget process should be thought of in terms of the two dimensions of the COSO internal control framework. That is, there is a need for budgets covering various levels of the enterprise and for specialized internal control areas.

Budgets, of course, are of little value unless their projected periodic values are matched against actual results, with budget performance monitored. As an important operations control, management should examine the performance reports, initiate responsibility reporting processes, and take necessary corrective actions, all roles that are related to the fundamentals of management.

Responsibility reporting is an operations control process requiring that all expenditures are traceable to some manager within the enterprise. In other words, management must be able to authorize or veto these budgeted expenditures. Responsibility reporting is an important operations control and parallels a requirement that all performance objectives should be traceable to some manager in the enterprise. Accordingly, the expenditures incurred by a manager and the organizational unit under his or her control in pursuing a performance objective need to be recorded. This COSO reporting dimension, then, would largely reflect the organizational structure of the enterprise.

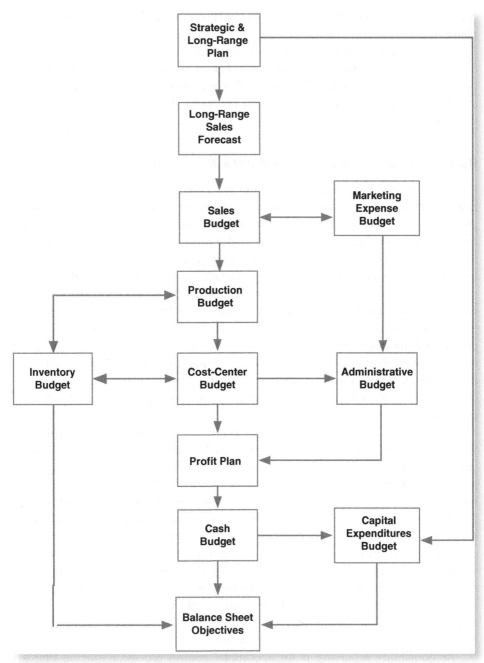

EXHIBIT 9.2 Budget Function Interactions

Effective planning and budget processes are important enterprise operations controls. The following sections discuss IT systems operations controls and procedures controls. The scope or types of these operations controls certainly are much broader, but our idea here is to introduce planning and budgeting, two important COSO operations control elements. The idea is to always relate all enterprise operations controls to the other two dimensions of the COSO. We should always consider the inactions and dependencies of any internal control element with other related internal control elements.

IT SYSTEMS OPERATIONS CONTROLS

IT operations represent a major component of COSO enterprise controls. Although we have thought of IT controls in terms of what we traditionally called application and general IT controls, this view should be much broader in today's world-wide pervasive IT systems and processes. Exhibit 9.3 is a picture of today's more typical IT control environment. We should think of each of these areas as a COSO operations controls. The following sections summarize these IT operations controls areas on a high level, but for more IT management control information, we recommend this author's book on IT security and controls.[1]

IT Policy and Governance Controls

The top component of this element and application control hierarchy highlights the importance of top-level IT policy and governance controls. IT policies are necessary for the protection and efficient operation of an enterprise and the productivity of all stakeholders. Yet it is also important to carefully align these policies with specific organizational needs and strategies.

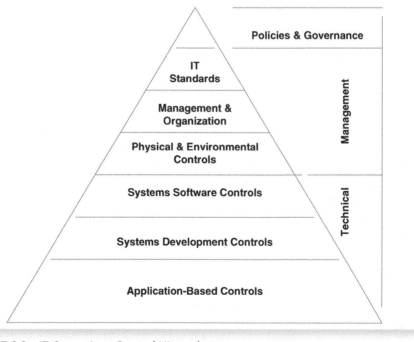

EXHIBIT 9.3   IT Operations Control Hierarchy

IT policies should be practical, adaptable, and effective. They are often best developed and implemented by a policy task force composed of senior IT management and key executives from every group or division affected by these IT policies as well as senior enterprise management. This creates accountable ownership of the IT policy management function, a group or function responsible for creating, communicating, monitoring, changing, and enforcing IT policy. Its first "task" should be to develop policies based on what the enterprise needs and then to establish processes and procedures for everything from software procurement and information security to compliance and disaster recovery. While there are many unique needs and requirements, an enterprise should consider developing IT policies covering the following areas:

- Controlling all levels and types of IT costs.
- Optimizing IT assets, with goals of improving productivity.
- Simplification and internal controls improvement of IT processes.
- Remaining organized and compliant with laws, regulations, and standards over time.
- Monitoring and enforcing IT security and employee compliance.

Enterprise IT policies should provide a link or an anchor point for other management and technical controls. When there is a question about any lower-level IT controls, as shown on Exhibit 9.3, there should be a clear path to an established and approved policy.

IT governance issues and practices operate at a different level and almost above established IT policies. There is no single definition of IT governance, and an Internet search shows that IT governance means different things to different people.

- IT governance is often used to describe the processes for deciding how money for IT resources should be spent. This IT governance process includes the prioritization and justification of IT investments. It includes controls on spending, such as budgets and authorization levels.
- IT governance is often used to describe many different aspects of IT changes. At the low level, it is sometimes used to describe project management and describes the management and controls of a portfolio of IT-related projects.
- IT governance is used to make sure that IT change management processes comply with regulatory requirements, both for governmental laws and rules and professional standards.
- IT governance is the process of aligning IT changes and expenditures to business requirements and expenditures. Sometimes it also covers the deployment of IT staff.
- IT governance is also used to describe the management and control of IT services. For example, service level agreements (SLAs), discussed in Chapter 13, are used to define levels of service that are acceptable to business and then used as a basis for monitoring services.
- IT governance makes sure that day-to-day problem fixing and support of all IT resources are aligned to business needs.

IT governance deals primarily with the connection between an enterprise's business focus and the IT-related management and operation of the enterprise. The whole concept highlights the importance of IT-related matters and emphasizes that strategic IT decisions should be owned by the most senior levels of corporate management, including the board of directors, rather than just senior IT management, such as the chief information officer (CIO). IT governance concepts have really evolved since the earlier days of enterprise IT operations, where senior management often handed over the authority and funding of IT operations to specialists, with such titles as CIO, and really did not aggressively manage IT resources from an overall management perspective.

IT Standards

COSO internal controls are a framework to provide management at all levels with some general guidance to support their IT governance policies and practices. One level down, standards exist to support the requirements of an enterprise's generally stated policies. Larger enterprises are in a position to develop their own IT standards, but many will adopt best practices or recognized professional practices as the basis for these IT standards. The ITIL set of best practices, discussed in Chapter 13, is an example of IT documents that can be established as an enterprise's IT standards.

Senior and IT management should establish standards within their IT organization, covering such areas as new systems development, software acquisition, documentation, and applications control procedures, among many other issues included in the Exhibit 6.2 hierarchy. Evidence should be in place to demonstrate that these standards and supporting procedures have been communicated and followed by all members of the IT organization. Although there are certainly many more issues here, examples of these IT standards might include

- **E-mail communications and social networking protocols**. Social networking software tools such as Facebook or Twitter, discussed in Chapter 13, can violate enterprise security rules and privacy practices, if used improperly. An enterprise also can experience many e-mail abuses, such as massive and unnecessary attachments connected to messages, excessive use of "cute" graphics, or the sharing of confidential data. Similar to the enterprise codes of conduct, an enterprise and its IT function should develop standards for social media and e-mail use and messaging.
- **IT security standards**. IT security and privacy concerns are major issues for all enterprises, and a wide range of standards and monitoring practices is needed. These can cover such areas as regular backups of key files and systems, controls over the issuance and maintenance of passwords, and physical controls over IT assets.
- **Systems development standards**. Although IT functions develop far fewer from-scratch programs and applications today and typically purchase necessary software packages, systems development standards are needed. Enterprises need to establish systems development life cycle (SDLC) process standards to develop and implement new IT applications. The SDLC processes are discussed as part of systems development controls, but standards are needed as well.

▪ **IT documentation**. Standards should specify the minimum level of documentation required for each application or IT installation. These standards should include different classes of applications, processes, and physical IT facilities.

These are just a few examples of the types of standards that senior management should expect to find when establishing general controls in an IT facility. For a larger enterprise, these standards may exist at multiple levels, with general standards issued through the CIO and more detailed standards in place for development and processing centers.

IT Management and Organization Controls

Effective IT organization and management processes are an important area of COSO operations controls. Whether a larger enterprise with multiple large-facility data centers or a smaller server system and a limited number of attached terminals, responsible management should have a good understanding of overall enterprise IT management controls, including provisions for an adequate separation of duties, financial management, and overall change management controls. Senior management should work with internal audit and its IT auditors to perform a preliminary review of the IT function's organization and management controls, as described in Exhibit 9.4.

EXHIBIT 9.4   IT Management Preliminary Survey Review Steps

1. Review the organizational chart and position titles to determine that an appropriate separation of functions exists. Resolve and correct any potential conflicts with IT management.
2. Obtain job descriptions of key IT personnel and review them for adequate and appropriate qualifications, task definitions, and responsibilities. Ensure that security and control accountability are appropriately assigned to key personnel.
3. Based on discussions within IT management, both inside and outside the IT organization, assess whether the IT organizational structure is aligned with business strategies to ensure expected IT service delivery.
4. Review documented IT policies and selected procedures for completeness and relevance, with specific emphasis on security, business continuity planning, operations, and IT customer service.
5. Inquire whether responsibilities have been assigned to keep the policies and procedures current, to educate/communicate them to staff members, and to monitor compliance with them.
6. Based on discussions with senior IT management, assess whether strategic, operational, and tactical IT plans are in place to ensure alignment with the organization's overall business plans.
7. Determine the existence of an IT steering committee and assess this committee's functions through a limited review of steering committee meeting minutes to assess its level of activity.
8. Assess whether IT planning and control linkages have been established through communication or reports to the audit committee.
9. Ensure that a formal methodology is used in the development of new systems or major enhancements to systems in production. The methodology should include formal steps for definition, feasibility assessment, design, construction, testing, and implementation, as well as formal approvals at every stage.

EXHIBIT 9.4 (*continued*)

10. Determine that processes are in place for making changes to application programs in production, including testing and documentation sign-off, and formal approvals to implement the change into production.
11. Ensure that responsibility for physical and logical security has been appropriately apportioned and that appropriate documented procedures exist.
12. Review procedures in place for operating and maintaining the network, in terms of device configuration and software parameter changes, and ensure that procedures for allocating and maintaining the network configuration are performed on a scheduled basis and under proper change management.
13. Review the business continuity and IT disaster-recovery plans to ensure that detailed plans for the recovery of operations have been prepared and that the plans are documented, are communicated to the appropriate personnel, and are properly tested on a periodic basis.
14. Review both the IT budget and actual costs, as well as performance, against those measures to assess financial performance. Discuss reasons for any variances.

These preliminary survey steps are not structured as a formal IT audit but are informal steps for senior IT managers to better understand their internal control processes in place. The objective of such a survey is to gain some background information to serve as a basis for scheduling other IT reviews or for determining the status of control issues that surfaced in prior reviews.

Although a preliminary IT internal control survey can cover a wide range of areas regarding IT organization and management issues, the need for an adequate separation of duties is vital in many controls and is often the most important control issue. The functions of initiating, authorizing, inputting, processing, and checking data should be separated to ensure that no individual can create an error, omission, or other irregularity and then authorize it as evidence. Traditional separations of duties within an IT environment are divided between systems development and operations, where operations personnel responsible for running production systems should have little or no contact with the development process.

IT Physical and Environmental Controls

In older, traditional IT environments, computer operations were often a prime area of internal control concerns. Computer operators then had considerable power to make changes or to bypass systems controls, such as overriding data file label protections, making changes to program-processing sequences, or inserting unauthorized program instructions into production applications. Although these override control violations are still possible today, the complexity of large computer operating systems, the often-complex connections between systems servers, and the sheer volume of work passing through a modern IT operations center make unauthorized operator override actions difficult. IT management often has greater risks to consider, and many once-common IT operations control improvement recommendations are no longer feasible. For example, older data center computers had a terminal monitor or even a console printer attached to record operator commands, but IT operations management often ignored these log reports, even though they may have been useful for tracing inappropriate operator activities. Today, this console activity is still recorded onto log files, but the sheer volume of that data makes a periodic human review of console log reports unrealistic; other tools and controls are available to help IT understand these operations controls, and control procedures should be established to gain an understanding of these specialized IT control procedures.

IT systems today are operating in a client-server or even cloud computing world, where powerful but very major server computers drive a wide range of terminals and storage devices. Computer operations centers are much more automated and efficient than they were not so many years ago. User terminals are protected by firewalls and are connected—through either cables or wireless connections—to complex enterprise-controlled networks or to the Internet. We have moved to the concept of what we call *cloud computing*, where the IT network is so vast and complex that it appears as if we are just connecting a device to a cloud in the sky to receive interconnections. There is more on cloud computing in Chapter 14.

IT management often face challenges in building and establishing controls in a smaller IT systems operations, ranging from networked client-server configurations to enterprise desktop systems. General control evaluation problems arise because smaller systems often are installed with limited staffs in a more "user-friendly" type of environment. IT management, however, too often looks for general IT controls in terms of the more traditional, larger mainframe IT environments, even though mainframe systems have been almost a thing of the past for many years now. That is, senior managers are often looking for the strong physical security, good revision, and proper separation-of-duties controls that often do not exist or are only partially implemented in typical smaller-system environments. This less formal approach was adequate when these small business or desktop systems were used primarily for single-office accounting or similar lower-risk applications. The large capacity and capability of smaller systems, the growth of the Internet, and the transition to client-server computing have made these smaller systems important parts of the IT control framework. When faced with evaluating controls in these smaller computer system settings, traditional management sometimes reverts to the traditional, almost "cookbook" types of internal control assessments. That is, it recommends that desktop systems be placed in locked rooms or that a small, two-person IT development staff be expanded to four, in order to ensure proper separation of duties. There may be situations where such controls are appropriate, but often they are not applicable in a smaller business setting.

Enterprises today implement increasing numbers of smaller client-server systems to support business units, for specific departmental computing, or provide IT for the entire enterprise. Despite their smaller size, these systems often represent significant general control concerns, and adequate general controls are necessary in order to place reliance on specific application controls.

Smaller systems can be implemented in a variety of ways, depending on the system configuration and the size of the enterprise, and both general and IT management should develop appropriate general internal control procedures to review their general controls.

IT Systems Software Controls

Virtually every computer system has some type of master program—often called an operating system—to perform such tasks as scheduling an application program to run and saving or storing the results of an application program and outputting the results to a printer or a display device. No matter what the size of the computer operation, these operating system master programs and related supporting programs control a system's operations. An enterprise needs systems software control processes to better manage and control its IT operations. Whether it be a Microsoft Windows operating system on a laptop computer or Linux controlling an office server system or some form of handheld device using Android, the operating system (OS) is a key component of any computer system operation, and its supporting systems software is essential to support enterprise IT operations.

An IT or computer OS is the master program that serves as the prime interface between all system hardware components and the users of that computer system, both people and sometimes other automated devices. An OS is responsible for the management and coordination of the many activities that are necessary to run certain applications on a computer system. Many senior managers first encounter an OS while using their laptops or desktop personal computers equipped with either Microsoft or Apple Macintosh OS programs. A version of Microsoft's Windows OS has been perhaps the most familiar to many. In its multiple versions, it can be both a major help and sometimes a source of frustration.

The origins of today's OS go back to the days of mainframe computers, when the then manufacturers of these devices—Burroughs, Control Data, Honeywell, IBM, Univac, and many others—each developed complex OS programs for their own systems. Each was fairly unique to that computer manufacturer and its individual machine models. As an example, although it was years ago, Univac, which was really the founder of large-scale computer systems, had its model 1100 and 494 series of mainframe machines. Each of these products had a unique OS that did not communicate with other Univac machines and certainly not with other mainframe system competitors. In those early days of mainframe computers, there were many such computer models and each was unique, and many of the machine OS controllers had innovative features in those early days of computer systems. As another example, Univac, in its 1100 series of computers, had facilities for real-time processing, a feature that took the market-dominant IBM many years to later introduce.

The concept of a mainframe OS really changed, however, when IBM introduced its System/360 series of computer and mainframe operating systems in the mid-1960s. The IBM System/360 was a family of mainframe computers available in widely differing capacities and price points and with a single operating system, OS/360, planned for every individual model. This concept of a single OS spanning an entire product line was crucial for the success of OS/360, and IBM's current mainframe operating systems, later called MVS and now z/OS, are distant descendants of this original system. Applications written for the OS/360 can still be run on some larger-scale modern IBM machines.

Exhibit 9.5 conceptually illustrates how an OS interacts with both computer resources and its applications. In the center, the computer system primarily consists of its central processing unit (CPU) and random access memory, as well as the external

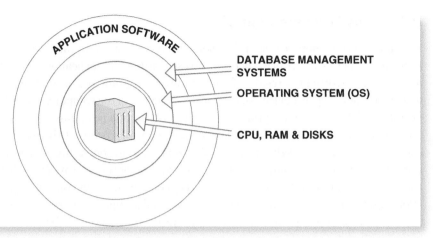

EXHIBIT 9.5   IT Operating Systems Architecture

storage devices. The CPU is the set of highly integrated circuits that define the logic of how the computer will operate. The OS give instructions to the CPU and manages these other computer resources. The next ring out are key software components, such as an Oracle database system and others. The applications are then found at the outer ring. Users and IT management primarily deal with these applications.

An enterprise needs some strong control procedures in place to manage and control its installed systems software, including operating systems, database management, revision control tools, security management, and other utilities. These are all necessary for a well-controlled IT operation that will support overall COSO operations objectives. A more detailed discussion of these issues, in a COSO internal control framework sense, can be found in Chapter 13.

IT System Development and Application Controls

IT applications are the tools that bring value to computer systems; they drive many, if not most, of today's enterprise business processes. These IT applications will range from the relatively simple, such as an accounts payable system to pay vendor invoices, to the highly complex, such as an enterprise resource management (ERM) set of multiple inter-related database applications to control virtually all enterprise business processes. Many IT applications today are based on vendor-purchased software, an increasing number come from Web-based services, some are developed by in-house systems and programming teams, and many others are based on spreadsheet or database desktop processes. Although the IT general control procedures, higher up on the Exhibit 9.3 COSO IT controls hierarchy, cover internal controls for all IT operations, specific control processes apply to each installed IT application. In order to establish effective COSO operations controls in specific areas of enterprise operations, such as accounting, distribution, or engineering, senior management should understand the controls over its supporting IT applications. These specific application controls can often be more critical to achieving overall internal control objectives than general IT controls are.

Application controls, however, are very dependent on the quality of overall IT general controls. For example, if there are inadequate general controls over an IT configuration management process, as will be discussed in Chapter 13, it will be difficult to rely on the controls built into a specific application that is dependent on strong configuration management processes. For example, even though an IT order-entry application is properly screening sales orders for valid credit approvals, the surrounding general controls must also be considered. Without IT configuration management update controls, in this example, the order-entry system's programs could be changed, without management's authorization, perhaps to override established credit approval controls.

A typical enterprise may use a large and diverse number of production IT applications. They will support a wide variety of functions within the enterprise, starting with accounting but including such areas as production, marketing, distribution, and others. These supporting applications may be implemented using a variety of IT technologies, such as centralized systems with telecommunication networks, Internet-based network systems, client-server applications, and even older mainframe batch-processing systems. Some of these applications may have been developed in-house, but increasingly large numbers of them are based on purchased software packages installed locally or accessed through Web-based service providers. In-house-developed applications may be written in a language such as C# (also called C-sharp) or Visual Basic, a database report-generator language such as SQL, or more typically today, the object-oriented language JAVA. Applications documentation may range from very complete to almost nonexistent, and management should understand this environment when assessing COSO IT operations controls.

Although members of management sometimes do not have a good understanding of IT general control issues, they are frequently interested in IT internal control issues covering specific applications. For example, an IT audit report finding of an incorrect discount calculation based on a foreign currency conversion problem in an accounts payable application is sure to draw attention. However, because of the relative complexity of many IT applications and because their controls often reside both within the application and in supporting user areas, appropriate overall application controls can often be a challenge.

Most enterprises today have installed a large number of IT applications operating on their main client server systems, as well as on local handheld wireless or local desktop systems or operating through the Internet to a cloud computing provider. Some of the applications may have been developed by the IT department through the use of purchased software, while others may have been fully developed in-house. Some may be closely tied or linked to other enterprise applications, while others may be almost free-standing. However, strong enterprise polices and standards should be in place, requiring that all such applications meet enterprise internal control standards.

An enterprise should have formal internal control processes in place to select, build, test, and then implement effective, well-controlled IT applications. Exhibit 9.6 outlines some of the objectives that IT management should consider and use when developing new IT applications. Because major IT applications can be so crucial to enterprise operations, senior management may often receive specific requests from the audit committee or CEO-level management to ensure that specific application controls are in place.

EXHIBIT 9.6 IT Applications Development Review Guidelines

1. All requests for new or revised applications should follow IT standards and receive prior authorization.
2. The application development process should include sufficient documentation, including evidence user interviews, to develop a firm understanding of needs.
3. All new application projects should receive a detailed statement of requirements, along with a formal cost-benefit analysis.
4. Project plans should be prepared for all IT department development work, as well as for individual application development projects.
5. Care should be given to ensuring that application development projects meet the long-range objectives of the enterprise.
6. The responsibilities for applications development work should be assigned with adequate time allowed to complete development assignments.
7. The applications development process should include sufficient user interviews to obtain a full understanding of requirements.
8. Attention must be given to internal controls, audit trails, and continuity procedures.
9. Adequate resource and capacity planning should be in place to ensure that all hardware and software are sufficient when the application is placed in production.
10. Sufficient attention must be paid to backup, storage, and continuity planning for the new application.
11. Adequate controls must be installed to provide strong assurances regarding the integrity of the data processes and output from the application.
12. The application should be built with adequate controls for the identification and correction of processing errors.
13. All application processing data and transactions should contain strong audit trails.
14. Adequate documentation should be prepared on a technical, as well as an application, user level.
15. Test data should be prepared following a predetermined test plan that outlines expected results and satisfies user expectations.
16. When data is converted from an existing application, strong control procedures should be established over the conversion process.
17. If it is a critical application, internal audit should be given an opportunity to participate in a formal pre-implementation audit.
18. There should be a formal sign-off and approval process as part of the completion of the application development process.

Processes should be in place for evaluating and testing internal controls as part of the SOx Section 404 internal controls process for identified key applications. This application control assessment is an important part of overall Section 404 evaluation, as discussed in Chapter 15. The results of understanding, documenting, and testing specific IT applications controls by IT audit may provide a basis for the external auditors in their SOx attestation processes.

There are many internal controls operational issues surrounding the development and use of IT applications, the key tools necessary for many, if not almost all, enterprise business processes. Using the COSO internal controls framework, these IT operations control processes link with and connect to other internal controls in the overall COSO framework. We have emphasized that the original COSO framework did not do that adequate of a job in providing guidance on IT controls. There is much more material in the new framework guidance materials, and we have tried to expand on some of these issues in this chapter. This is an important area to consider when implementing the COSO internal control framework and establishing effective internal controls.

OPERATIONS PROCEDURE CONTROLS AND SERVICE CATALOGS

Our last element of the COSO internal control framework is an element of operations controls that we have called *operations procedures*. The words here are ours and not COSO's, but *internal control element* refers to the printed and even verbal rules and procedures that set the rules for every element and type of internal control process. Operating procedures are detailed and typically written instructions to achieve uniformity in the performance of a specific function. They are the rules. Well-written operating procedures can be used to satisfy compliance requirements. They are recommended for all business processes and, in particular, those that pose potential risks to the health and safety of personnel.

Well-managed business enterprises in the past once issued detailed, printed operational procedures that were designed to cover all of the rules to handle their then often manual processes of the past. Enterprises had teams of personnel charged with developing and issuing procedure manuals. The problem was that business changes often occurred faster than there was time to issue procedure revisions, and there was often too much material to allow a responsible manager to absorb it. This author, for example, led a project to reengineer the printed procedural manual processes for a major retail organization. At that time and before the days of effective automation processes, a new store manager received some 12 three-ring binders of company and store procedures, spanning more than 36 inches of shelf space. Many were out of date and just did not provide very good guidance. They tended to be only used to "get" someone for violating an important rule but were otherwise a costly burden. As a final step in his project of now many years ago, this author met with the CEO of that then large US retail enterprise and recommended that the firm eventually drop its procedure books and move to an Internet-based system. The CEO and his CIO then dismissed the proposal, saying that the Internet was "not trustworthy." The rest is history.

Most enterprises today develop their operating procedures through public and private Internet resources. An Internet search will yield many examples of how to develop effective operating procedures here. Enterprise IT functions usually publish their procedures and other service offerings through a private website available only to authorized stakeholders. A user can then go to this website to search for a specific procedure or service, such as requesting a new laptop system, requesting a change in benefits, or adding a new employee to a department. The service catalog site groups services by category and allows for searching (especially when hundreds or thousands of services are available). The user selects a desired service and sees the description and details. The user enters any pertinent information, such as contact information or service-specific questions and submits the request for service. The request requires approval and goes through routing, service level management, and other processes necessary to fulfill the request. The user may return to the site later to check on the status of a request or to view overall metrics on how well the organization is performing the services it provides.

An IT service catalog is an important and valuable function and governance tool for many enterprises. Because IT management sets standards and controls what resources should be listed as IT services on its catalog and because that catalog outlines the options available to an enterprise IT user community, a well-organized and controlled service catalog can be an important element of effective COSO internal controls and IT governance.

To be effective, an enterprise IT service catalog must be understood, embraced, and used by the business. IT service catalogs became a "hot" new concept a few years ago, but all too often, IT departments have invested countless hours to create service catalog documentation in a static or fixed format that few customers have ever read or used. Ultimately, many of these static service catalogs are rarely seen or read by either end users or business decision makers—and thus they often have little to no impact.

In order to build an effective IT service catalog, IT management, as well as enterprise business unit managers, should determine what services and procedures to "publish" to end users via the service catalog. The business unit managers and IT analysts typically should determine what questions are to be asked of their catalog users, any approvals necessary for a request, and what other systems or processes are needed to fulfill the request. Once the service is defined and the fulfillment process organized, these people or a more technical employee would build the requisite functionality into the service definition and then publish this to the service catalog.

Customer service is not a new term for IT operations. However, in the earlier days of IT systems and IT operations, the IT function often all but decided what and when to implement. IT's high costs and user dissatisfaction with poor service and systems that did not meet needs led to a massive rethinking of an IT function's service to its users. The growth of personal computer systems and the Internet has changed these concepts over the years. Today, many IT functions and enterprise management are realizing that they are essentially a customer service function, providing systems support and other IT facilities to all aspects of their enterprise organization. The IT service catalog has become a key feature for helping to build and support IT customer service. However, in order to ensure a successful and customer-focused IT service initiative, IT organizations should follow strong enterprise IT guidelines for building and developing an IT service catalog that documents IT offerings and serves as an important COSO operations control.

IMPORTANCE OF COSO OPERATIONS CONTROLS

This chapter has looked at the COSO internal control operations objectives. To properly and effectively implement the COSO internal control framework, we always need to consider the three-dimensional nature of this model, when control elements of any side must relate to those in other dimensions.

Although the revised COSO internal control model can be expanded, we have focused on only three elements of COSO operations controls: planning and budgeting controls, IT operations controls, and operations procedures, along with service catalogs. This list of operations controls could be expanded to other types of operations controls, but these have been selected as examples of key control areas. An understanding of building and monitoring operations controls is a very important element in the overall COSO internal control framework.

 ## NOTE

1. Robert Moeller, *IT Audit, Control, and Security* (Hoboken, NJ: John Wiley & Sons, 2010).

CHAPTER TEN

COSO Reporting Processes

T HIS CHAPTER LOOKS AT ANOTHER view and a different side of the revised COSO internal control cubical framework, one of the three categories on reporting objectives that is often shown on the top side of the COSO framework model diagrams. Exhibit 9.1 shows the flipped-over COSO framework from this different perspective, and this chapter reviews the reporting objectives of COSO internal controls.

As we discussed in Chapter 9 and earlier chapters, the real strength of the COSO internal control framework is that it describes internal control objectives in a three-dimensional sense, where each control objective and principle must relate to, and interact with, other related internal controls. The reporting control objective is important because virtually all elements of an enterprise must provide input to or develop their own internal and external reporting processes. These reports may range from internal performance reports to fulfilling external regulatory reporting requirements.

This chapter reviews the reporting requirements component of the COSO internal control revised framework and discusses why accurate and timely reporting processes are important to an enterprise in order to achieve an effective internal control environment. The chapter also discusses why accurate and timely reporting is important for all elements of internal controls, from control environment factors to monitoring activities, and why this reporting should serve as a communications facility to all units of an enterprise.

 ## COSO REPORTING OBJECTIVES

Reporting objectives pertain to the preparation of reliable reports at all levels within an enterprise. These reporting objectives may relate to financial and nonfinancial reporting and to internal and external reporting. Internal reporting objectives are driven by internal requirements in response to a variety of potential needs, such as an enterprise's strategic directions, operating plans, and performance metrics at various levels of an enterprise, as well as specific management needs and preferences. External reporting objectives are driven primarily by regulations and/or standards established by accounting bodies and other standard-setting organizations. An enterprise may also be involved in external marketing and public relations–types of external reporting.

An enterprise needs to establish and achieve external financial reporting objectives in order to meet its overall external reporting requirements, whether SEC Form 10K reports, external news releases to the investment community, marketing-related contracted fulfillments, or many others. Reliable financial statements are a prerequisite for gaining access to capital markets and may be critical for the awarding of contracts or dealing with suppliers. Investors, analysts, and creditors often rely on an enterprise's financial statements to assess performance against its peers, as well as when considering the firm as an alternative investment. Management reporting on the effectiveness of internal control over external financial reporting should be part of an enterprise's external nonfinancial reporting objectives.

Management also may report external nonfinancial information in accordance with regulations; standards, including enterprise reporting on internal controls; and operational processes. For example, when management operates in accordance with the ISO standards, as discussed in Chapter 18, it needs to publicly report on its compliance with these ISO operations. An enterprise may engage an independent auditor to review and/or report on its concurrence with such ISO standards. In that situation, the enterprise would typically arrange for an annual review and certification to demonstrate adherence to such a standard, and any reviewer would rely on many levels of external reporting to support such conclusions.

The reporting controls element of the COSO framework operates in conjunction with the COSO operational control element discussed in Chapter 9, as well as with the compliance objectives discussed in Chapter 11. The reporting control element also has linkages with the COSO internal control element, ranging from the control environment to monitoring activities. We have looked at COSO reporting controls in terms of internal and external financial and nonfinancial internal controls.

Reports and reporting controls are of little value to an enterprise unless they capture and demonstrate a flow of information. As will be discussed in the following sections, here are the reasons that internal and external information reporting control activities, as outlined in the COSO framework, must be in place:

▪ To *identify* all data and information elements to be included in reports.
▪ To *capture* the data and information needed to be included in reports.
▪ To *process* these materials before releasing reports, using IT systems and other necessary facilities.
▪ To *distribute* reports to proper and designated people and entities in a timely and agreed-on manner.

These concepts of identify, capture, process, and distribute are key internal control elements necessary to support overall control objectives and will be used in our discussions on COSO internal control reporting objectives in the following sections.

COSO EXTERNAL FINANCIAL REPORTING CONTROLS

The most important external financial reports for most publicly held enterprises are their annual and interim financial statements, as well as earnings releases. In addition, an enterprise is required to file a large number of governmental and other regulatory reports that may reference financial matters. These reports directly affect the control environment on the COSO internal control framework and link with business-level entity controls on this revised COSO control framework.

The quality and integrity of external financial reporting controls are perhaps the major issues that launched the development of the original COSO framework and then the SOx legislation. Public investors and government regulators historically relied on published enterprise financial reports, but those reports were sometimes misleading, were sometimes not issued in a timely manner, or occasionally were just fraudulent. Weak financial accounting standards and loose internal controls led to questionable external financial reports. Bad decisions were then made, based on those reports, but SOx rules and other factors now require an enterprise to devote more care to developing and issuing accurate, well-controlled external financial reports.

A strong assumption in external financial reporting is that the internal controls for external financial reporting—which are subject to scrutiny and testing by senior management and internal audit and are revised as considered necessary—support the integrity and reliability of an enterprise's financial statements. There are inherent limitations in the effectiveness of systems of internal control covering these external reports, including the possibility of human error and the circumvention of overriding controls. Accordingly, even an effective internal control system can provide only reasonable assurance with respect to financial statements.

All elements of the revised COSO internal control framework—up, down, and across—are important for establishing effective internal controls of the development and issuance of external financial reports. In the prior paragraphs, we summarized some important but general internal controls for external financial reports. Although certain documents, such as legal agreements or product specifications, are very important, critical, external financial reports are the ones receiving the most attention. Their content is the basis for government financial reporting, as well as for public press releases of earnings and financial conditions. Errors here can lead to legal actions, as well as to public embarrassment.

Using accepted accounting standards, an enterprise's financial management is responsible for the preparation of these reports. They will then first be reviewed by internal audit for the adequacy of the internal controls surrounding the reports and then audited by external audit for their release. However, whether it is a unit sales office for sending in the correct supporting transactions, IT operations for loading the correct files, or accounting department personnel for reconciling report details, many people in an enterprise have responsibility for the preparation and delivery of accurate financial reports. An enterprise should emphasize the importance of the financial reports and have a policy statement supporting this financial reporting. Exhibit 10.1 is an example of such a policy statement, based on our example company, Global Computer Products.

Global Computer Products   **Financial Reporting Policy**

Global Computer Products management is responsible for the preparation of complete and accurate annual and quarterly consolidated financial statements, in accordance with generally accepted accounting principles, and for maintaining appropriate accounting and financial reporting principles, policies, and internal controls designed to assure compliance with accounting standards, laws, and regulations.

It is Global Computer Products policy that employees and others acting on our behalf have a responsibility for the accuracy, thoroughness, and timeliness of actual and forecasted financial information and for compliance with Global Computer Products' internal controls over financial reporting, disclosure controls and procedures, document retention, and auditing policies. We ensure compliance with these policies through our internal and independent auditors and by monitoring the integrity of our financial management and reporting systems.

EXHIBIT 10.1 External Financial Reporting Policy

Well-controlled and accurate external financial documents are very important and crucial for any enterprise's formal financial reporting. Any type of factual or timing error, even if unintentional, may affect investment markets, will be a major embarrassment for the enterprise and its senior management, and may result in governmental inquiries or actions. Errors or internal control shortcomings should simply not be allowed.

External financial reports will (or, at least, should) receive a lot of attention from senior financial management, their external auditors, and others before their release. Certain internal controls necessary for these external financial reports also apply to internal and nonfinancial reports and will be discussed in the following sections, and strong attention should be given to external financial report internal controls in the following areas:

- Checking and double-checking report accuracy.
- Obtaining reviews and formal approvals from responsible management, external auditors, and other parties before issuance.
- Paying close attention to report filing times and issuing reports on schedule.
- Establishing strong cross-reference links to all items in reports to allow ease in tracing back to supporting details.
- Maintaining strong revision controls over all issued reports.

Many enterprises still function almost entirely in a "paper-driven" environment or, more typically, a combination of both electronic and hard-copy environments for their external financial reporting. This is usually a direct result of the need to maintain information on all aspects of external reporting activities, resulting in such a significant increase of retained information that it has become difficult for an enterprise to function as effectively as it did prior to the introduction of the Internet and the wide acceptance of electronic communications. A very important consideration for an enterprise evaluating or considering technologies is to first implement the necessary foundational components and then add other functionality as required by the business units, enabling the enterprise to fully adopt the new technologies and modify the business processes as required without adversely affecting day-to-day operations.

We should always keep in mind that enterprise management is responsible for the preparation, integrity, and fair presentation of its published financial statements and all other information presented in external financial reports. Prior to their issuance, these financial reports should have been audited by an independent accounting firm, which has been given unrestricted access to all financial records and related data, including the minutes of all meetings of the board of directors and committees of the board. Management needs to believe that all representations made to the external auditor during its audit were valid and appropriate.

Although the external auditor's report accompanies the audited financial statements, management is responsible for establishing and maintaining effective internal control over external financial reporting for financial presentations in conformity with auditing standards. The system of internal controls should contain monitoring mechanisms, as defined in the revised COSO framework, and actions should be taken to correct deficiencies identified.

COSO INTERNAL FINANCIAL REPORTING CONTROLS

The COSO reporting control segment for *internal* financial reporting covers the vast array of reporting processes that management needs for a wide range of activities, such as budget performance, time and labor status, capital investment analysis, production cost schedules, and a wide variety of others. While people tend to think of external reports to include such documents as an earnings statement that is part of a 10K report or a press release delivered to the outside world, there is a much wider range of internal financial reports that is needed to support ongoing business operations, as well as to provide support for the external financial reports.

Although strong internal controls over all internal and external, financial, and non-financial reports are always important, particular attention should be given to establishing effective internal controls over internal and external *financial* reports. However, we have moved away from the printed paper reports of earlier years and should generally think about these reports and their supporting information processes as an electronic document management system (EDMS). An EDMS is one of those "all-encompassing" terms referring to the internal document-capture technologies that include scanning, indexing, optical character recognition (OCR), as well as digital document creation, and management technologies, including document services, workflow processes, and other work management tools beyond just actual printed reports.

EDMS processes provide management with strong internal controls and access to electronically stored internal or external financial reports from common user interfaces

Document Imaging	Document Library Services	Workflow Routing	Forms Processing	Records Mgmt. Applications
Individual Application Services				
Database Services			Storage Device Drivers	
Operating Systems				

EXHIBIT 10.2   EDMS Technology Building Blocks

that typically use industry standard Internet browser technology. Effective EDMS processes provide distributed functionality and an ability to maintain standard desktop configurations for other office and business–related applications. The overall structure of EDMS technologies for external financial reporting can be viewed as a set of building blocks, as illustrated in Exhibit 10.2.

This exhibit really says that internal controls for an enterprise's external financial reports, as well as for any reporting structures, are based on the enterprise's IT resources, as discussed in Chapter 13, and shown as part of other COSO internal control framework elements. The lowest level in this EDMS exhibit is the IT operating system, with database services and storage device drivers installed onto servers at just above the operating systems layer. The selection of the EDMS database that is used is typically at the discretion of the IT organization but has become standardized and can almost be considered a "commodity item," rather than a specialized IT tool. The block in the chart for database services refers to a mix of automated and manual tools for database administration. For example, an enterprise should have specific tools for configuration management that identify and connect various processes.

The third layer encompasses EDMS application components and services that typically include software solution configuration tools, application programming interfaces, and application components integrating the applications reporting components with the database services, along with providing the components that integrate the storage environment with the overall solution. Storage device drivers or services are at the same level as the database services. These are software tools to connect the selected storage technology to the system and make the storage space available for the selected EDMS solution.

The next layer in the Exhibit 10.2 "building block" consists of the individual EDMS server applications. Early in the development and maturity cycle of EDMS technologies, end-user organizations were required to provide database administration and resources to manage data relationships and develop reporting tools. Current versions of enterprise EDMS solutions have shifted the database administrative functions back to the vendor with the end-user organization responsible for daily application maintenance and periodic server maintenance. Most enterprise EDMS solution providers today supply their products with technical support, including system installation, initial configuration, application updates/patches, and other tools. This major shift from requiring significant technical resources at the end-user level to offering vendor-supported solutions has been achieved through the use of standard technology components configured to address specific environments and business needs.

These are core building blocks that are needed to build an effective EDMS and supporting processes for enterprise reporting. More information about each of these areas can be found through Internet resources. These are all elements of the foundational building blocks that are necessary to establish an enterprise's EDMS processes and build effective COSO internal control reporting controls. The top level of Exhibit 10.2 shows some key components of EDMS processes that are necessary for effective reporting controls and overall document management.

Document Imaging

Most enterprise reports and documents are generated through system-generated screens or printed reports. There is a need to have strong internal controls over these established IT systems with reports that have been tested for accuracy and have error-correction mechanisms where necessary. The COSO control environment and internal control activities are important here, but COSO information and communication elements are key to helping provide accurate and well-controlled reporting.

Although most reporting today is done through online IT resources, paper documents still have not and probably never will go completely away. Various types of inspection and receipt reports, as well as reports from overseas operations, may be produced on paper and sent in. Although they are just a small aspect of reporting control processes, an enterprise needs a facility to digitize whatever paper input documents it has to create appropriate reports.

These reports can be generated through the use of document-imaging technologies that enable an enterprise to scan hard-copy documents into its IT system and store them in digital format. Document-imaging technologies enable users to index or enter paper documents into a system, using a form of storage technology to save a digital version of the document. A document-imaging system needs input, identification, storage, and retrieval control components for its stored documents.

The input components typically consist of multiple single-sided and/or double-sided document scanners or facsimile input devices. The scanning stations are used to convert hard-copy documents into a digital format for subsequent storage and management in the document-imaging system. The identification and indexing components allow users to identify or index this digital information, enabling them to be retrieved at a later date, and all types of information required by the end-user organization to fully be tracked with all necessary report data. The storage part of the system consists of various components connected to the document-management or workflow server and are used to store, retrieve, and manage digital information. The retrieval component of the system consists of the user issuing a request for information that is then processed by the server. After these requests are processed, the information is retrieved from the appropriate storage media connected to the server.

Document imaging is not an important component of an EDMS process, because most of us today are all but paperless. Nevertheless, an enterprise needs document-imaging resources to covert and manage what paper documents it has for effective controlled reporting.

Document and Report Library Services

We should preface in our discussion here on COSO reporting controls and internal financial reports that we will make numerous references to the use and control of enterprise documents. These documents are the same as the *reports* outlined in the COSO framework. While COSO uses the term *reports*, we feel the reference to documents is more appropriate for the many forms and formats used today. Document and library service technologies enable an enterprise to manage its digitally born reports. These library service processes control the authoring, check-in/out, and/or version control of documents being developed, managed, or stored. This enables collaborative development whenever desired, along with a mechanism to store/manage digitally born document libraries. The basic capabilities of these technologies include allowing authorized users to:

- Load or import digitally born documents directly into enterprise systems and processes.
- Enter relevant supporting data associated with the document or the report.
- Create virtual folders linking various documents together.
- Check information in/out of a document repository.
- Make changes and check the modified information back into the repository.
- Manage whether original documents are updated or replaced during the update operations.
- Establish security levels for groupings of documents.

The management portion of document/library service technologies should include the ability to restrict access to certain documents or groups of documents to only authorized users. Along with security controls, these technologies enable users to be granted different levels of access. For example, the author of a document might only grant read access to users outside a specific organization, while granting "check-in/out" control to others who are working on updating the document. As the other users prepare to update the document, they would "check" the document out of the library, update the information, and then "check" the document back in.

Document/library service technologies ensure that any authorized user attempting to check the document out (1) would not be allowed to check it out, and (2) would be notified that someone already has a copy being updated. On completion of the update cycle, the system automatically updates the version number of the document and makes it available to all authorized users.

Similar to document imaging, there are four basic processes associated with document/library services technologies: (1) importing documents and reports, (2) report document identification and indexing, (3) document archival and storage, and (4) report document management and retrieval. These terms cover many aspects of COSO reporting controls and may vary, depending on various perspectives, such as records management vs. content management vs. archival management, but the underlying functions remain the same, with slightly different terminology and/or descriptions.

The document and report import components consist of enabling users and other connected IT systems to import digitally born information into their EDMS. This digitally born information can be any format/structure and can be loaded into the system in original or native format. Digital data does not need to be modified prior to being stored and should include all relevant indexing associated with the information. These indexing and identification components allow users to identify or index and track this digital information, enabling it to be retrieved at a later date.

Reporting Control Workflow Technologies

Workflow functionality processes are another building block commonly incorporated into enterprise EDMS processes and is important for reporting internal controls. Workflow technologies provide different levels of routing, tracking, and administration processes for reporting documents. Administrative document workflow processes are typically used by enterprises where their document reporting requirements do not change or change very infrequently. Ad hoc workflow provides the ability for a user to create a "work process map" for a specific piece or type of external report. Production workflow covers the typical regular automated system, such as planned vs. actual activity reports, and incorporates administrative workflow and ad hoc workflow capabilities, along with providing extensive tracking and logging capabilities.

Workflow reporting processes provide for the automation of business document management and reporting tools to better enable and meet user reporting requirements, typically through graphical user interfaces (GUI) and other tools. This workflow capability to control various business document and reporting processes enables mission-critical, content-centric business applications to operate in an environment that would otherwise be cumbersome to implement and manage. Specialized software products are available for document workflow management, with EDMS vendors offering software engines tied to other various workflow products and internal IT systems. The maturity of an enterprise's workflow technology and associated trends is based on the separation of the processing rules from work routing. In some environments, workflow scripts should be tightly integrated to specific activities, making the routing, editing, approval, and submission of document content manageable at the user level.

Workflow computing is the automation of document and other processes performed throughout an organization. A workflow application automates the sequence of actions, activities, or tasks used to run a designated process. This includes tracking the status of each occurrence of all new or revised documents and providing tools to manage them.

Although we have just touched on workflow documentation internal control concepts here, it should become an important area of internal control significance for many enterprises. We only need to think of what is meant by a document in terms of COSO internal control reporting controls. Going beyond the paper reports of the old days, e-mail messages, Twitter and Facebook communications, photographs, and a wide variety of other media formats can be considered as documents to be reported, following the COSO reporting controls designation.

In this section, we have highlighted workflow technologies as a key step leading to building effective EDMS processes, and these are important components for establishing COSO reporting controls. We have listed only a few general features of workflow processing technologies here, but a Google search will show a wide range of workflow technology software offerings. Vendors have different approaches, but an enterprise should consider implementing workflow technologies as a key element of its EDMS processes. Exhibit 10.3 summarizes some of the values and features of using an EDMS process for workflow report and document management.

Following are some of the benefits and advantages of using an EDMS process to improve enterprise document-reporting internal controls:

- **Reduce document delivery and queue time.** Information can be routed electronically using email or as Web-based communications, eliminating document mailing and transport activities.
- **Minimize duplication.** A single copy of a document can be made available to all authorized users, with controls to restrict unauthorized copies.
- **Decrease data input keying requirements.** Forms processing and e-forms can gain access to current data via lookups and can export forms' data directly to business applications.
- **Reduce document storage and retrieval expense.** A single EDMS repository reduces the need to store multiple copies, and standardized indexing and integration with business applications allows users to instantly gain access to needed documents or other information.
- **Improve access to records and information.** Authorized users can search across departments and affiliated business units to gain access to documents maintained by other authorized units with a single search query. Workflow processes then can automatically notify internal or external users when needed information has arrived or has been processed.
- **Automate or improve business processes.** Workflow procedures can be used to move information from one step to another. Rules-based routing can automatically determine needed activity and work steps to automatically update business applications, create additional documents or workflow, and communicate with internal and external users.
- **Improve customer service.** Retained or in-process information can immediately be available for access. Accessed information can be faxed or emailed to the customer from the desktop.
- **Improve regulatory compliance.** Technologies can create audit trails of access and activity. Compliance with Records Retention Schedules can be automated and improved. Incoming documents can be automatically classified and stored in the system.
- **Improve quality of data.** Workflow systems' use of automated filling and validation capabilities can reduce the potential for missing or misplaced data.
- **Share information with external entities.** Authorized external users can directly gain access to existing information collections.
- **Increase information security.** Documents and information stored in an EDMS can be protected from unauthorized access by security requirements.

EXHIBIT 10.3 EDMS Advantages for Enterprise Document Workflow Management

Document Forms Processing Internal Controls

Not many years ago, organizations of all types and sizes used a wide variety of paper forms. Their recorded information was stored for archival purposes, as well as to serve as input documents for entry into other IT systems. How quickly things have changed. With very few exceptions, paper documents for business purposes have all but gone away or are designed to easily convert to electronic formats.

The creation and utilization of electronic forms enables an enterprise to collect data in a standardized format and automatically enter or load the data into an EDMS solution. Electronic forms are typically created using either a forms design package or through the use of standard HTML editors.[1] Forms design packages typically not only include the forms design components, but also enable organizations to "tag" or identify each field on the form and relate that data to a database or an application that would receive and further process the information. These forms management tools also enable enterprises to validate and/or perform edit checks on the forms as they are being completed to simplify data entry.

Although IT departments once designed many unique forms, due to the needs of an application and the whims of the responsible IT analysts, most EDMS solutions today incorporate some level of forms design and/or management as a portion of the standard product offering. In many cases, the use of forms design and management tools is replacing the older style of programmed forms that were used in the 1990s. Using these newer tools, enterprises are able to quickly develop and deploy forms-driven data entry across the Internet without significant development efforts.

There are multiple tools available for developing effective business forms, including online forms display, word processors, terminal emulators, legacy application components, and so on. These tools are used to gain access to existing host applications and perform office-related activities as required to complete necessary work. Effective reporting processes should be sufficiently sophisticated to support video, audio, and other forms of information in the workflow system. These objects become the work item to be processed during the normal course of business.

It is not at all an objective of this chapter to provide a tutorial on effective IT systems forms design. However, to create "user friendly" forms that seek to improve internal control processes, an enterprise and its IT function should strive for forms design legibility and readability. Legibility is often a concern only in the use of type size and line art. Legibility, however, is not the same as readability, which is a measure of the ability to understand the written message. Readability deals with a form or a document's grammar, structure, and usage. Readability is normally associated with messages displayed on a report or a form, while legibility is how the material is presented, and how easily we can recognize and identify a report's messages or presentations. Legibility can also extend to how easily we can recognize and identify the intended use of a graphic. An enterprise can achieve user friendliness in its forms design by applying the principles of design: contrast, balance, proportion, harmony, rhythm, movement, and unity in its use of effective internal control reporting.

An enterprise should establish standards for all of its business forms, whether electronic or even paper. Many such standards may seem almost trivial, but all forms and their supporting systems should include such things as standard document titles, revision references where applicable, and identifying date formats. Titles should be consistent and informative, and dates should be reported not just as yyyy/mm/dd for some and mm/dd/yy for others. This is just an example, but a good internal control environment requires a consistent look and feel for all enterprise documents.

Application Records Management Reporting Controls

Reporting processes create a large number of various formats of reports. Some of these signal immediate concerns and have little use for retention beyond immediate needs. But for most reporting processes, there is a need to both distribute reports to only authorized persons and to store the reported data for archival purposes. As a key component of COSO reporting controls, an enterprise should consider establishing a records and information management (RIM) process as part of its internal controls procedures.

Although there can be many automated and manual variations here, a RIM is a management process responsible for the efficient and systematic control of the creation, receipt, maintenance, use, and disposition of enterprise records, including processes for capturing and maintaining evidence of and information about business activities and transactions in the form of records. Records, whether IT-based or in some other medium, have value and add to the intrinsic worth of the enterprise.

Enterprise records need to be managed in a manner that they can be available for access and use in the course of daily business functions throughout the organizational environment. Records are recorded information, regardless of the medium or the characteristics, that are made or received by an enterprise in pursuance of legal obligations or in the transaction of business. IT and general management, however, should establish standards regarding how a record is distinguished from other nonrecord material, such as a convenience file or a draft. How records are managed throughout their life cycles can be formalized into the policies and practices of the RIM program.

A records life cycle consists of discrete phases covering the life span of a record or a record type from its creation to its final disposition. IT systems usually play a key role in record creation, and systems backup and retention policies are key components for record backup retention.

Legal and regulatory requirements often dictate needs for records retention. For example, an enterprise should keep records in such areas as correspondence regarding a product failure, internal notes regarding the matter, and reports that are generated for public and regulatory scrutiny. Once a record is created, RIM controls should regulate its access and distribution. Software should identify the official record, versions, copies, and distribution.

Throughout the record's life cycle, issues such as security, privacy, disaster recovery, emerging technologies, and mergers are addressed by IT and managers responsible for organizational RIM programs. Document management professionals can be instrumental in controlling and safeguarding the information assets of the entity. They should understand how to manage the creation, access, distribution, storage, and disposition of records and information in an efficient and cost-effective manner using RIM methodology, principles, and best practices in compliance with records and information laws and regulations.

COSO EXTERNAL NONFINANCIAL REPORTING CONTROLS

External nonfinancial reporting refers to any types of reports that will be seen by persons outside of the enterprise. These can run the gamut of report types and styles, including:

- **Government-mandated regulatory reports**. Whether it is a tax form or fulfilling some regulatory requirement, enterprises are faced with numerous forms that must be completed. There are legal requirements for the correct and accurate completion of such reports. Care must be taken to review, complete, and retain backup versions of such forms accurately. Errors and omissions can result in legal penalties.
- **Reports to certification and standards-setting bodies**. Depending on their business activities, enterprises are required to file a large number of external reports to standards-setting and regulatory bodies. Again, care must be taken to comply with the rules to avoid embarrassment or legal penalties.
- **Product training materials and supporting documentation**. Most individuals have purchased some personal or home-based product and have run into the frustration of trying to understand its installation instructions. There is a need for accuracy and strong quality control in all such documents.
- **Product descriptions and price lists**. Although not part of our classification of external *financial* reports, many external reports can have strong financial implications. Essentially, the same internal control reporting processes that were outlined for external financial reports apply here as well.
- **Advertising and marketing materials**. Enterprises typically release a large number of nonfinancial documents and other report-like materials. These reports and materials represent the enterprise to the outside world. Although an online marketing rebate coupon seems a far cry from external financial reports, the coupon's content, logos used, and the nature of the coupon offer represents the overall enterprise.

The typical business enterprise produces a large and varied number of external nonfinancial reports that are used for regulatory, marketing, and other purposes. Management should always remember that these reports represent the overall enterprise and have legal, ethical, and reputational consequences if they are released in an incorrect, sloppy, or uncontrolled manner. COSO external nonfinancial reports are important elements in the COSO internal control framework.

COSO INTERNAL NONFINANCIAL REPORTING CONTROLS

Our last category of COSO reporting controls covers everything else, the many operational, management status, statistical, and management reports that are needed for all aspects of an enterprise's operations. Managers need internal control reports that often include a lot of detail. An enterprise, along with its IT function, should design management control reports that highlight significant problems, as compared to less serious issues. Control reports shouldn't be flat, with all lines of information appearing to be equally important. They should emphasize critical internal control issues. Every business enterprise should have internal control procedures—such as management control reports—in place to prevent, or at least to quickly catch, errors. A business is the natural target of all sorts of dishonest schemes and scams by its employees and managers, its customers, its vendors, and others, and these internal nonfinancial reports are important internal control components.

Although the nonfinancial reports that an enterprise may generate and issue cover a large variety of types of nonfinancial reports, there is a need for a record management plan to better control the many nonfinancial, as well as internal financial, reports that may be generated by an enterprise as part of its internal control processes. As we have referenced throughout this chapter, an enterprise needs to establish a document-management system to put in place effective reporting controls.

A document-management system refers to the use of an IT system and supporting software to store, manage, and track IT systems-generated documents and the electronic images of paper-based information captured through the use of a document scanner. An enterprise needs to establish effective and consistent processes to manage its many nonfinancial reporting processes. It is essential that all reporting documents be designed with effective internal controls. They should have the following attributes:

- **Strong reporting approval processes**. Before any enterprise report is released and distributed within the enterprise and its organizational units, it should be subjected to strong internal and quality control procedures.
- **Check in/check out and locking procedures**. Reporting distribution controls are needed. Internal reports should be distributed to authorized persons on a need-to-know basis.
- **Version controls**. Similar to all IT software, as well as many internal control processes, there is a need for version controls over internal processes. This may be as simple as the use of date stamps or may be much more complex.
- **Roll backs**. Reporting systems should be designed so that, if necessary, at least one earlier version can be recalled.
- **Audit trails**. All reports should be designed with clear audit trails, an essential internal controls requirement, such that reporting details can clearly be traced back to supporting details. This may require effective reporting design or strong and easy-to-use reporting documentation.

Internal nonfinancial reports are significant tools that are often key to running and managing an enterprise. There can be many variations here, but an enterprise needs to establish strong internal controls over the many reports that it uses internally to generate its business processes.

 ## IMPORTANCE OF COSO REPORTING CONTROLS

Although the COSO internal control framework is a three-dimensional set of internal control relationships, many professionals have tended to look at the COSO framework only from its front-facing side, containing components that range from the control environment through monitoring. The top side of that framework and its reporting controls element is particularly important as well. Whether it is periodic financial reporting, internal system status messages, or other systems communications, an enterprise needs effective reporting controls.

There has been almost too much of an emphasis in COSO on reporting controls in the sense of the computer system–generated reports of past years, where management reviewed these large, multi-page reports and took corrective actions, as appropriate. Management used these paper-based reports and often had to make any corrections or adjustments through other manual input procedures.

Today, enterprise financial and other internal controls reporting is usually based on online systems and may follow multiple formats. Enterprises should give consideration to the following key points to establish effective reporting controls:

- **Verify all aspects of a report's content and accuracy**. Outside parties, in particular, will potentially be looking at every number and supporting reference in external financial reports. It is essential that all enterprise reports, both internal and external, are accurate and fairly presented. The matters reported should closely link with other elements of the internal controls, such as at a business unit level. More important, the senior managers responsible for these reports should be aware of and should understand the reported financial results.
- **Secure proper levels of approval before report release**. The rush and flurry of activities before the release of a critical and anticipated report can sometimes result in reporting errors that must be corrected. Strong review and revision controls are needed.
- **Establish strong revision and security controls over released reports**. These are really more IT issues that should apply to all processes, but particularly strong attention should be given to controls over all reports, with an emphasis on external financial reports. Unauthorized access to financial reports before their official release could result in insider trading and embarrassment to the responsible enterprise.

Internal reporting controls are a key component of the overall COSO framework. Whether they are traditional paper reports, online screens, e-mail messages, or other formats, an enterprise should strive to establish effective reporting controls. Part of this process is the need for strong IT controls, as will be discussed in Chapter 13, as well as general management controls to manage the format and accuracy of the many nonfinancial but significant reports that an enterprise may generate.

 NOTE

1. HTML—Hypertext Marking Language. This refers to the automated tools used to build Internet documents.

CHAPTER ELEVEN

COSO Legal, Regulatory, and Compliance Objectives

W E HAVE TAKEN THE REVSED COSO internal controls framework, shown in Exhibit 3.2, and have rotated this cubical framework to better describe the three-dimensional, interconnected nature of this internal control framework model. Exhibit 9.1 looked at another view of this important framework model, and this chapter looks at legal standards, and regulatory compliance controls that are important elements of the revised internal controls framework.

These internal controls have had an impact on all other dimensions of both the original and the newly revised COSO internal control framework. For example, compliance controls are important for many aspects of the control environment and certainly affect many internal control activities. Looking at another dimension of the framework, compliance controls are crucial in every level of the enterprise.

IMPORTANCE OF ENTERPRISE COMPLIANCE CONTROLS

Members of senior management and their boards of directors develop strategies and set the rules for operating in compliance with laws and regulations for their business operations. However, whether compliance here includes paying taxes, operating in accordance with human resource salary and benefit agreements, correctly labeling and advertising products, following local regulations, or following safety and environmental standards, enterprises across almost every industry face a wave of rules and regulations that require their compliance with these rules. These compliance rules cover every aspect of business operations and require the management and monitoring from many people in the enterprise. In many cases, these various compliance rules may be so extensive that they may challenge the viability of some business models.

Enterprises today are up against an almost "perfect storm" with the multitude of legal and regulatory issues they face in their efforts to achieve appropriate levels of COSO internal control compliance. In the United States, federal and state governments and industry groups continue to issue new regulations, as well as data and systems protection standards and so on, that an enterprise must adhere to. In addition, existing regulations and standards are continually undergoing updates, sometimes making their compliance requirements more prescriptive and rigorous.

Successful managed enterprise COSO compliance requires that all business units recognize these issues in their areas of operations and then establish internal controls and monitoring procedures to ensure that they are following the appropriate rules. With the exception of such areas as the beef and pork meat slaughter and meat-cutting industries, where inspectors are almost always on site to observe processes and ensure compliance, most compliance procedures are self-administered, with the managers directly in charge of an area responsible for compliance there. Each responsible manager may then report compliance in his or her direct reports, and outside reviewers, such as internal auditors, will check and verify compliance from time to time.

A CEO or others responsible are often called on from time to time to assert their enterprise's compliance with laws and regulations. Such an assertion is difficult because there are so many rules that we may be expected to follow, but there should be internal control monitoring and reporting systems in place such that a CEO can assert that the enterprise is *substantially* in compliance with appropriate laws and regulations.

We are using the term *substantially* here when we think of the US individual income tax code as an example. The actual legislation covers many pages and pages of often complex rules and proscribed accounting practices. As individuals, we usually pay our taxes by using specialized software or with the help of a tax adviser. However, if our tax returns are the least bit complex, despite the help we receive, we may not be 100 percent in compliance with all of those tax rules. Yet any indiscretions may be minor, and we as individuals and the taxing authorities will generally be satisfied that we have correctly paid our income taxes.

In order to maintain compliance with the many rules that an enterprise faces, processes should be established throughout the enterprise to assure substantial COSO internal controls compliance. This requires strong information and education processes such that stakeholders in appropriate areas are knowledgeable of the rules, systems, and processes to monitor compliance with these requirements, and both self-assessment processes and such things as internal audits to assess compliance.

Although many different compliance issues cover a vast swath of typical enterprise operations, the following sections discuss COSO internal controls in three broad areas: internal control compliance issues associated with products, productions, and other regulations; internal control legal issues; and compliance procedures with professional standards. Processes should be in place to link these compliance controls with other elements of the COSO internal control framework.

REGULATORY COMPLIANCE CONTROL ISSUES

Depending on the industry or the area where they operate, every enterprise faces a series of national and local governmental regulations. Using the US government as an example, there are many business regulations in place with objectives to protect employees' rights, protect the environment, and hold corporations accountable for the amount of power they have in this business-driven society. Some of these regulations stand out more significantly than the others because of their relevance to every US employee and consumer. The following are four general areas where regulations are in place in almost every country in the world that can have an impact on enterprise internal controls and operations:

1. **Employment and labor.** Enterprises worldwide face a wide and varied mix of employment laws. These pertain to minimum wages, benefits, safety and health compliance, work for noncitizens, working conditions, equal opportunity employment, and privacy regulations—and cover the largest area of subjects of all of the business regulations. In the United States, several employment regulations stand out as heavy hitters among the others. The Fair Labor Standards Act, applied by the Wage and Hour Division, sets the minimum wage for workers in the United States. As of 2010, decisions made by the division affect more than 130 million workers, according to the Department of Labor. The Employee Retirement Income Security Act ensures that employees receive the retirement plan options and health-care benefits to which they are entitled as full-time employees. There are also several required benefits, including unemployment insurance, Workers' Compensation Insurance, and employee Social Security assistance. The Immigration and Nationality Act ensures that only US citizens and individuals with work visas can be hired, and every business must keep on file eligibility forms for applicable employees. These are just a few US examples, and when we move over to Asia or the European Union (EU), there are many other and often very different regulations.

2. **Environmental.** What has become to be known as the carbon footprint of businesses on the environment is regulated by the EU and the US Environmental Protection Agency alongside with state agencies. The EPA enforces environmental laws passed by the federal government through educational resources, frequent inspections, and local agency accountability. The rules here are often very complex, where an EPA hearing officer will look at some area and then make what sometimes seems like an almost arbitrary ruling.

3. **Privacy.** Sensitive information is usually collected from employees and customers during hiring and business transactions, and privacy laws prevent businesses from disclosing this information freely. Information collected can include the person's Social Security number, address, name, health conditions, credit card and bank numbers, and personal history. Not only do various laws exist to keep businesses from spreading this information, but people can sue companies for disclosing sensitive information.

4. **Safety and health.** The US Safety and Health Act of 1970 requires that employers provide safe and sanitary work environments through frequent inspections and a grading scale. An enterprise must meet specific standards in order to stay in business. These regulations have changed frequently throughout the years, alongside the changing sanitary and workplace standards. In accordance with this act, employers must provide hazard-free workplaces, preventing employees' physical harm and death, through a number of procedures.

The above are just a few of the many broad areas, with a US emphasis, in which an enterprise faces regulatory requirements. These generally all cover specialized areas in an enterprise, and the management team in any specific area of operations should be made responsible for understanding the rules and establishing legal compliance in each given area. For example, an enterprise director of human resources should assess the rules and implement procedures to assure compliance with HR related compliance rules.

Different people should be given responsibility in other broad areas of regulatory rules. Production operations management, if that is the nature of the business, should have responsibility for compliance with shop floor health and safety rules. The idea is to distribute the regulatory requirements to those closest to the issue who would have knowledge to better understand and implement the requirements.

In order to better review and monitor these issues, an enterprise should consider establishing a Regulatory and Public Policy Committee, as part of its overall internal control structure, with a responsibility for overseeing enterprise policies and programs that relate to regulatory and compliance matters, business operation risks related to business continuity, privacy and security, and public policy and corporate citizenship, including public issues of significance to the enterprise and its stakeholders that may affect enterprise operations, performance, or reputation. This should be a very senior or even board-level group, with high COSO compliance oversight responsibilities. Committee activities could include the following:

- Review and provide guidance to senior management and the board audit committee about legal, regulatory, and compliance matters concerning current and evolving regulations in all major area of business operations, including competition and antitrust, privacy, security, employment, and immigration laws.
- Schedule an annual meeting with the audit committee to review privacy, security, business continuity, and operational risks relevant to the company's computerized information system controls and security.
- Review and provide guidance to the full board and the senior management about the current status of enterprise policies and programs that relate to corporate citizenship, including human rights, environmental sustainability, corporate social responsibility, and charitable giving and political activities and expenditures.
- Review and manage legislative and regulatory trends and public policy developments that may affect the company's businesses, as well as the enterprise's public policy agenda and its position on significant regulatory matters.

Our point in this section is that an enterprise in today's business environment faces numerous regulatory issues. Virtually all of these have an internal control impact. Senior management needs to get the word out to all front-line managers and other responsible persons that it is their job to directly install and manage regulatory compliance controls in their areas of operations. More senior management can provide supporting assets or training when necessary, but the front-line people who are more directly involved with these regulatory matters should exercise their best efforts to operate in compliance with them.

INTERNAL CONTROLS AND LEGAL ISSUES

The corporate legal counsel—an enterprise's in-house lawyer—is a front-line liaison between the board, the general management, and all other stakeholders, representing them on legal concerns. The general counsel, along with any supporting legal staff, is a group that represents and supports the enterprise for a wide variety of internal control issues.

For most enterprises, the general counsel is responsible for trying to assure that its company is acting within the law. However, many enterprises have also turned to their general counsel to provide advice that goes beyond legal compliance. A proposed course of action may raise reputational issues for an enterprise, and the general counsel is expected to spot such issues and have a view about them. In addition, the general counsel may be asked for his or her judgment on people. For example, when an enterprise is hiring a new senior manager, that person may frequently interview with the general counsel.

An enterprise's general counsel provides advice on the legal environment and legal responsibilities. That knowledge of how the legal environment is developing should give the general counsel a basis on which to offer valuable advice in planning transactions or taking other business initiatives. For the general counsel to be an effective legal advisor, the CEO and other senior managers must be sure that their general counsel is included early in the planning and decision-making process and is viewed as a partner in the business process. A general counsel should help mold these transactions or initiatives so that they meet legal requirements and do not transgress into areas that would damage the corporation's reputation.

In some enterprises, the general counsel serves as the chief compliance officer, with strong dotted-line connections to such functions as internal audit and credit. The idea here puts the general counsel in charge of many internal control functions. The problem with this arrangement, however, is that the general counsel's function can become embroiled in such issues as a shareholders' lawsuit that will divert its attention from day-to-day internal control issues.

However, an enterprise general counsel should have an important role in helping to establish effective internal control processes. Governance and compliance are areas of conduct and analysis that should primarily be of concern to the CEO and financial and marketing officers, as well as to the board, but not primarily to legal officers. The reason members of the general counsel should have a strong advisory role in governance and compliance internal controls issues is that good lawyers are often best equipped to synthesize governance and compliance issues within the context of a financial, tax, or some other corporate framework. That is why dealing with these issues has become a lawyer's function, and why a first-rate general counsel can ensure that they are continuously scrutinized at the right level.

Legal and regulatory controls are an important element of the COSO internal control environment. Enterprise executives should work with their general counsel to establish an understanding of the requirements here and to establish appropriate compliance procedures. This is an area of potentially high risk to enterprise executives. There can be a regulation at a small subsidiary location that, when revealed by the press or others, blows up in the face of senior executives, with questions along the lines of "Why didn't you know about this violation?" Both good information and strong internal control processes are essential.

COMPLIANCE WITH PROFESSIONAL AND OTHER STANDARDS

In addition to legal regulations and accounting standards, an enterprise must operate in compliance with many other standards, some required by various standards-setting bodies, others by such ethics matters as truthfulness in advertising, and still others tied to promises made by enterprise executives. Violations of many of these types of standards do not have legal or regulator consequences but, even worse, can be a public embarrassment to the enterprise and its key executives. Compliance with some of these standards is fairly easy to monitor and manage. For example, Chapter 18 discusses the importance of ISO international standards that cover such areas as internal controls, quailty standards, IT security, and other matters. Compliance with these standards can be an important business attribute for an enterprise, and compliance with each should be available for assessment by an outside reviewer. A compliance failure here can be damaging to the company, but nearly as damaging, if not as devastating, is a failure in a SOx internal control assessment or an unfavorable external audit opinion.

Our point here is that an enterprise faces many other areas where compliance with many rules and standards is essential. Product advertising is an area where an enterprise must be compliant with good standards. For example, in the United States, under the Federal Trade Commission Act, advertising must be truthful and nondeceptive, advertisers must have evidence to back up their claims, and advertisements cannot be unfair. "Deceptive," according to the FTC, means an ad contains a statement or omits information that is likely to mislead consumers who are acting reasonably under the circumstances and that is "material"—that is, important to a consumer's decision to buy or use the product. "Unfair" means an advertisement causes or is likely to cause substantial consumer injury, which a consumer could not reasonably avoid, and it is not outweighed by the benefit to consumers.

Although we usually think of product advertising in terms of consumer products, they can affect an enterprise's overall commercial products as well. The advertising may not be all that false, but the underlying product may turn out to be deficient. As a result,

EXHIBIT 11.1 Compliance Prevention and Remediation Program

Compliance Prevention			Compliance Remediation				
Compliance Program Design	Compliance Education	Violation Case Management	Data Collection and Management	Recovery and Risk Scoring	Due Diligence Research	Monitoring	Investigations
Implement rules, controls, and procedures	Manage compliance programs to train enterprise stakeholders	Implement systems to report suspected violations and inappropriate conduct	Develop policies to ensure adequate documentation to support compliance initiatives	Tier and flag violations based on risk	Research and analyze violations for issues of concern	Install continuous monitoring processes to flag potential compliance violations	Investigate and suspend compliance failure and activities in preparation for taking corrective actions

the bad advertising claims will appear in various trade publications, and customers will reject the product, a compliance failure.

Faced with many different types and levels of compliance requirements, an enterprise needs a general program of prevention measures to limit any compliance failures and then remediation efforts to correct matters if there is a potential compliance violation. Exhibit 11.1 outlines some general steps in a compliance remediation program. Whether product quality standards, advertising, environmental concerns, or any of the many compliance requirements facing an enterprise, compliance standards should be well known when implemented, and processes should be in place to monitor compliance with those standards and to take corrective actions where appropriate.

Depicted as the foundation block on our earlier Exhibit 9.1 description of the COSO internal controls framework, effective compliance prevention and remediation processes are essential at all levels. This again is an area where the three-dimensional COSO internal control framework is very important. Efforts should be made to achieve regulatory compliance over all internal control elements and throughout the enterprise.

CHAPTER TWELVE

Internal Control Entity and Organizational GRC Relationships

A LL TOO OFTEN, ENTERPRISE MANAGERS looked at the original COSO internal control framework by viewing only the front-facing elements and all but ignoring the upper and side components of the framework model. To provide a better introduction to this internal control framework model, Chapters 9 through 11 discussed the key internal control elements usually shown on the top side of the COSO framework. We also sometimes forget that important internal control organizational elements are usually depicted on the right side of the framework.

This chapter flips that framework model around again and focuses on organization-level internal controls, ranging from total enterprise entity-wide internal controls down to issues in operating departments and units. The idea here is that enterprise internal controls should be consistent throughout, but their level and focus may vary at different levels.

These separate organization-level internal controls also translate into a set of governance processes for an enterprise. This chapter discusses the importance of having strong governance processes in place over all aspects of an enterprise. An expression that really did not exist with the original COSO framework, *governance, risk,* and *compliance,* or GRC, are important concepts for building and establishing effective internal controls. This chapter relates GRC concepts to the COSO internal controls framework. Although it is important to describe organizational internal controls as a consistent process, starting with very senior levels of management, things sometimes can break down when we introduce international internal control elements into the mix.

INTERNAL CONTROLS FROM AN ORGANIZATIONAL GRC PERSPECTIVE

For many, the COSO internal control's three-dimensional framework, where everything relates to everything else, is difficult to grasp. For this chapter, we have flipped the

COSO internal controls framework once again to show organizational and governance controls as the front-facing set of control elements in Exhibit 12.1. Although a word or two may have changed from our other views of this framework, due to our editorial discretion, this is the same internal control framework that was shown in Exhibits 3.2 and 9.1 but from a different perspective.

The important concept here is that an enterprise must have consistent internal controls installed at each organization level. These controls will not be the same at each level of operations, but they should follow a consistent theme. For example, an enterprise purchasing department may develop and issue some very specific and detailed standards and procedures for selecting and bidding for production parts and equipment.

As another example, an enterprise division–level unit often will not be purchasing the same production piece parts but may have a need to select an overall product family that meets product and quality requirements. Similarly, an overseas business unit purchasing similar production parts may be required to follow different rules, due to such factors as local regulations and consumer preferences. Each organization level, however, should follow the same broad internal control activities covering its enterprise-wide purchasing policies.

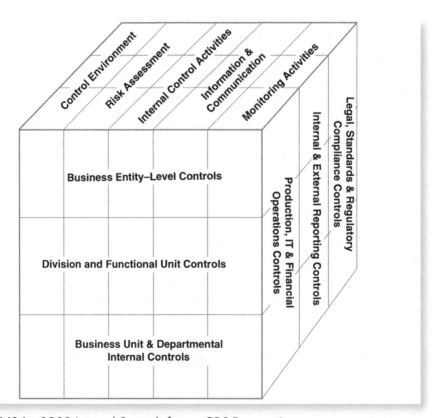

EXHIBIT 12.1 COSO Internal Controls from a GRC Perspective

The COSO internal control framework and its supporting guidance materials do not really directly address GRC issues, because the main objective of the COSO internal controls framework is to ensure accurate and well-controlled financial statements. However, good GRC processes are important here, particularly for implementing organization-level internal controls. These controls must be linked with other dimensions of the COSO framework model.

ENTERPRISE GOVERNANCE OVERALL CONCEPTS

Although its concepts have been with us for many years, enterprises did not talk much about governance issues until shortly after the many financial scandals and business failures in the early part of this century, with companies such as Enron, WorldCom, and Pharmalot as prime examples.[1] These were other events that occurred about the same time as the passage of the Sarbanes-Oxley Act (SOx), discussed in more detail in Chapter 15, and caused many to ask why these corporate executives, board members, and others were so careless and sometimes greedy in managing their enterprises. A general consensus at that time began to take place that business enterprises needed better governance practices to help prevent some of these things from happening again. In addition, they needed to better accept enterprise-wide risks and comply with the many rules and regulations facing the modern enterprise. The need for strong GRC practices arose, a concept that was not part of our language at the time of the original COSO internal control framework.

Business professionals had not even heard about this now increasingly familiar GRC acronym until early in this century. The G in GRC stands for *governance* and concerns the entire enterprise. In short, governance means taking care of business, making sure things are done according to an enterprise's standards, regulations, and board of directors' decisions, as well as governmental laws and rules. It also means clearly setting forth the stakeholder expectations of what should be done so that all stakeholders are on the same page with regard to how the enterprise is run. The R in GRC is *risk*. Everything we do and all aspects of business operations involve some elements of risk. When it comes to an individual running across a freeway or a child playing with matches, it's pretty clear that certain risks should just not be taken. When it comes to business, however, risk factors become a way to both help protect existing asset values and create values by strategically expanding an enterprise or adding new products and services.

Finally, C in GRC is *compliance* with the many laws and directives affecting businesses and citizens today. Sometimes, people will also extend that letter C to include *controls*, meaning that it is important to put certain controls in place to ensure that compliance is happening. For example, this might mean monitoring a factory's emissions or ensuring that its import and export papers are in order. Or it might simply mean establishing good internal accounting controls and effectively implementing legislative requirements, such as the SOx rules, briefly discussed in Chapter 2. Putting it all together, GRC is not just what you have to do to take care of an enterprise, but is a paradigm to help grow that enterprise in the best possible way.

All enterprises, and corporations in particular, historically have not thought of GRC as a combined set of principles. As much as an enterprise managed or cared about any of these three combined GRC areas, they were often managed as separate areas or concerns. Risk management is a classic case here. Enterprises thought of risk management in terms of insurance coverage and managed their risks through an insurance department that often had little to do with other enterprise operations. Similarly, we always had a need to comply with all levels of established rules, including the rules that were put in place to help govern the enterprise, but we have not historically combined them to form GRC concepts. GRC is an increasingly recognized term that reflects a new way in which enterprises today are adopting an integrated approach to these aspects of their businesses.

Going beyond just the acronym GRC, it is important to remember the expression represents core disciplines of governance, risk management, and compliance. Each of the disciplines consists of the four basic GRC components: strategy, processes, technology, and people.

Exhibit 12.2 illustrates this GRC concept. Governance, risk management, and compliance principles should be tightly bound to tie these principles together. The diagram also shows that internal policies are the key factors supporting governance, that external regulations drive compliance principles, and that what we call an enterprise's risk appetite is a key element of risk management.

Risk appetite refers to the amount and type of risk that an enterprise is prepared to pursue, retain, or take. For example, one individual investor who speculates in what are often call very risky "penny stocks" has a high appetite for risk, while an investor holding generally safe money market funds has a low appetite for risk. This same analogy can be translated to many enterprise business decisions.

The Exhibit 12.2 triangle also shows the components of strategy; effective processes; technologies, including IT; and the people in the enterprise that are needed to make all of this work. Off to the left side, the exhibit says that an enterprise requires management attention and support, and that correct ethical behavior, organizational efficiency, and improved effectiveness are keys.

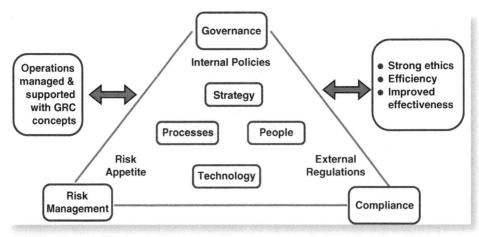

EXHIBIT 12.2 GRC Concepts

These three GRC principles that support IT governance should be thought of in terms of one continuous and interconnecting flow of concepts, with neither the G, the R, nor the C more important or significant than the others.

Enterprise Governance and Internal Controls

Corporate or enterprise governance is a term that refers broadly to the rules, processes, or laws by which businesses are operated, regulated, and controlled. The term can refer to internal factors defined by the officers, the stockholders, or the constitution of a corporation, as well as to external forces such as consumer groups, clients, and government regulations.

Moving down from senior corporate levels into many areas of enterprise operations, we can define *enterprise governance* as the responsibilities and practices exercised by the board, senior executive management, and all levels of functional management in many areas, with the goals of providing strategic direction, ensuring that objectives are achieved, ascertaining that risks are managed appropriately, and verifying that the enterprise's resources are used responsibly. Governance is the process of establishing rules and procedures within all levels of an enterprise, communicating those rules to appropriate levels of stakeholders, monitoring performance against those rules, and then administering rewards and punishments based on an enterprise's compliance with those rules.

A well-defined and enforced set of enterprise governance principles provides an internal controls structure that, at least in theory, works for the benefit of everyone concerned by ensuring that the enterprise adheres to accepted ethical standards and best practices, as well as to appropriate formal laws, rules, and standards. Although enterprise governance, in more recent years, has received the most attention because of high-profile scandals involving the abuse of corporate power and, in some cases, alleged criminal activity by corporate officers, there is much more to consider here.

Although it is difficult to describe all of the concepts of enterprise governance in a few short paragraphs or a single picture, Exhibit 12.3 shows enterprise governance concepts with an executive group in the center and their interlocking and related responsibilities for establishing controls, a strategic framework, performance, and accountability. The exhibit shows some of the key concepts within each of these responsibility areas. For example, for the strategic framework, there are the elements of planning corporate and business activities, risk management, business continuity, IT and network, and internal audit plans.

GRC Risk Management Components

An effective risk management program is a key component of enterprise GRC principles. Risk management should be part of the overall enterprise culture, from the board of directors and very senior officers down throughout the enterprise. There are four inter-connected steps in effective enterprise risk management GRC processes, as shown in Exhibit 12.4 and as follows:

1. **Risk assessment and planning.** An enterprise faces all levels of risks, whether global issues, ranging from national economic or currency crises to product market

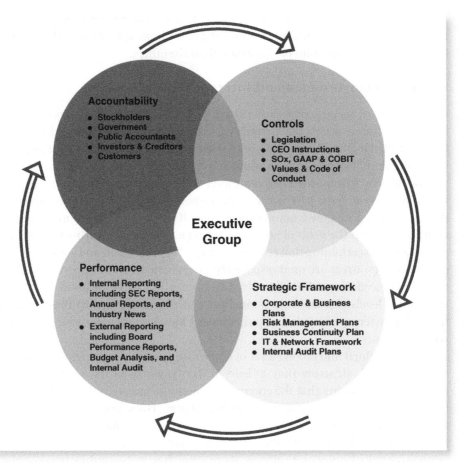

EXHIBIT 12.3 GRC Governance Elements

competition factors, and on to weather-related disruption at local operations. We cannot plan or identify every type of risk that might affect an enterprise, but there should be an ongoing analysis of these various potential risks that may face an enterprise.

2. **Risk identification and analysis.** Rather than just planning for the possibility of some risk event occurring, there is a need for more detailed analysis on the likelihood of these risks coming to fruition, as well on their potential impact. There is a need to quantify the impacts of the identified risks and to determine mitigation strategies in the event the risk event occurs. Mitigation refers to assessing the best way to manage or eliminate an identified risk. The final factors associated with these risks should also be identified. An identified risk will be much more significant if we can identify the total costs to the enterprise if the identified risk occurs.

3. **Exploit and develop risk response strategies.** Essentially in parallel with risk identification, an enterprise should develop plans and strategies to return to normal operations and then recover from a risk event. This may include an analysis of risk-related opportunities. For example, if there is an identified risk that some older

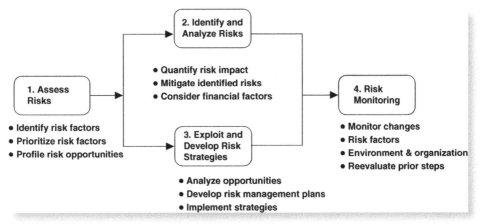

EXHIBIT 12.4 Risk Management Overview

factory production equipment may fail, an opportunity may be to abandon that production line and install new equipment, using a newer technology and possibly even at a newer or alternative location.

4. **Risk monitoring.** Tools and facilities should be in place to monitor the identified, as well as other newer, risks and their possible occurrence. A smoke detector or a fire alarm is an example here, although most risk-related monitoring requires a wide series of special reports, established and measurable standards, and a diligent human resources function. The idea is to keep ahead and to reenter these prior risk management steps as necessary.

Risk management should create value and be an integral part of organizational processes. It should be part of decision-making processes and be tailored in a systematic and structured manner to explicitly address the uncertainties an enterprise faces, based on the best available information. In addition, risk management processes should be dynamic, iterative, and responsive to change, with the capability to make repeated improvements and enhancements.

BUSINESS ENTITY–LEVEL INTERNAL CONTROLS

Although many enterprise internal controls cover processes at lower levels in the enterprise hierarchy, such as those for departments, business units, or production facilities, there are needs for entity- or enterprise-wide internal controls as well (see Exhibit 12.5). These are the types of statements of policy internal controls that managers, employees, and other stakeholders are expected to follow throughout the enterprise as part of normal business operations.

An enterprise board of directors and its audit committee often have a key role in establishing entity-level internal control policies, but these policies are initiated only through high-level board meeting resolutions. Members of senior management then

EXHIBIT 12.5 Enterprise Considerations for Their Scope of Compliance Activities

Scope of Compliance Area	Area for Considerations
Strategy	▪ As an enterprise develops its strategies, it must determine which regulations are more relevant.
	▪ Compliance sustainability needs to be an integral part of any compliance strategy.
Organization	▪ The organizational structure must be established to meet the specific requirements (or intent) of each regulation (e.g., Sarbanes-Oxley recommends that the chief executive officer and the president be two different people).
Processes	▪ Key processes must be documented and practiced.
	▪ Audits or reviews must take place to ensure that documented processes are effectively being used to address compliance/regulation requirements.
Applications and data	▪ Applications must be designed, implemented, and continuously tested to support the requirements of each regulation.
	▪ Data must be properly protected and handled according to each regulation.
Facilities	▪ Facilities must be designed and available to meet the needs of each regulation (i.e., some regulations may require records to be readily available at an off-site location).

take these very general board resolutions and translate them into specific procedures that appropriate members of the enterprise management can translate into specific policies and procedures. The role of the board of directors in establishing effective COSO internal controls is discussed further in Chapter 19.

Beyond devising board resolutions, the CEO and other members of senior management have a very important role in establishing effective internal control practices for the entire enterprise. These procedures are often communicated through the actions and words of senior management, what is known as the *tone at the top*. Others are communicated through enterprise-wide internal control policies. In this chapter, we will look at two of them: enterprise codes of conduct and mission statements.

The Importance of the Tone at the Top

What a CEO and other senior-level executives say and do is quickly and informally communicated to other members of the enterprise, who will act based on those observed words and deeds, despite formal procedures that try to give a different message. That tone-at-the-top message is communicated through formal press releases but, more important, through internal messages and actions as well.

Communication is a key factor here, and the CEO who talks about such things as the importance of new product innovations, fair hiring, and having fair relationships with vendors sends a message throughout the organization. Employees and supervisors at all levels will tend to say things like, "We don't do that—that's not our company policy," when faced with a decision contrary to the CEO's tone-at-the-top message.

These tone-at-the-top messages can cause even more disruption in an enterprise when the CEO says one thing and does another. As a personal example, this author worked some years ago as a project/program manager for a small consulting corporation serving the insurance industry. The company was small enough that the CEO frequently spoke at company meetings and often talked about the importance of fair practices and good ethics in our project dealings.

These events happened some years ago, but one of the company's vice presidents, a long-time buddy of the CEO, promoted his staff assistant to a manager-level position. During a short period of time, he promoted, promoted, and promoted her again until she reached the junior executive level. At a small company, the whole episode was the talk of many company managers, but there was no word from the CEO or the vice president buddy. Eventually, a woman with human resources responsibilities protested the whole matter to the CEO. She and the fast-track assistant suddenly resigned, but the vice president buddy of the CEO stayed in his job. The CEO held a series of staff meetings to try to explain why these two people had suddenly resigned.

When this author publicly asked the CEO whether possibly the vice president may also have violated some ethics rules as part of this whole affair, the CEO waffled. He did not "walk the talk" of his message of fair hiring practices. The whole matter created a level of cynicism among the company's project and program managers. This author, who asked the hard questions of the CEO, was certainly no longer a favorite of the executive team, and soon left for greener pastures.

This simple example shows how an executive-level tone at the top is a very important element in governance and business entity-level internal controls. CEOs and other senior executives should take care to give clear messages about enterprise objectives and internal control practices. When appropriate, those messages should link with an enterprise's mission statement and code of conduct, as discussed in the following sections.

Mission Statements

Every enterprise, no matter how big or small, should have a formal mission statement to describe its overall objectives and values. Properly developed, a mission statement is a high-level internal control that should be a source of direction—a compass—to let employees, customers, stockholders, and other stakeholders know what the enterprise stands for and what it does not. Though once little more than a nice but tired-sounding slogan, effective enterprise mission statements have become very important for promoting strong organizational ethics and good corporate governance. Effective mission statements can be a great asset to an enterprise, allowing it to better achieve organizational goals and purposes.

Although it was many years ago, the Johnson & Johnson Tylenol crisis that happened in the early 1980s provides a good example of the importance of a strong corporate mission statement as a compass to provide direction. Johnson & Johnson, a major medical products provider, manufactures a popular pain-reliever medication called Tylenol. In the past, such medications were sold in stores over the counter in screw-top bottles. Someone in the Chicago area opened a series of these Tylenol bottles, adulterated their contents with cyanide poison, and replaced the bottles back on the store shelves. Several people who purchased this tainted Tylenol subsequently died from cyanide poisoning. An investigation into the cause of these deaths quickly pointed to Johnson & Johnson and the poison-tainted Tylenol.

This whole matter put Johnson & Johnson under enormous pressure. The corporation knew that it had extremely strong quality control processes in place that would prevent such poison contamination from occurring within its own manufacturing facilities. Johnson & Johnson also knew that the contaminated products had appeared only in the Chicago area, while Tylenol was found on store shelves worldwide. A total product recall would be extremely expensive. However, Johnson & Johnson did not go through a long series of internal investigations and quickly did the right thing. It recalled all Tylenol from store shelves worldwide and subsequently re-released it in a newly designed, sealed package. When asked why it was able to make such an expensive recall decision so quickly, even though Johnson & Johnson knew it was not at fault, the corporation stated that there was no need for a delayed decision. The Johnson & Johnson Credo, its mission statement, dictated that decision. That Johnson & Johnson Credo, found on its website at www.jnj.com/connect/about-jnj/jnj-credo, states very strongly that the company's first responsibility is to supply high-quality products to its customers. At the time of the Tylenol crisis, everyone at Johnson & Johnson knew this, the credo had been posted widely in enterprise facilities, and there was no need for a decision. The whole unfortunate matter really highlighted the importance of a strong mission statement for an enterprise.

A strong corporate mission statement is an important element in any ethics and corporate governance initiative. Although most enterprises will not face a crisis on the level of Johnson & Johnson, with its tainted Tylenol in the 1990s, a stronger anchor of this sort might have helped some enterprises better avoid the accounting scandals around the turn of this most recent century that led to SOx.

Working with any ethics officer function and senior management, an enterprise should evaluate any mission statement that may exist today or can help rewrite or launch a new one, if needed. Stakeholder ethics surveys, discussed in the following section, will highlight potential problems in any existing mission statement. If employees or other stakeholders are not really aware of any existing corporate mission statement, or if they view it as little more than a set of meaningless words, there is a need to revisit and revise that document. A poorly crafted mission statement can often do more harm than good, creating cynical and unhappy organizational members who resist change. If the enterprise has no mission or values statement, there can be considerable value to assembling a team to develop a statement that reflects the enterprise's overall values and purposes. If an existing statement was met with cynicism during the ethics survey, it is time to rework and revise that statement. However, any revised statement should be carefully crafted and delivered. If it is just rolled out with no preparation, it may be viewed with even more cynicism. A good mission statement is also a good starting point for the senior management's "tone at the top" messages in today's corporation.

A mission statement should make a positive statement about an enterprise and inspire enterprise stakeholders to harness their energy, passion, and commitment to achieve goals and objectives. The idea is to create a sense of purpose and direction that will be shared throughout the enterprise. Again going back some years ago, perhaps one of the best examples of a mission statement was expressed by U.S. president John F. Kennedy in the early 1960s:

> This nation should dedicate itself to achieving the goal, before this decade is out, of landing a man on the moon and returning him safely to Earth.

Those simple words describe a mission and a vision much better than an extensive document of many pages might. Sometimes called values statements or credos, examples of these statements can be found in the annual reports of many enterprises. Some are lengthy, while others seem to be little more than fluff. The best are closer to the above Johnson & Johnson credo or the moon landing statement in their style.

Once an enterprise has developed a new mission statement or has revised an existing one, it should be rolled out to all enterprise members with a good level of publicity. Using a tone-at-the-top approach, senior managers should explain the reasons for the new mission statement and why it will be important for the enterprise. It should be posted on facility billboards, in the annual report, and in other places to encourage all stakeholders to understand and accept this mission statement. That mission statement, however, should not simply stand by itself; a series of other key steps is needed to build an effective ethics and compliance function.

Sometimes, an internal auditor might argue that "I'm an internal auditor—I just review the internal controls that are in place. What do I have to do with launching an ethics function?" This is very true, and internal audit should always be involved with reviewing and commenting on the controls that others have established. However, the unique nature of ethics and compliance programs and their relationship to the overall enterprise points to an area where internal audit can take an even more active role in helping to implement these important organizational processes.

Enterprise-Wide Codes of Conduct

While a mission statement is a keystone to hold together the overall structure of corporate governance, the code of conduct provides the supporting internal control guidance for enterprise stakeholders. Although codes of conduct have been in place at major corporations for many years, SOx requires that registrants must develop such a code for their senior financial officers to promote the honest and ethical handling of any conflicts of interest and compliance with applicable governmental rules and regulations. Even if an enterprise does not come under SOx rules, there are also many benefits to developing and issuing an appropriate code of conduct that covers all stakeholders.

A code of conduct should be a clear, unambiguous set of rules or guidance that outlines rules or what is expected of enterprise stakeholders, whether officers, employees, contractors, vendors, or any others. The code should be based on both the values and the legal issues surrounding an enterprise. That is, while all enterprises should have code of conduct prohibitions against sexual and racial discrimination, a defense contractor with many contract-related rules issues might have a somewhat different code of conduct than a fast-food store operation does. However, the code should apply to all members of the enterprise, from the most senior level to a part-time clerical employee. For example, a code of conduct rule prohibiting erroneous financial reporting is the same whether directed at the CFO for incorrect quarterly financial reporting or the part-timer for an incorrect or fraudulent weekly time card.

A Web search can yield examples of codes of conduct for many major corporations. An enterprise's code rules should be written in a clear manner such that the points can be easily understood by all. Exhibit 12.6 lists some examples of code of conduct topics. While this list does not apply to all enterprises, these topics are appropriate for many modern enterprises today. The key is that messages delivered in the code must be clear and unambiguous. This author led a project to develop and implement a code of conduct for a large US corporation some years ago. The following is an extract of the words or rules from that code of conduct on a section covering "Company Assets":

> We all have a responsibility to care for all of the company's assets including inventory, cash, supplies, facilities, and the services of other employees and computer systems resources. If you see or suspect that another employee is stealing, engaging in fraudulent activities, or otherwise not properly protecting company assets, you may report these activities to your manager or to the ethics office.

These words are an example of the tone and style of a good code of conduct. It places the responsibility on the recipient of the code, tries to explain the issues in an unambiguous manner, and suggests expected responses and actions. Enterprise codes of conduct look different for almost every enterprise in terms of style, format, and size. Some enterprises publish rather elaborate documents, while others are very bare bones.

An enterprise's code of conduct is an important component of the internal control structure and should be a *living document.* It has little value if it has been developed, has been delivered to all stakeholders with much hullabaloo, and then is essentially filed and forgotten after that initial launch. Codes of conduct in the past sometimes received only token acceptance from the senior officer group, with a feeling that it was really for the staff and not for them. The reported financial scandals that led up to SOx really highlighted this discrepancy. Both Enron and WorldCom had adequate corporate codes of conduct, but their corporate officers did not feel that these rules applied to them.

The senior management group should then formally acknowledge that they have read, understand, and will abide by the code of conduct. With the management team standing behind it, the enterprise should next roll out and then deliver the code of conduct to all enterprise stakeholders. This can be done in multiple phases, with delivery to local or more major facilities first, followed by smaller units, foreign locations, and other stakeholders. Rather than just including a copy of the code with payroll documents, an enterprise should make a formal effort to present the code in a manner that will gain attention. An enterprise should strive to get all stakeholders to formally acknowledge

EXHIBIT 12.6   Examples of Code of Conduct Topics

The following are topic areas found in a typical enterprise code of conduct. The actual code should have specific internal controls–related rules and guidance in each of these areas.

  I. Introduction

      A. **Purpose of this Code of Conduct:** A general statement about the background of the code of conduct, emphasizing enterprise traditions.

      B. **The Enterprise's Commitment to Strong Ethical Standards:** A restatement of the mission statement and a supporting message from the CEO.

      C. **Where to Seek Guidance:** A description of the ethics hotline process.

      D. **Reporting Noncompliance:** Guidance for whistleblowers—how to report.

      E. **Your Responsibility to Acknowledge the Code:** A description of the code acknowledgment process for all stakeholders.

  II. Fair Dealing Standards

      A. **Enterprise Selling Practices:** Guidance for dealing with customers.

      B. **Enterprise Buying Practices:** Guidance and policies for dealing with vendors.

  III. Conduct in the Workplace

      A. **Equal Employment Opportunity Standards:** A strong commitment statement.

      B. **Workplace and Sexual Harassment Policies:** An equally strong commitment statement.

      C. **Alcohol and Substance Abuse:** A policy statement in this area.

  IV. Conflicts of Interest

      A. **Outside Employment:** Limitations on accepting employment from competitors.

      B. **Personal Investments:** Rules regarding using enterprise data to make personal investment decisions.

      C. **Gifts and Other Benefits:** Rules regarding receiving bribes and improper gifts.

      D. **Former Employees:** Rules prohibiting giving favors to ex-employees in business.

      E. **Family Members:** Rules about giving business to family members, creating potential conflicts of interest and problematic family member-employee relationships.

  V. Enterprise Property and Records

      A. **Enterprise Assets:** A strong statement on the employees' responsibility to protect assets.

      B. **Computer Systems Resources:** An expansion of the enterprise assets statement to reflect all aspects of computer systems resources.

      C. **Use of the Enterprise's Name:** A rule that the enterprise name should be used only for normal business dealings.

      D. **Enterprise Records:** A rule regarding employee responsibility for records integrity.

      E. **Confidential Information:** Rules on the importance of keeping all enterprise information confidential and not disclosing it to outsiders.

      F. **Employee Privacy:** A strong statement on the importance of keeping employee information personal and confidential from outsiders and even other employees.

      G. **Enterprise Benefits:** Employees must not take enterprise benefits where they are not entitled.

(Continued)

EXHIBIT 12.6 (*continued*)

VI. Complying with the Law

    A. **Inside Information and Insider Trading:** A strong rule prohibiting insider trading or otherwise benefiting from inside information.

    B. **Political Contributions and Activities:** A strong statement on political activity rules.

    C. **Bribery and Kickbacks:** A firm rule against using bribes or accepting kickbacks.

    D. **Foreign Business Dealings:** Rules regarding dealing with foreign agents in line with the Foreign Corrupt Practices Act.

    E. **Workplace Safety:** A statement on the enterprise's policy to comply with OSHA rules.

    F. **Product Safety:** A statement on the enterprise's commitment to product safety.

    G. **Environmental Protection:** A rule regarding the enterprise's commitment to comply with applicable environmental laws.

that they will abide by the enterprise's code of conduct. This can be accomplished by an Internet or telephone response type of system, where every enterprise stakeholder is asked to respond to these three questions:

1. Have you received and read a copy of the code of conduct? Answer yes or no.
2. Do you understand the contents of the code of conduct? Answer yes if you understand this code of conduct or no if you have questions.
3. Do you agree to abide by the policies and guidelines in this code of conduct? Answer yes if you agree to abide by the code and no if you do not.

The whole idea is to require every employee and stakeholder to acknowledge acceptance of the enterprise's code of conduct. Responses should be recorded on a database listing the employee name and the date of his or her review and acceptance or nonacceptance. Any questions from number 2 can be handled through the whistleblower program described next. The idea is to have everyone—all of the stakeholders—buy into the code of conduct concept and agree to its terms. If someone refuses to accept the code because of questions, supervisors or others should discuss the matter with that person to gain eventual resolution. The final issue here is that the enterprise should expect all employees to agree to accept and abide by the enterprise's code of conduct. Following that code of conduct is just another work rule, and consistent failure to abide by these rules should be grounds for termination.

The whole concept behind this code acknowledgment requirement is to avoid any "I didn't know that was the rule" excuses in the future when code violations are encountered. It is a good idea to go through the code acceptance process on an annual basis or at least after any revision to the code document. The files documenting these code acknowledgments should be retained in a secure manner.

Enterprise codes of conduct are an important component of enterprise internal controls. Although COSO primarily mentions them as just a topic, management should give special attention to launching and then managing an effective code of conduct for the enterprise.

DIVISIONAL AND FUNCTIONAL UNIT INTERNAL CONTROLS

We have discussed how internal controls should be established and implemented for the overall enterprise, using codes of conduct and mission statements as examples. Enterprise divisions and their functional units need to establish internal control policies and procedures that are specific for their operating units but that also follow overall enterprise standards. Depending on the nature of the business, these functional unit internal control standards may cover many areas but typically cover such topics as

- Departmental cash management and budgeting.
- Travel and expense reporting.
- Capital equipment requisitions and budgeting.
- Safety and environmental policies.
- Job descriptions.
- Employee evaluation procedures.
- Requisition and use of company automobiles.

Our list here can go on and on, but it is important for an enterprise to develop specific policies and, where needed, detailed procedures covering all areas of its operations. Major corporations once had specialists on board charged with developing these procedures. These people have now gone away from many enterprises as cost savings measures. Corporate policies and procedures were once published on 8½ by 11 sheets, inserted in notebooks placed in a manager's office. Updates were published from time to time, and the manager was expected to file and understand these changes when required.

These notebooks were not all that effective. Changes were slow to get out, revisions were often not filed, and the books were so poorly indexed that it was almost impossible to find any references. This author was once part of a large retail organization where its published manager-level procedures occupied some four feet of shelf space in thick notebooks. It was almost impossible to find anything, and purging and rewriting procedures were a major effort.

Because of the need to improve these paper-based procedures, business unit demands for improved documentation, and cost pressures, many larger enterprises have automated their business procedures into what is called an *IT service procedures catalog*. Many software tools are available to build such a function, and an enterprise service procedures catalog is an important internal control and governance tool, essential for providing a foundation for defining procedures and communicating them to business stakeholders.

To be effective, an enterprise IT service procedures catalog must be understood, embraced, and used by the business. All too often, IT departments have invested countless hours to create service catalog procedures documentation in a static or fixed format that few users have ever read or used. Ultimately, many of these static service procedures catalogs are rarely seen or read by either end users or business decision makers—thus, they often have little to no impact.

In order to build an effective IT service catalog, IT management, as well as enterprise business unit managers, should determine what services to "publish" to end users via the service catalog. The business unit managers and IT analysts typically should determine what questions are to be asked of their catalog users, any approvals that are necessary for a request, and what other systems or processes are needed to fulfill the request. Once the service is defined and the fulfillment process organized, these people or a more technical employee would build the requisite functionality into the service definition and then publish this to the service catalog.

IT service procedure catalogs are common offerings in many enterprises today, but they should be much more than just a long list of application file names, similar to what can be found in a Windows-based operating system directory list. The types of items listed should be tailored to the enterprise and its objectives. As an example, Exhibit 12.7 shows a front-facing or home page of a procedures catalog for the IT division of a sample company called Compliance & Control Systems. After logging in with an assigned user ID and password, the employee or other authorized stakeholder user would receive this type of a home page. It lists the various systems support and applications areas available to a user. For example, an authorized user might then click on applications monitoring services. These could be special tools to enhance other user-assigned procedures, and the (5) notation indicates the number of other related applications available in this category. Although not shown here, a click in this spot would retrieve a list of these procedures.

Other request options can also be displayed as part of such a procedures catalog sample page, with links to other pages, including:

- **Policy and procedures service requests.** This would be a catalog listing of the status of user requests to gain access to some newly issued enterprise procedures.
- **Problem ticket status.** Stakeholders encountering problems in understanding any type of procedure or service would file some type of a problem ticket document.
- **Training history.** The home page would report on the status of training programs available to this user ID.
- **Department contact links.** In addition, a general help link would be useful.

Because any such procedures catalog will not cover all user requests, the enterprise should have a ticket process in place where users can both file special requests and verify the status of any filed tickets. In addition, accurate records should be maintained for training activities. It is important to demonstrate that certain employees have received training for key applications and that they have completed the requirements of that training.

An IT service procedures catalog can be the cornerstone for improving internal controls in many enterprises. By defining and publishing portfolios of business-relevant policies and procedures, an enterprise division or functional unit can more effectively communicate its business rules and establish a framework for communication throughout the business. And by making the service procedures catalog operational and transactional, an enterprise business unit can help standardize service fulfillment processes, manage consumption, and drive continuous improvement.

Information Technology Division

Global Computer Products

Division IT Procedures Catalog

User-ID:	**Password:**

FIND a Service: _____.   A–Z Listing | Recently Added | Print Version

- **Application Services (5)**

  Application Monitoring Services, Call Center Management (Operator Services), Custom Application Development

- **Communication/Collaboration Services (23)**

  ActiveSync Wireless Messaging Services (iPhone, Windows Pocket PC, Palm, smartphone), BlackBerry Wireless Messaging

- **Connectivity Services (10)**

  Paging Network Support, Cable Management - Inter/Intra Building Connectivity, Consolidated Network Monitor

- **Enterprise Applications IT Support (3)**

  Business Intelligence Services, Enterprise Application Services, Enterprise Directory Services

- **Hosting Services (7)**

  Co-Location Services, Database Hosting Services, Google Search Engine Service, Mainframe Hosting Services

- **Infrastructure Services (13)**

  Active Directory Development and Testing Services, Active Directory Management and Operations Services, Desktop

- **Professional Services (5)**

  Consulting Services, General IT Security Services, IT System Security Assessment and Authorization Relationships

- **Support Services (10)**

  Deskside Support Services, eDiscovery Services, Media Sanitization Service, Messaging and Infrastructure Support

- **Training Services (3)**

  Custom IT Training, IT Training Facilitation (Classroom Rental), IT Training,

  Please contact the Global Computer Products IT Service Desk if you need any additional information about services in this catalog.

EXHIBIT 12.7   Global Computer Products Procedures Catalog Home Page

DEPARTMENT- AND UNIT-LEVEL INTERNAL CONTROLS

Going beyond higher-level policies and procedures, an enterprise needs to develop and distribute a wide range of more detailed internal control procedures that affect employees and stakeholders in their day-to-day work activities. These are often the almost mundane procedures that all employees, and in particular lower-level folk, need to understand to complete their daily work activities. These include such matters as rules for completing a weekly time and hours report, requesting vacation time, or requesting travel reimbursements.

Exhibit 12.8, a flow chart, describes the process for requesting petty cash, the small cash balance activities for such matters as purchasing coffee and donuts for a staff morning meeting. The whole idea is to keep such processes simple and easy to understand. The amounts are small, and if anything were to go wrong here, the internal controls exposure would not be that great.

These detail-level flowcharts and procedures should be consistent with the more upper and senior level of internal controls. Going back to the COSO internal controls framework, efforts should be made to link these detailed procedures with other elements

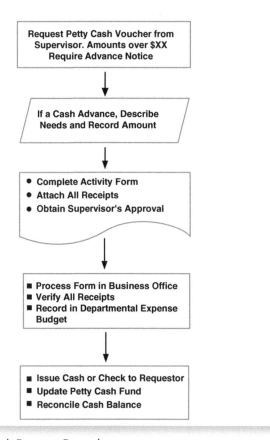

EXHIBIT 12.8   Petty Cash Request Procedures

of the internal controls framework, where appropriate. For example, procedures should be developed for control activities, on one dimension of the framework, and for financial reporting controls on another dimension. A complete and comprehensive set of business unit–level documented procedures is necessary to establish an overall effective internal controls environment.

 ## ORGANIZATION AND GRC CONTROLS IN PERSPECTIVE

This chapter has introduced internal controls from the perspective of the right-hand side of the COSO framework when viewed from its traditional Exhibit 3.2 image. Internal control activities should cover all elements of an enterprise, from senior management levels to detailed, almost desk, procedures. There is little value in senior management embracing some control procedures if they are not documented and followed at a detailed departmental level. Even more important, the procedures in place at detailed levels should be embraced through all levels of the enterprise.

Although there may be some exceptions where more senior executives should have and deserve certain perks, an enterprise should try to develop level playing fields for the rules covering many internal control activities. Exceptions to rules, in which some classes of employees can ignore established procedures that apply to everyone else, will only cause problems and improper behavior.

This chapter has also discussed GRC, a concept that was perhaps imbedded in the COSO internal control framework and now is still not emphasized as much as perhaps it should be. COSO internal controls have their main emphasis on accurate external financial reporting and the necessary enterprise internal controls to enable those financial reports. Strong enterprise GRC concepts really cover an almost bigger set of issues but should be essential to developing internal control structures.

 ## NOTE

1. There are many Internet references about the failures of these companies. See Robert Moeller's *Sarbanes-Oxley Internal Controls*, published by John Wiley & Sons in 2008, for more information.

CHAPTER THIRTEEN

COSO, Service Management, and Effective IT Controls

W E HAVE DISCUSSED HOW THE original COSO internal control framework originated during the days of centralized mainframe computer systems, with many key financial systems based on batch-processing and paper report output. We almost forget that the Internet, as a powerful business tool, was just in its infancy then, and earlier cell phones were about the size and weight of a brick but had few functions except for making and receiving voice calls. The revised COSO internal controls framework has tried to correct this IT materials deficit, but it still remains a framework that primarily describes effective financial reporting internal controls and still does not fully recognize today's IT controls and their importance to the COSO internal controls framework.

This chapter emphasizes the importance of IT general controls, the control procedures that go beyond just individual applications, and covers overall enterprise IT processes. In addition, the chapter outlines some key IT service management concepts that are elements of information technology infrastructure library (ITIL) best practices. Not an IT technical discussion, this chapter has an objective of bringing these IT internal control objectives to the attention of today's enterprise business executive who is striving to adopt COSO internal controls.

 IMPORTANCE OF IT GENERAL CONTROLS

Enterprise IT processes today cover many areas, ranging from an IT application to control an enterprise's accounting general accounting ledger to numerous laptop and handheld systems and connections to the all-pervasive Internet. Although it was once the realm of "IT geeks," today's business executive should have a strong understanding of IT internal control techniques covering these many technologies and processes. The lines of separation are sometimes difficult, but we generally think of IT controls on two broad levels: application controls that cover a specific process—such as an accounts payable application to pay invoices from purchases—and what are called general IT controls, controls that cover all aspects of IT operations and are necessary for specific application controls to be effective.

IT general controls cover broad areas of the overall IT environment, such as computer operations, access to programs and data, program development and program changes, network controls, and many others. The concept of IT general controls goes back to the early days of centralized mainframe computers, when management and its IT auditors looked for such things as an access control lock on a computer center door as a general control that covered all processes and applications operating within that earlier-era centralized IT operations center. Today, we often think of the set of processes that covers all IT operations for an enterprise as the IT infrastructure. Because of the many possible variations in business systems, equipment, and IT techniques here, there is really no one right or wrong set, but an enterprise should establish and implement a set of best practices that will serve as guidance for establishing IT general controls best practices.

This chapter will consider IT infrastructure controls from a revised edition COSO internal controls perspective, including some key governance, management, and technical IT general controls. We should think of IT controls in terms of both the controls within a specific application and what are called *general controls*, the pervasive controls surrounding all IT systems operations. IT general controls cover all information systems operations and include:

- **Reliability of information systems processing.** Good controls need to be in place over all IT systems operations. Discussed throughout this chapter, these controls often depend on the nature and management of the specific size and type of systems used.
- **Integrity of data.** Processes should be in place to ensure a level of integrity over all data used in various application programs. This is a combination of the general operations controls in this chapter, as well as specific application controls.
- **Integrity of programs.** New or revised programs should be developed in a well-controlled manner to provide accurate processing results. These control issues include the overall process of application program development and are part of ITIL best practices, discussed later in this chapter.
- **Controls over the proper development and implementation of systems.** Controls should be in place to ensure the orderly development of new and revised information systems.
- **Continuity of processing.** Controls should be in place to back up key systems and to recover operations in the event of an unexpected outage—what was once called *disaster recovery planning* and is often known today as *business continuity planning.*

This chapter discusses general controls over in-house information system operations, ranging from client server-systems to desktop or wireless operations, as well as older, larger mainframe computer system operations that still exist in a few environments. Although there are differences between the sizes and the management of these different systems, all should be subject to the same general control needs.

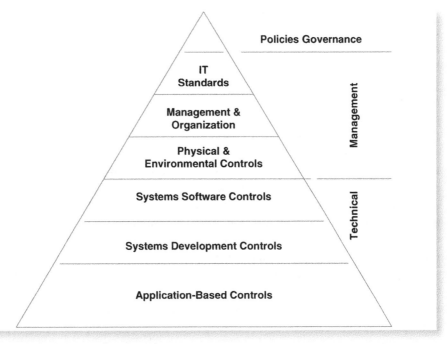

EXHIBIT 13.1   IT Controls Hierarchy

For some non-IT managers, it can be a bit confusing about what we mean by general and application controls. This is true today because we often do not think of a separate application but simply a process embedded in the laptop device. As another approach to looking at IT general and application controls, Exhibit 13.1 describes an IT control hierarchy. At the top of this triangle configuration are IT policies defining the overall enterprise IT organization. Some of these general control requirements will be discussed in the following sections, while others involving the audit committee are found in Chapter 19. Moving down this Exhibit 13.1 hierarchy are general controls for IT standards, organization of the IT function, and physical and environmental controls. The next level down in the hierarchy brings two categories of technical-level general controls—systems software and systems development general controls, followed by application based controls at the base of the controls hierarchy.

Understanding and reviewing IT general controls and making appropriate recommendations for improvements or corrective actions are key areas for building and developing appropriate IT internal controls. Strong IT general controls are important, and effective application controls are of little value unless they are supported by strong IT general controls.

 ## IT GOVERNANCE GENERAL CONTROLS

The concept of IT governance is a key component of the COSO internal control framework, where enterprise governance issues are a major component of the foundation of that internal controls framework. While COSO talks about a wide range of enterprise governance controls, such as the importance of an active audit committee and senior management tone at the top, these same high-level internal control messages apply to the IT function just as well.

IT internal controls at a governance level involve ensuring that effective IT management and security principles, policies, and processes are in place, along with appropriate compliance measurement tools to assess and measure those controls. Effective IT governance controls require an active audit committee that goes beyond just financial reporting issues and reviews a wide range of enterprise issues including IT infrastructure operations. Key issues from IT audits, as well as internal control findings and recommendations that involve IT-related issues, should be reported to the audit committee in such a way that they can understand and comprehend these IT internal controls issues. The enterprise IT audit function and the overall IT audit group should present their recommendations and issues in such a manner that board members can easily understand IT audit's concerns and issues.

IT governance internal controls can also present concerns because sometimes top-level enterprise governance issues are not actively communicated and promoted to an enterprise's IT functions. This was particularly true back in the days of legacy mainframe systems, when many of the IT staff worked behind the locked doors of the IT operations facility and did not have that much day-to-day contact with other enterprise activities. This same isolation, however, can still exist today, when there is often a separation between the IT function and other enterprise activities.

IT MANAGEMENT GENERAL CONTROLS

The Exhibit 13.1 IT controls hierarchy diagram shows three levels of IT management controls: standards, organization and management, and physical and environmental general controls. Following high-level policies, these should be considered in a top-down manner. That is, IT standards should follow top-level policies and should have good IT organization and management controls at the next level down. The third level of IT management general controls is the overall category of IT physical and environmental controls.

Although we are describing these as levels of COSO internal controls, management should recognize that these are not separate internal control domains, but all are related to one another on many levels. In addition, an enterprise often will not have just one IT function but may have multiple units that differ by geographic location, line of business, or IT technology. Senior managers should always look for certain minimum control requirements in each of these areas but should realize that some IT general controls may differ across different environments.

IT Standards

In the COSO internal control framework, standards exist to support the requirements of an enterprise's often generally stated policies. While larger enterprises are in a position to develop their own IT standards, many will adopt best practices or recognized professional practices as the basis for their IT standards. The ITIL set of best practices, discussed later in this chapter, is an example of the IT documents that can be established to form the basis of an enterprise's IT standards.

IT function management is the best resource to develop standards over its own internal processes. These standards should cover activities within the IT organization, such as for testing requirements before initiating applications changes, as well as user requirements for purchasing new IT hardware and software assets. Responsible senior managers should look for established standards within their IT organization, covering such areas as new systems development, software acquisition, documentation, and applications control procedures, among many other issues. Some of these IT standards may be very precise and technical, but the non-IT executive should be able gain a general understanding of their objectives. Evidence should also be in place to demonstrate that objectives have been communicated to, and followed by, all members of the IT organization and appropriate users. Examples of IT general controls standards include

- **E-mail communications protocols.** Whether they are massive and often unnecessary attachments connected to messages, an excessive use of "cute" graphics, or the sharing of confidential data, an enterprise can experience many e-mail abuses. An enterprise and its IT function should develop standards for e-mail use and messaging.
- **Systems development standards.** Although IT functions develop few "from scratch" programs and applications today and typically purchase software packages, systems development standards are needed, even if a new application is built from table components in a purchased software package. Enterprises need to establish what are called systems development life cycle (SDLC) process standards to develop and implement net IT applications.[1]
- **IT applications documentation.** Standards should specify the minimum level of documentation required for each application or IT installation. These standards should include different classes of applications, processes, and physical IT facilities. Software today is usually purchased from outside vendors, who often supply voluminous amounts of sometime difficult-to-comprehend on-line documentation. An enterprise IT function should take this material and rework it to a level that can be more easily used by the enterprise.

The above are just a few examples of the types of IT standards that an IT function should implement and establish to develop and build effective general controls in its IT facilities. For a larger enterprise, these standards may exist at multiple levels, with general standards issued through the CIO and more detailed standards in place for development and processing centers. IT operations management should document and understand these standards and, when appropriate, perform compliance tests to assess procedures against these IT standards and supporting processes.

When establishing standards for the overall IT organization and its operations, both IT and general management should recognize the three-dimensional level of the COSO internal controls framework. That is, some IT standards should be applicable to the entire enterprise, while others may concern only individual operating units or functions. All too often, larger enterprises establish standards, and particularly IT standards, that are worded as if they apply to all units. On closer inspection or through internal audit reviews, it often becomes apparent they really cannot reasonably apply to all. A standard on database maintenance may apply to larger operating units, for example, but may be difficult for a sales office whose database is a small office system.

IT Organization and Management

Effective IT organization and management processes are an important area of general controls. Whether a larger enterprise with multiple, large facility data centers or a smaller business with a server system and a limited number of attached terminals, IT management should have a good understanding of overall management controls, including provisions for an adequate separation of duties, financial management controls, and overall change management controls. These types of reviews are frequently performed by the enterprise's IT internal audit function, and senior management should, with its IT internal auditors or directly, perform such a preliminary review. Suggested review steps are described in Exhibit 13.2, and the review should be tailored to cover various enterprises' IT operating units.

This type of a survey should be structured informally to better understand the IT-related internal control processes in place. If it is a first-time exercise, this survey of the IT organizations should be documented by internal auditors, with a copy sent for their reference to responsible members of management. The idea here is that this is not a formal IT audit but a process to gain some background information to serve as a basis for scheduling other IT audit reviews or for determining the status of control issues that surfaced in prior reviews.

Although a preliminary survey can cover a wide range of areas, regarding IT organization and management issues, the need for an adequate separation of duties is a vital element in many controls and is often perhaps the most important control issue or concern. The functions of initiating, authorizing, inputting, processing, and checking data should be separated to ensure that no individual can both create an error, an omission, or another irregularity and then authorize this evidence. Traditional separation of duties within the IT environment is divided between systems development and operations, where operations personnel who are responsible for running production systems should have little or no contact with the development process.

IT Physical and Environmental System General Controls

In older, traditional IT environments, computer operations were often a prime area of internal control concern of both external auditors and IT internal audit. Computer operators then had considerable power to make changes or to bypass system controls, such as overriding data file label controls, making changes to program-processing sequences, or inserting unauthorized program instructions into production applications. Although it is still possible to do this today, the complexity of large computer operating systems, the often intricate connections between system servers, and the sheer volume of work passing through a modern IT operations center make unauthorized operator override

EXHIBIT 13.2   IT General Controls Preliminary Survey Review Steps

1. Obtain basic information about the environment through initial exploratory discussions with IT management.

2. Review the organizational chart and the position titles to determine that an appropriate separation of functions exists. Discuss any potential conflicts with IT management.

3. Obtain job descriptions of key IT personnel and review them for adequate and appropriate qualifications, task definitions, and responsibilities. Ensure that security and control accountability are appropriately assigned to the correct personnel.

4. Based on discussions with management, both inside and outside the IT organization, assess whether the IT organizational structure is aligned with business strategies to ensure expected IT service delivery.

5. Review documented IT policies and selected procedures for completeness and relevance, with specific emphasis on security, business continuity planning, operations, and IT customer service.

6. Inquire whether responsibilities have been assigned to keep the policies and the procedures current, to educate/communicate them to staff members, and to monitor compliance with them.

7. Based on discussions with senior IT management, assess whether strategic, operational, and tactical IT plans are in place to ensure alignment with the organization's overall business plans.

8. Determine the existence of an IT steering committee, and review this committee's functions through a limited review of steering committee meeting minutes.

9. Assess whether IT planning and control linkages have been established through communication or reports to the audit committee.

10. Ensure that a formal methodology is used in the development of new systems or major enhancements to systems in production. The methodology should include formal steps for definition, feasibility assessment, design, construction, testing, and implementation, as well as formal approvals at every stage.

11. Determine that processes are in place for making changes to application programs in production, including testing and documentation sign-off, and formal approvals to implement the change into production.

12. Ensure that responsibility for physical and logical security has been appropriately apportioned and that appropriate documented procedures exist.

13. Review procedures in place for operating and maintaining the network, in terms of device configuration and software parameter changes, and ensure that procedures for allocating and maintaining the network configuration are performed on a scheduled basis and under proper change management.

14. Review the business continuity and IT disaster-recovery plans to ensure that detailed plans for the recovery of operations have been prepared and that the plans are documented, are communicated to the appropriate personnel, and are properly tested on a periodic basis.

15. Review the department's IT budget and its actual costs, as well as performance against those measurements, to assess financial performance. Discuss the reasons for any variances.

actions more difficult, and many once common IT operations control improvement recommendations are no longer feasible today. For example, older business data center computers had a terminal monitor or even, years ago, a console printer attached to record operator commands, and IT auditors traditionally recommended that these console logs be reviewed on a regular basis. These logs were often ignored by IT operations management even though they were useful for tracing inappropriate operator activities. Today, this console activity is recorded onto log files, but the sheer volume of that data makes a periodic human review of console log reports all but totally unrealistic; other tools and controls are available to better understand operations controls.

Today, IT systems are operating in a client-server world where powerful but very major server computers drive a wide range of terminals and storage devices. Computer operations centers are much more automated and efficient than they were not that many years ago. User terminals are protected by firewalls but connected—through either cables or wireless connections—to complex enterprise-controlled networks or to the Internet. This concept is known today as *cloud computing*, in which the network is so vast and complex that it appears we are simply connecting a device to a cloud in the sky to receive interconnections.

Members of IT management, as well as internal audit, should define, implement, and test their physical and environmental internal IT controls. However, an important first step in better understanding IT operations' general controls is to clearly define the planned internal controls' objectives. All too often, management may ask IT, as well as internal audit, to "review the computer system controls" in some data center, without delineating any clear objectives for the review. Management's memories do not fade that fast, and that request by management for a review and an assessment may be based on IT controls as they once existed in older legacy systems. The following questions should be considered when planning any internal controls review of IT physical and environmental system controls:

▪ What is the purpose of the information system operations review?
▪ Which specific controls and procedures are expected to be in place?
▪ How can evidence be gathered to determine whether controls work?

Based on the results of this exercise, responsible members of management should develop a set of control objectives specifically tailored for the planned review, rather than just using a standard set of internal control questions. Whether IT or any other review, the IT internal control objectives that are identified depend on the purpose of the assessment review.

 ## CLIENT-SERVER AND SMALLER SYSTEMS GENERAL IT CONTROLS

Senior managers with a knowledge of IT general controls that dates from their experience in past years tend to think of those IT general controls in terms of larger, more centralized system configurations. Although many enterprises today have installed many of their IT applications on smaller department-level systems, laptops, or wireless devices, we still tend to think of enterprise IT resources in terms of the corporate IT function, with its multiple servers, database processors, and network management tools or even the classic mainframe. IT management and its internal auditors often face challenges in establishing and recognizing enterprise general controls for today's smaller IT operations that range from networked client-server configurations to enterprise desktop systems to handheld device wireless systems. General controls evaluation problems arise because smaller systems are often installed with limited staffs in a more "user-friendly" type of environment. Many senior traditional managers, however, typically look for general IT controls in terms of the classic larger mainframe IT environment, discussed in previous sections. That is, management is sometimes looking for the strong physical security, good IT revision, and proper separation of duties that often just do not exist or are only partially implemented in the typical smaller systems environment. This less-formal approach was perhaps adequate when these small business or desktop systems were used primarily for single office accounting or similar low-audit-risk applications. The large capacity and capability of smaller systems today, the growth of the Internet, and the transition to client-server computing has made these smaller systems important parts of the IT controls framework. When faced with evaluating controls in these smaller computer systems' settings, managers have sometimes reverted to the traditional, almost "cookbook" types of controls.

Enterprises are implementing increasing numbers of smaller client-server systems to support business units and specific departmental computing or provide IT for the entire enterprise. Despite their smaller size, these systems can often represent significant general control concerns. Management should understand the general IT controls surrounding smaller computer systems; adequate general controls are necessary in order to place reliance on specific application controls.

Smaller systems can be implemented in a variety of ways, depending on the system configuration and the size of the enterprise. A common configuration for these smaller systems is known as a client-server system, where each local network workstation is a *client*, and a centralized processor, which contains common shared files and other resources, is called the *server*. There may also be specialized servers for such tasks as storage management or printing. Workstation users submit requests from client machines to a server, which then serves that client by doing the necessary processing.

This client-server architecture, however, goes beyond just a workstation and a server. An application that queries a centralized database can be considered the client, while the database that develops the view of the database is the server to all workstations requesting database service. Similarly, an application program can request services from an operating system communications server. Exhibit 13.3 shows a client-server system's sample configuration, where a single server handles requests from multiple clients across a network. This client-server configuration, though very general, represents the typical IT system of today.

Smaller business IT systems can follow many configurations, with most following the basic client-server configuration. However, all of these systems should be controlled and managed following good COSO internal controls. Senior and IT management should implement and install general controls over client-server systems with many of the

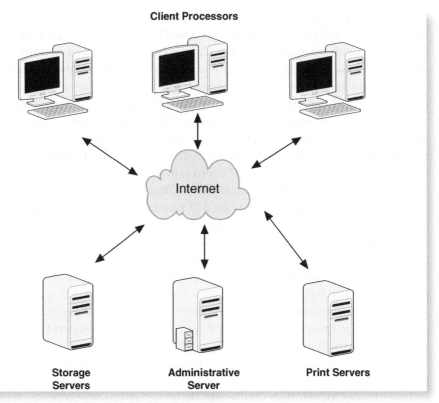

EXHIBIT 13.3 Client-Server System Configuration

internal control procedures found in a classic, larger enterprise system. That is, there is still a need for systems security, integrity, and backup procedures. These types of smaller business systems will generally have the following common characteristics:

▪ **Limited IT staff.** The small business IT system, whether a single Internet-connected desktop system or a series of units tied to a server, will have a very limited dedicated IT staff, if any. A desktop system designed to provide accounting reports for a small company may be maintained by a single person. A small business or server system may have a manager/administrator and perhaps one or two system administrators as its total IT department. Such a small IT operation creates an internal controls risk because it is dependent on a separate small consulting firm for much of its IT support, and requirements for such functions as backing up critical files may be ignored. However, a small staff size will not in itself create internal control concerns. IT audit should be able to look for compensating controls, just as it does when reviewing a smaller accounting department, in which a classic separation of duties is lacking.

▪ **Limited programming and systems development capability.** The typical small business IT system makes extensive use of purchased software packages. The only "programming" needed may be for installing and updating purchased software, maintaining configuration parameter tables, and writing simple retrieval programs.

▪ **Limited environmental controls.** Small business systems can generally be plugged into normal power systems and operate within a fairly wide range of temperatures. Because of these limited requirements, they are sometimes installed without important, easy-to-install environmental controls, such as backup drives or electrical power surge protectors. Although some small business computer installations or file servers may be housed in formal, environmentally controlled computer rooms, this is not a necessary attribute of these systems.

▪ **Limited physical security controls.** Because of less need for environmental controls, these systems are often installed directly in office areas. The level of IT auditor concern regarding physical security controls depends on the type of equipment and the applications being processed. IT audit may sometimes recommend that physical security be improved, particularly where critical applications are being processed. In many other instances, however, this lack of physical security controls should not present a significant internal control problem.

▪ **Extensive telecommunications network.** Virtually all desktop systems today are tied to the Internet. Data and applications can be easily uploaded or downloaded. In addition, materials can be easily downloaded through the common, easy-to-use USB devices. A combination of controls and policies should be established to protect the enterprise.

These characteristics certainly do not *define* a smaller business IT system but only explain some common attributes. However, they should help IT audit to better decide on the control procedures to be used. When in doubt, however, responsible managers should consider the system to have the internal control characteristics of a larger, more complex IT system.

Senior management should always remember that IT internal control concerns do not go away or can be waived just because the installed IT business system is small and informal. Just as a proper separation of duties in accounting controls is important, whether in a major corporation's purchasing department or in a small restaurant, IT general controls should be installed and be operating effectively in all IT operations.

ITIL SERVICE MANAGEMENT BEST PRACTICES

A concept that was not part of the original COSO internal controls framework, what is called the IT infrastructure is an almost preferred way to implement and understand all aspects of IT general and application internal control processes today. The IT infrastructure includes all of the IT services necessary to manage and control IT processes, such as hardware, software, related resources, and the people who operate and manage IT.

An installed IT infrastructure will be very different across large and small enterprises, due the relative size of their operations and the overall nature of their business. Because of the many possible variations in the types and sizes of IT systems and the facilities that may be needed, there is really no one right or wrong set here, but an enterprise should establish and implement a set of best practices to serve as guidance for establishing its IT general controls.

An important internal control concept here, however, covers how the IT application reports and other IT resources are delivered to their business users. Every business IT function supports a wide-range of IT service management processes that include such areas as problem management—how IT resolves issues with its business users—or configuration management, how IT keeps track of installed software and equipment versions. IT service management covers a wide range of internal control issues, and rather than specific process rights and wrongs, there are some well-recognized best practices that an enterprise should follow.

This section looks at IT infrastructure general controls based on the worldwide recognized set of best practices called the Information Technology Infrastructure Library (ITIL). ITIL was first developed in the 1980s by the British government's Office of Government Commerce (OGC), formerly called the Central Computer and Telecommunications Agency. It is an independent collection of best practices that was first widely recognized in IT operations in the United Kingdom, followed by the European Union community (EUC), next by Canada and Australia, and now is increasingly common in the United States. ITIL is a detailed framework of significant IT best practices, with comprehensive checklists, tasks, procedures, and responsibilities designed to be tailored to any IT organization. Dividing key service delivery processes between those covering IT service delivery and those for service support, ITIL has now become the de facto standard for describing many fundamental processes in IT service management, such as configuration or change management.

The ITIL "library" of technical publications, all published by the British OGC,[2] are tightly controlled, similar to the ISO international standards publications discussed in Chapter 18. ITIL best practices are an important part of IT internal controls. Our intent here is not to provide a detailed description of ITIL's service management components but to give senior managers a high level of understanding of some of its components. An understanding of ITIL will help management and its IT resources better implement and understand key IT general controls.

ITIL service delivery best practices cover the IT infrastructure—the supporting processes that allow IT applications to function and deliver their results to systems users. All too often, responsible managers have focused their attention on the application development side of IT processes and ignored important supporting service delivery processes. An enterprise can put enormous effort, for example, into building and implementing a new budget forecasting system, but that application will be of little value unless there are good processes in place, such as problem and incident management, to allow the users of this budget forecasting system to report system difficulties. Also needed are good capacity and availability processes to allow the new application to run as expected. These ITIL processes are all part of the IT infrastructure, and a well-designed and controlled application is of little value to its users without strong service support and delivery processes in place. Enterprise managers understand these enterprise processes as a means of building better IT internal controls.

Although fairly common elsewhere in the world, ITIL best practices are now widely recognized in the United States as well. The ISACA website, introduced in

Chapter 18, has numerous reference materials that tie ITIL best practices into the COBIT framework. The following paragraphs provide an overview of some ITIL service delivery processes that are important for COSO internal controls, including such areas as capacity or service level management best practices. Similar to the broad guidance in the COSO internal controls framework, ITIL does not specify standards for building and managing IT controls but suggests new ways to implement and operate infrastructure IT general controls that should have already been in place.

ITIL service delivery strategies can be viewed as a continuous-activity life cycle, sometimes shown as three embedded process activity rings. The outer ring defines continual service improvement processes. That is, an ITIL-ready organization should have continual service processes in place that encompass all of its other service management processes to receive input from outside IT customer sources. There are three independent, linked processes within this continual service improvement process—service design, transition, and operations best practices—which are illustrated in Exhibit 13.4 and will be discussed in the following sections. In the center of these is the service strategy process, the IT organization policies and practices that are also described in the COSO internal control framework control environment element.

ITIL processes have traditionally been split between those covering service support and service delivery. Service support processes help make IT applications operate in an efficient and customer-satisfying manner, while service delivery processes improve the efficiency and performance of IT infrastructure elements. There are five ITIL service support best practice processes, which range from release management best practices

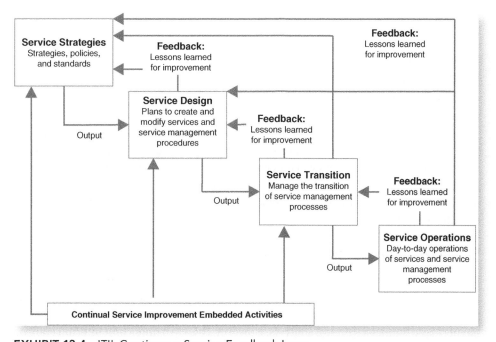

EXHIBIT 13.4 ITIL Continuous Service Feedback Loop

for placing an IT component into production to incident management, for the orderly reporting of IT problems or events. ITIL service support processes cover good practices for any IT enterprise, whether a centralized operation using primarily classic legacy mainframe systems as its IT central control point or highly distributed client-server operations. Because of the many possible variations in an IT operations function, ITIL does not proscribe the details of "how" to implement service support processes, but rather it suggests good practices and ways to manage input and relationships between these processes. There is no order or precedence among each. They can be considered and managed separately, but all of them are somewhat linked to one another. It shows that the service management areas of service delivery and support, along with security management, provide a linkage between the business operations and IT technology and infrastructure management.

Although there are many separate but interrelated elements of ITIL, this chapter discusses only two of ITIL's service life-cycle components to explain these important IT internal control concepts. These ITIL best practices suggest preferred IT operation approaches to run IT production systems in a manner that will promote efficiency and will deliver high-quality, well-controlled services to the ultimate user or customer of these services.

The upper-left corner of Exhibit 13.4's diagram of ITIL processes shows a function called Service Strategies. This component describes ITIL service management policies, strategies, and standards that provide input and direction to the other ITIL service design, transition, and operation processes. Those latter three also provide input to service strategies to establish continuous process improvements.

As a best practice, ITIL suggests that the IT management team should first ask some hard questions about its IT-serviced function, including

- Which of our IT services or service offerings are the most distinctive?
- Which of our services are the most profitable?
- Which of our customers and stakeholders are the most satisfied?
- Which of our activities are most different and effective?

The above are not the types of questions that IT management typically asks, but they are the types of questions that senior management should consider when evaluating the adequacy and efficiency of enterprise IT operations and internal controls. The idea is to encourage the enterprise IT function to move away from a resource that simply maintains IT processes to one that provides valuable and cost-effective services to the overall enterprise.

Financial Management for IT Services

ITIL introduces a best practices process that is often ignored by both IT and financial managers: financial management for IT services. This is an area that has been avoided by many IT professionals, who argue that they are not accountants and need not worry about classic financial internal controls. However, this is an important internal control area of potential concern and an ITIL best practice.

In its earlier days, the IT function in most enterprises was operated as a "free" support service, with its expenses handled through central management and costs allocated to benefit users. There was little attention given to IT-related costs in those early days. If a department wanted some new application, it would pressure management to purchase the package and would add any additional necessary people to manage it. Over time, IT enterprises began to establish charge-back processes, but these were too often viewed as a series of "funny-money" transactions, where no one paid too much attention to the actual costs and pricing of IT services.

Today, the costs and pricing of IT services are or should be a much more important consideration. The well-managed IT function should operate more as a business, and ITIL financial management is a key ITIL process to help manage the financial controls for that business. The objective of the ITIL service strategy financial management process is to suggest guidance for the cost-effective stewardship of the assets and resources that are used in providing IT services. IT should be able to account fully for its spending on IT services and to attribute these costs of the services delivered to the enterprise's customers by using the following three separate subprocesses associated with ITIL financial management:

1. **IT budgeting.** This is the process of estimating and controlling the spending of money for IT resources. Budgeting consists of a periodic, usually annual, negotiation cycle to set overall budgets, along with the ongoing day-to-day monitoring of current budgets. Budgeting ensures that there has been planning and funding for appropriate IT services and that IT operates within this budget during the period. Other business functions will have periodic negotiations with IT to establish expenditure plans and agreed-on investment programs; these ultimately set the budgets for IT.

2. **IT accounting.** These processes enable IT to account fully for the way its money is spent by customer service and activity. IT functions do not always do a good job in this area. They have a wide variety of external costs, including software, equipment lease agreements, telecommunications costs, and others, but these costs are often not that well managed or reported. They have enough data to pay the bills and evaluate some specific area costs, but IT functions often lack the level of detailed accounting that can be found in a large manufacturing enterprise, as an example. The manufacturing cost accounting or activity-based accounting model has applicability there.

3. **Charging.** Pricing and billing processes are established to charge customers for the services supplied. It requires sound IT accounting and needs to be done in a simple, fair, and well-controlled manner. The IT charging process sometime breaks down in an IT function, because the billing reports of IT services are too complex or technical for many customers to understand. IT needs to produce clear, understandable reports of the IT services used, such that customers can verify details, understand enough to ask questions regarding service, and negotiate adjustments, if necessary.

Financial management for IT supports the service strategy process through defined IT costing, pricing, and charging procedures. Although generally not operated as a profit center, the financial management process allows both IT and its customers to better think of IT service operations in business terms. The financial management process may allow IT and overall management to make decisions about what, if any, functions should be retained in-house or outsourced to an external provider.

The financial management process allows for accurate cost–benefit analyses of the IT services provided and enables the IT enterprise to set and meet financial targets. It also provides timely reporting to the service level management process, such that customers can understand the charging and pricing methods used. Of all of the ITIL service support and delivery processes, financial management is one ITIL best practice that frequently gets short shrift. IT people have a technical orientation and tend to think of financial management as an *accounting issue*, almost beneath them. On the other hand, finance and accounting professionals tend to look at these issues as too technical and beyond such transactions as equipment lease accounting or facility space charges.

Service Delivery Service Level Management

Service level management is the name given to the process of planning, coordinating, drafting, agreeing, monitoring, and reporting on formal service level agreements (SLAs) between both IT and the providers and recipients of IT services. SLAs represent a formal agreement between IT and both providers of services to IT and IT end-user customers. When the first ITIL service level best practices materials were first published in 1989, an SLA was an interesting but not very common concept. Today, many enterprises have introduced them—although with varying degrees of success—and senior management should be familiar with and should understand the importance of SLAs when establishing effective internal IT infrastructure controls.

As an example of a SLA, when IT contracts for an outside provider, such as for disaster recovery backups, the arrangement should be covered by a formal contract, in which the disaster recovery provider agrees to provide certain levels of service, following some time response–based schedule. The governing contract here is an SLA between IT and the provider of continuity services. SLA agreements between IT and its customers are even more important here, from an internal control perspective. We have used the term *customer* here, as the older and still common term for IT users. There are many groups in an enterprise that use IT's services, and as customers, they have expectations of certain levels of service and responsiveness. These arrangements are defined through an SLA, a written agreement between IT and its customers defining the key service targets and responsibilities of both parties. The emphasis should be on agreement, and SLAs should not be used as a way of holding one side or the other for ransom. A true partnership should be developed between the IT provider and the customer for a mutually beneficial agreement; otherwise, the SLA could quickly fall into disrepute, and a culture of blame might prevent any true service quality improvements from taking place.

In an SLA, IT promises to deliver services per an agreed-on set of schedules and understands there will be penalties if service standards are not met. The goal here is to maintain and improve on service quality through a constant cycle of agreeing to, monitoring, reporting on, and improving the current levels of IT service. SLAs should be strategically focused on the business and on maintaining the alignment between the business and IT.

The SLA process is an important component of IT operations' internal controls. If an enterprise does not use formal SLAs, senior management and IT should consider establishing formal SLA processes. SLAs can create a totally new environment within IT, where all parties will better understand their responsibilities and service obligations, using the SLA as a basis for resolving many issues.

Service Delivery Capacity Management

ITIL capacity management ensures that the capacity of the IT infrastructure is aligned to business needs to maintain the required level of service delivery at an acceptable cost through appropriate levels of capacity. By gathering business and technical capacity data, this process should result in a capacity plan to deliver cost-justified IT capacity requirements for the enterprise. In addition to a prime objective of understanding an enterprise's IT capacity requirements and delivering against them, capacity management is responsible for assessing the potential advantages that new technologies could have for the enterprise.

The capacity management process is generally considered in terms of three subprocesses covering business, service, and resource capacity management. Business capacity management is a long-term process to ensure that future business requirements are taken into consideration and then planned and implemented as necessary. Service capacity management is responsible for ensuring that the performance of all current IT services falls within the parameters defined in existing SLAs. Finally, resource capacity management has more of a technical focus and is responsible for the management of the individual components within the IT infrastructure. The multiple types of input into these three capacity management subprocesses include:

- SLAs and SLA breaches
- Business plans and strategies
- Operational schedules as well as schedule changes
- Application development issues
- Technology constraints and acquisitions
- Incidents and problems
- Budgets and financial plans

As a result of these multiple types of input, the capacity management process—often under a designated capacity manager—will manage IT processes, develop and maintain a formal capacity plan, and make certain that capacity records are up-to-date. In addition, the capacity manager must be involved in evaluating all changes to establish the effect on capacity and performance. This capacity evaluation should happen both when changes are proposed and after they are implemented. Capacity management must pay particular attention to the cumulative effect of changes over a period of time that may cause degraded response times, file storage problems, and excess demand for processing resources. Capacity management processes in an enterprise IT function are joint responsibilities of network managers, the application managers, and the system manager. They are responsible for translating the business requirements into the required capacity to be able to meet these requirements and to optimize IT performance.

Smaller enterprise IT facilities, of course, will usually not be able to justify a full- or even part-time capacity manager. However, some resource within the IT organization should have the responsibility for capacity management issues. It is an important service design issue.

The implementation of an effective capacity management process offers IT the benefits of an actual overview of the current capacity in place and the ability to plan capacity in advance. Effective capacity management should be able to estimate the impact of new applications or modifications, as well as provide cost savings that are in tune with enterprise operation requirements. Proper capacity planning can significantly reduce the overall cost of ownership of an IT system. Although formal capacity planning takes time, internal and external staff resources, and software and hardware tools, the potential losses incurred by an enterprise that has no capacity planning can be significant. The lost productivity of end users in critical business functions, overpaying for network equipment or services, and the cost of upgrading systems that are already in production can more than justify the cost of capacity planning. This is an important ITIL process, and IT management should consider the capacity management processes in place when establishing IT infrastructure internal controls.

Service Delivery Availability Management

Enterprises today are increasingly dependent on their IT services being available 7 days per week and 24 hours a day (24/7). In many cases, when those IT services are unavailable, the business stops as well. It is therefore vital that an IT function manage and control the availability of its services. This can be accomplished by defining the requirements of the business regarding the availability of the IT services and then matching them with the possibilities of the IT enterprise.

Availability management depends on multiple types of input, including requirements regarding the availability of the business; information on reliability, maintainability, recove rability, and serviceability; and information from the other processes, incidents, problems, and achieved service levels. The objectives of the availability management process are to:

- Produce and maintain an appropriate and up-to-date availability plan that reflects the current and future needs of the enterprise.
- Provide service and guidance to all other areas of the enterprise on IT availability–related issues.
- Ensure that service availability achievements meet or exceed targets, by managing service- and resource-related availability performance.
- Assist with the diagnosis and resolution of availability-related incidents and problems.
- Assess the impact of all changes on the availability plan and the performance and capacity of all services and resources.
- Ensure that proactive measures are implemented wherever those actions are cost-justifiable.

Availability management activities can be described as planning, improving, and measuring actions. Planning involves determining the availability requirements to find out if and how IT can meet them. The service level management process, discussed previously, maintains contact with the business and will be able to provide the availability expectations to availability management. The business may have unrealistic expectations with respect to availability, without understanding what this means in real terms. For example, business users may want 99.9 percent availability, yet may not realize that this will cost five times more than providing only 98 percent availability. It is the responsibility of the service level management and the availability management process to manage such expectations.

Exhibit 13.5 shows this availability-and-cost relationship. It does not cost very much just to keep basic IT systems running, if that is all the enterprise will receive. Both senior management and IT should keep this relationship in mind when reviewing controls and making recommendations.

An IT function can be designed either for "availability" or "recovery." When the business cannot afford a particular service's downtime for any length of time, IT will need to build resilience into the infrastructure and ensure that preventative maintenance can be performed to keep services in operation. In many cases, building "extra availability" into the infrastructure is an expensive task that can be justified by business needs. Designing for availability is a proactive approach to avoiding downtime in IT services.

When the business can tolerate some downtime of services or a cost justification cannot be made for building additional resilience into the infrastructure, designing for

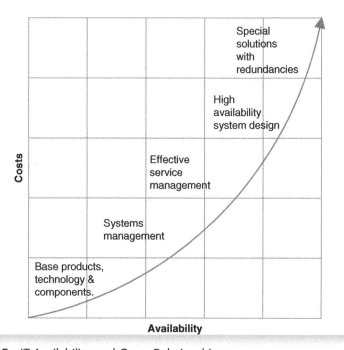

EXHIBIT 13.5 IT Availability-and-Costs Relationships

recovery is the appropriate approach. Here, the infrastructure will be designed such that in the event of a service failure, recovery will be "as fast as possible." Designing for recovery is a more reactive management approach for availability. In any event, processes such as incident management need to be in place to recover as soon as possible in case of a service interruption.

The main benefit of availability management is that it is a structured process to deliver IT services according to the agreed-on requirements of the customers. This should result in a higher availability of the IT services and increased customer satisfaction. This covers an area where IT auditors can often ask some hard questions as part of their IT general controls reviews.

 SERVICE DELIVERY BEST PRACTICES

The preceding paragraphs have described just a few of the ITIL service management life-cycle processes. ITIL service management outlines processes for launching, managing, and controlling all levels of IT services, with an emphasis on establishing customer satisfaction. ITIL guidance goes beyond just the COSO framework configuration of internal controls and includes managing IT costs, establishing measurements and metrics, and putting into effect other quality-improvement measures.

The IT infrastructure is an important internal control review area. All too often, we have concentrated our attention on the application controls and the IT general controls of the past. In today's world of complex processes supporting the IT infrastructure, ITIL processes describe some excellent areas for management and IT attention. When reviewing and establishing COSO internal controls for any IT enterprise, whether a major corporate-level IT operation or the smaller function found in many of today's enterprises, the effective senior manager should concentrate on reviewing controls over key IT infrastructure processes. ITIL service management life-cycle processes are increasingly being adopted by IT functions worldwide. The emphasis on service raises the importance of IT resources and its supporting infrastructure to the overall enterprise and its customers and stakeholders.

The ITIL service management processes introduce an expanded and improved approach for looking at all aspects of the IT infrastructure and IT-related internal controls. These processes are not independent and freestanding. While every ITIL process can somewhat operate by itself, they each depend on the input and support from other related processes. We have tried to show these interdependencies in several of the process descriptions, and a manager reviewing the controls over any of the ITIL processes must think of these controls in relation to other related processes.

The ITIL service management life cycle is a series of interrelated best practice processes that supports the management of the IT infrastructure and the management of the enterprise. IT applications are in the center of this puzzle and are a key central area of internal control concerns. Although our previous discussions of the separate but interrelated ITIL processes tend to call for a very large IT function, with multiple levels of staff and management resources, these ITIL best practices apply to a much smaller enterprise as well.

In order to be ITIL-compliant, an enterprise does not need multiple levels of support staff. Rather, it needs to think of the various service support and service delivery processes from an ITIL best practices perspective. A smaller IT function may not need to establish separate incident management and problem management functions, for example, but must think of each as a separate process with unique control procedures. Even if it is a very small IT function, each ITIL process area should be treated as a separate area for process improvement.

Responsible senior managers should give this area particular care when creating and building COSO IT internal controls. The size and scope of the area being audited and the scope of operations should always be considered. This author thinks of the early days of IT controls, back when many applications were developed in-house for production applications. To promote an adequate separation of duties, many audit guidance materials recommended there be a separation of duties between people who operate the computer and those who program it. Otherwise, in those days of far simpler systems, there was a risk that an individual of fraudulent intent might change an application program (e.g., to write himself an unauthorized check) and then produce this personal check when operating the system. This was a good control in the early days of IT but is not as relevant today. Today, senior managers should think about the adequacy and appropriateness of IT controls in terms of the controls built into individual applications, as well as the infrastructure process controls discussed in this chapter.

 NOTES

1. For more information on IT general control standards, see Robert Moeller's *IT Audit, Control and Security* (Hoboken, NJ: John Wiley & Sons, 2010).
2. ITIL publications are available from the UK agency called The Stationery Office (TSO) and can be found through www.tsoshop.co.uk.

CHAPTER FOURTEEN

Cloud Computing, Virtualization, and Wireless Networks

S ENIOR MANAGERS WHO ARE WORKING with IT systems and processes for any length of time and building effective COSO internal control processes understand that IT technologies and their supporting processes are changing on a continual basis. Some of these changes—such as the move to wireless configured laptop or even handheld computers from desktop devices tied or wired to a network—do not have that significant of an impact on enterprise internal controls. Others do. This chapter discusses three areas where IT is changing and where enterprise management may need to take somewhat different approaches in its understanding of COSO internal controls.

This chapter begins with a discussion of the internal control implications of enterprise wireless networks, both public and private. Enterprise managers can often easily gain access to their e-mail messages or get current business news off their handheld or laptop devices and the Internet. These facilities provide a significant convenience to all system users, but they do present some control and security threats if an enterprise's network is not properly protected through firewalls and other security controls. An enterprise's senior manager may be quite happy to be able to gain access to e-mail messages or change an airline flight reservation over a wireless network, but those connections should be secure. This chapter will also briefly look at some wireless network security and internal control issues.

An IT configuration approach called *cloud computing* has been rapidly growing and evolving in recent years. Although the term sounds almost exotic to many people, it has become a significant concept today with our growing dependency on Web-based applications for many business processes, rather than applications downloaded to home office servers. Known as Web services or Software as a Service (SaaS), the concept has been widely embraced by many software vendors today. Cloud computing is a concept in which many different IT applications supported by multiple vendors and operating on multiple servers operate together out of what looks like a large fuzzy Internet cloud.

This chapter introduces cloud computing concepts and discusses some security and control concerns that may affect COSO internal controls.

On a somewhat different level, *storage management virtualization* is another evolving IT infrastructure technology with COSO internal control implications. The term refers to the connections between a computer's central processor and the supporting mass storage devices. In past years, IT managers and auditors thought of a computer system in terms of its physical configuration—the disk drives and other peripheral devices that were connected to a computer's central processing unit (CPU). These were once attached through an often complex network of hard-wired cables. However, starting early in this century, software tools known as *storage virtualization* were introduced to manage large server sites, and today virtualization concepts have been introduced to all levels of computer processors. File virtualization can introduce strong efficiencies to IT operations; however, there can also be some internal control risks if mass storage relationships are not properly managed and backed up. This chapter will also briefly introduce storage virtualization as an element of COSO internal controls.

This chapter discusses these three newer and still evolving IT technical areas that may affect senior managers in their understanding and assessment of COSO IT internal controls. These three IT-related areas may not be all that familiar to many senior managers today but will quite possibly be for COSO IT internal control concerns going forward. Of course, the landscape here is always changing, and senior managers should always be aware of these and other newer technology-driven internal control issues and should modify their understanding to accommodate and assess these and other new internal control areas. Effective senior managers should always take a strong lead in their enterprises in understanding newer IT technology-based processes and then translating them to reviews and assessments of internal controls.

INTERNAL CONTROLS FOR IT WIRELESS NETWORKS

Computer system components, such as terminals or printers, have traditionally been connected from their central processor units (CPUs) or major server devices through cables or transmission wires. When an employee moved from one office to another, it was often historically necessary for a maintenance crew to string the necessary computer system and network cables to the new office location. Although they originally could not transmit IT data, radio or wireless communications tools began to have a significant impact on the world as far back as World War II, when wireless information could be sent overseas or behind enemy lines easily, efficiently, and reliably. Since then, transmission standards have been developed, and wireless networks have grown significantly. Using local transmission stations, wireless networks first became common for local emergency services, such as the police or fire departments, which used wireless networks to communicate important information quickly.

By the late 1980s, local area networks (LANs), based on networks of wired IT components, were very common IT system configurations. Shortly thereafter in the early 1990s, processes and standards were developed for wireless LANs, where each system was a point in a network. Standards were developed in the early 1990s to implement wireless local area networks (LANs). These originally required communication cards between a central computer and local terminals, but they eventually expanded to broad networks with connections to remote transmission stations and the Internet.

Wireless systems and wireless LANs have some internal control risk vulnerabilities, because their data is carried as radio signals instead of wires and are subject to snooping. From a reliability standpoint, it is difficult to predict the dependable coverage of a wireless network radio inside a building because building construction features, such as steel beams and heavily plastered walls, severely weaken radio waves. Even outside of structures, predicting coverage accurately and dependably is difficult, owing to radio propagation issues. Much more troubling is that wireless LANs, by their very nature, broadcast their data into space, where they can be intercepted by anyone with the ability to listen in at the appropriate frequency. These features also facilitate itinerant use of wireless LANs and enable interlopers to easily enter such networks with the same privileges as authorized users, unless there are appropriate security controls in place.

Not all networks, and certainly not all wired networks, are secure. However, when a traditional LAN operates over cables within a relatively secure physical perimeter, the level of security provided by the physical construction usually is sufficient. Adding wireless transmission capabilities adds security vulnerabilities and the need for additional systems controls, such as the necessity to authenticate every network user. An IT security specialist, as well as an enterprise's internal auditors, should look for the following internal control and security characteristics in all wireless applications:

- **Confidentiality.** An application should contain a level of protection against interception or eavesdropping to provide assurance that messages sent are readable only by the intended recipients.
- **Authenticity.** Protections against spoofing or impersonation controls should be in place to ensure that messages originate from the claimed entity.
- **Integrity.** Controls should provide protection from transmission errors and/or willful modification of messages to provide assurance that a message has not changed in transmission.
- **Availability.** Assurances should be in place that application data will be available when and where it is required, as a protection against denial of service or poor reliability.

Wireless networks and LANs are important and should be included in any IT management review and assessment of COSO internal controls. The following sections discuss some key internal control characteristics of wireless networks that are important for IT wireless systems' general controls. With its emphasis on external financial reporting, neither the original nor the revised COSO internal control framework specifically addresses such matters as wireless networks. However, effective controls here should be part of the COSO framework's control environment elements, with linkages, in particular, to other organization units.

Key Components of an IT Wireless System

A wireless IT system is almost a generic name, but the overall configuration of any such system can cause some confusion. Many wireless systems are set up as an open system configuration, in which any entity that can pick up the wireless signal can potentially gain access. This is often the type of wireless system that a business executive will encounter when logging on to the Internet from a hotel room or in some public places such as coffee shops, using standards such as Wi-Fi, Bluetooth, or related protocols that can connect to a wired network and can relay data between the wireless devices, such as computers or printers, on the network.

Many wireless systems in offices or homes are limited in their proximity. Within their borders, however, they may connect to a variety of devices, such as local LANs, a cell phone network, and personal hand-held devices. From a general management perspective, two key controls in this wireless system configuration are the placement of two crucial wireless internal control components: routers and firewalls.

> **Wireless system routers.** A key component of all networks, including wireless, a router is an electronic device used to connect two or more computers, or to the Internet, by cable or wireless signals. A router allows several computers to communicate with one another and with the Internet at the same time. A wireless router performs the functions of a router but also acts as a wireless access point to allow access to the Internet or a computer network without the need for a cabled connection. It can function as a wired or a wireless LAN. Some routers also contain wireless antennae that allow connections from other wireless devices.

> **Wireless firewalls.** A firewall is a type of one-way door, where transactions and activity can exit but cannot enter through the door. It is an internal system, implemented with hardware, software, or a combination of both, that is designed to prevent unauthorized access to or from a private network. Firewalls are frequently used to prevent unauthorized Internet users from gaining access to private networks connected to the Internet, where all messages entering or leaving the intranet pass through an installed firewall. This important network control examines each message and blocks those that do not meet the specified security criteria. A firewall is considered a first line of defense in protecting private information.

> **Wireless network vulnerabilities and risks.** There are multiple internal control risks associated with any wireless network, including the risk of eavesdropping on system activities, illicit entry into the network enabled by a failure of user authentication, and denial of services. A major systems integrity concern here is the risk of eavesdropping. By their nature, wireless LANs intentionally radiate their radio signal network traffic into space, and once this is done, it is impossible to control who can receive the signals. The key control here is to encrypt all such messages. Wireless message standards allow for such encryption, but appropriate standards are not always installed. As a key internal control over wireless networks, enterprise IT security specialists should determine that encryption standards have been installed and that they have been applied to critical applications.

The implementation of internal controls to ensure message integrity is also important for wireless systems. Network messages are transmitted as small packets of data that are then reassembled to deliver the correct message. Transmission software provides standards that should protect the integrity of all messages. While the technical details here may be beyond many people's understanding, a concerned manager should meet with the communications software specialists who are responsible for the enterprise's wireless networks and discuss the software default standards that have been implemented that emphasize message integrity and provide controls over illicit entry into the network.

Our discussion here is not intended to provide detailed information on wireless networks but is meant to alert the enterprise executive that wireless networks include some COSO internal control vulnerabilities. We emphasized only the closed wireless networks that are more common for a business enterprise. Over time, we will almost certainly see a much greater concentration of the public, open wireless network connections that are common in some public places to provide access to the Internet and other sites. Because these wireless systems are based on radio signal messages, we may see an increased use of perpetrators trying to get around whatever security rules have been established for them and attempting to gain improper access.

Wireless Network Security Concerns

Security is a major issue with many, if not most, enterprise wireless networks. Anyone within the geographical network range of an open, unencrypted wireless network can potentially "sniff" or read the network traffic, gain unauthorized access to internal network resources and to the Internet, and then possibly send spam messages or attempt other illegal actions using the wireless network's Internet addresses. Although these threats reflect issues that have long troubled many types of wired networks (it is possible for individuals to plug their laptop computers into available Ethernet communication jacks within a site and get access to a local network), this usually does not pose a significant problem, because many enterprises today should have reasonably good physical security controls. However, radio signals bleed outside of buildings and drift across property lines, making network physical security largely irrelevant.

Establishing effective wireless security procedures is a challenge to both IT network administrators and certainly responsible senior managers. Good IT process and technology internal controls are often easily confused, and particularly so with wireless information security management issues. However, many of the same business processes that establish strong risk management practices for physical assets and wired networks also work to protect wireless resources. The following cost-effective best practice guidelines enable enterprises to establish proper security protections as part of an overall wireless strategy. This list includes areas that represent good IT wireless internal control practices and objectives. An interested senior executive should work with IT management and internal audit to better understand and evaluate enterprise wireless security processes in a COSO internal control framework environment.

- **Wireless security policy and architecture design.** Enterprise security policy, procedures, and best practices should include wireless networking as part of the overall security management architecture to determine what is and is not allowed with wireless technology.

▪ **Treat wireless access points as untrusted.** Access points need to be identified and evaluated on a regular basis to determine whether they need to be designated as untrusted devices before wireless clients can gain access to internal networks. This determination requires the appropriate placement of firewalls, virtual private networks, intrusion detection systems, and authentication between access points or the Internet.

▪ **Access point configuration policies.** Enterprise administrators need to define their standard security settings before the wireless systems can be deployed. These include guidelines over IDs, wireless keys. and encryption,

▪ **Access point discovery.** Administrators should regularly search outward from a wired network to identify unknown access points. Such a search may identify rogue access points operating in the area—often a major concern in densely populated locations.

▪ **Access point security assessments.** An enterprise should perform regular security reviews and penetration assessments to identify poorly configured access points and default or easily guessed passwords.

▪ **Wireless client protection.** Wireless clients—typically, user departments—should establish good security practices. An enterprise IT function can establish good wireless procedures, but the actual users should also follow good practices.

The overall objective of this section is to highlight some evolving internal control area vulnerabilities that may affect an installed COSO internal control IT framework. IT wireless systems are nothing really new, but today they are becoming almost standard components of the internal controls in many system configurations.

 ## CLOUD COMPUTING AND COSO INTERNAL CONTROLS

Although some enterprise executives who grew up in the pencil-and-paper days of old may have felt that certain members of their IT systems and development staffs have had their "heads in the clouds" for years, those clouds are now part of IT, and cloud computing is a newer and evolving concept that is important to many IT operations. Also closely related is the concept of Software as a Service, a cloud computing approach to the way that enterprises build and use IT applications.

A cloud symbol is often used to refer to the Internet. The idea behind this Internet cloud is that users there do not need knowledge of, expertise in, or control over the technology infrastructure "in the cloud" that supports them. This term originated in the telephone industry, where, up until the 1990s, data and even early Internet circuits were hard-wired between destinations. Then, long-haul telephone companies began offering wireless virtual private network (VPN) service for data communications. The growth of these wireless networks and the Internet's World Wide Web concepts enhanced the way that we think of IT services.

Cloud computing is more than just the Internet. It is the way we think of the services that Internet-resident applications provide. Because it is impossible to determine in advance precisely the paths of Internet traffic, the cloud symbol has been used to denote that which was the responsibility of the service providers, as well as the network infrastructure. The concepts of software products or services on the Internet—that is, SaaS—soon followed. While cloud computing and SaaS concepts are not really part of the revised COSO internal controls framework guidance materials, they are important concepts for building effective, integrated IT internal controls.

To provide some background on how we got here, in the early 2000s, Microsoft launched what we now know as Software as a Service, or SaaS, through the development of what it called Web Services. IBM later released what it called the Autonomic Computing Manifesto, which described automation techniques such as self-monitoring, self-healing, self-configuring, and self-optimizing in the management of complex IT systems, along with heterogeneous storage, servers, applications, networks, security mechanisms, and other system elements that can be virtualized across an enterprise.

Other software vendors picked up on these concepts by offering their IT products as services on the Internet, rather than as applications that resided on individual customers' servers. A good example—and an early product type leader—is the provider of customer relationship management (CRM) software, SalesForce.[1] This supplier of customer and sales tracking software tools does not sell its products as a set of programs loaded on proprietary CDs for customer use. Rather, all of the SalesForce programs and documentation is found on the Internet, and customers pay for their software only when they use the product. The SalesForce applications are used as a service to customers.

Exhibit 14.1 shows this cloud computing concept. We have highlighted several vendor names that currently offer SaaS products today, including Amazon, Google, and Microsoft, as well as SalesForce. This is only a limited example of SaaS current applications, and there certainly will be many more to follow. Some of the benefits of SaaS applications in a cloud computing environment and from a COSO internal control perspective are:

- **Reduced infrastructure costs, due to centralization.** With the SaaS application in the cloud, there is no need to maintain application change management and other controls for those applications in the cloud.
- **Increased peak load capacities.** The cloud providers, such as Amazon or Google, have massive server farms with enormous capacities—their load capacities are almost infinite.
- **Efficiency improvements.** These help systems that are often underutilized.
- **Consistent performance.** This will be monitored by the provider of the service.
- **Application and IT services resiliency.** Cloud providers have mirrored solutions that can be used in a disaster scenario, as well as for load-balancing traffic. Whether there is a natural disaster, requiring a site in a different geographic area to pick up the overload, or simply heavy traffic, cloud providers should have the resiliency and capacity to ensure systems sustainability to recover from some unexpected event.

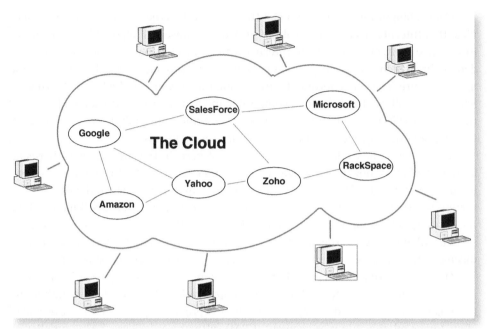

EXHIBIT 14.1   Cloud Computing Concepts

Although the COSO internal controls remain unchanged, senior managers should take a different approach in reviewing internal controls for SaaS applications, as well as for understanding COSO internal controls and IT security in a cloud computing environment. Web and other infrastructure services are increasingly being delivered in a cloud environment, and there is a need to rethink some audit and control considerations.

Reviewing Cloud Computing Application Controls

As IT professionals should realize, even though an application is operating in an SaaS environment, the need to assess and review its application internal controls does not go away. The SaaS-based application should continue to have the same audit trails, error-checking procedures, and other good practices that would be found with any well-controlled IT application. A senior manager can almost expect that a business application run under a major vendor, such as Google, with many often worldwide users, can be expected to have adequate internal controls.

Cloud computing represents a major change in the way applications are run and managed, and while there are only a limited number of vendors providing service-based software applications today, that number of service providers can be expected to increase. There is an implicit level of trust in the services provided by many vendors under the SaaS clouds, but care should be taken that IT and business management applications using SaaS applications are well controlled.

IT management should attempt to help demonstrate to direct and indirect users of cloud computing that they can have a strong level of trust in the software services and infrastructure that make up the cloud for an enterprise. Some of the key assurance issues that should be addressed are

- **Transparency.** Service providers should be able to demonstrate the existence of effective and robust security internal controls, assuring customers that their information is properly secured against unauthorized access, change, and destruction. Key questions for any service provider providing SaaS applications are
  - What types of service provider employees have access to customer information?
  - Is a segregation of duties between the provider's employees maintained?
  - How are the files and the data for different customers' information segregated?
  - What controls are in place to prevent, detect, and react to any security and control breaches?
- **Privacy.** Cloud computing service providers should provide assurances that privacy controls are in place that will prevent, detect, and react to breaches in a timely manner, with strong and periodically tested lines of communication.
- **Compliance.** In order to comply with various laws, regulations, and standards, there can be cloud computing concerns that data may not be stored in one place and may not be easily retrievable. It is critical to ensure that if data is demanded by authorities, it can be provided without compromising other information. When we use cloud services, there is no guarantee that an enterprise can get its information when needed, or that a service provider may claim a right to withhold information from authorities.
- **Trans-border information flow.** With cloud-generated information potentially stored anywhere in the cloud, the physical location of the information can become an issue. The physical location dictates jurisdiction and legal obligation. There are many legal issues here yet to be solved.
- **Certification.** Cloud computing service providers should provide their customers with assurance that they are doing the "right" things. In the future, we should see independent third-party audits and/or service auditor reports that will become a vital part of any cloud computing service provider assurance program.

Strong and effective standards will help enterprises gain assurance about their cloud computing supplier's internal controls and security. At present, there are no publicly available, generally recognized cloud computing standards. With no defined set of such standards, an IT manager who is responsible for cloud applications should request that the enterprise's cloud service provider demand strong internal control assurances in these three key areas:

1. **Events.** The service provider should regularly document and communicate changes and other factors that have affected SaaS system availability.
2. **Logs.** The service provider should provide comprehensive information about an enterprise's SaaS application and its runtime environment.
3. **Monitoring.** Any such surveillance should not be intrusive and must be limited to what the cloud provider reasonably needs in order to run its facility.

Cloud computing represents a newer and interesting opportunity to rework security and IT controls for a better tomorrow, and IT internal control standards should soon follow. As limited internal control guidance have been published, we can expect to see much more in the future, as SaaS applications and cloud computing grow and mature.

Cloud Computing Security and Privacy Challenges

The use of SaaS applications operating in a cloud computing environment shifts a wide range of challenges and responsibilities from primarily an enterprise's IT function to an environment where some responsibilities are assumed by the cloud computing service provider, while others still are the responsibility of the enterprise's IT function. This is a challenge for IT management as well, which must understand the security and privacy components of its selected service providers.

Cloud computing and the use of SaaS applications are still new evolving trends in a COSO internal controls framework concept. An increasing number of vendors are offering suites of SaaS applications, and vendors such as Google and Amazon are building huge, multiserver cloud computer complexes, but there is not an established set of recognized best practices across these various service providers. In some respects, the trend of enterprises to shift some of their in-house IT resources to cloud service providers has, in perhaps a strange sort of manner, some similar elements to the move to IT service bureaus in the early 1980s.

Going back to the mid to late 1970s, an increasing number of enterprises decided they needed to move from their manual or unit record punched-card processes to one of the then new mainframe computer systems. Many enterprises added systems development programming staffs and installed mainframe computer systems, often with very disappointing results. A frequent problem was that these new mainframe systems did not have the capacity to process the volumes of enterprise data and, when they did, experienced computer system maintenance or down-time problems on their mainframe systems.

A solution for many at that time was to convert their computer system programs and operations to what was called a service bureau—a large centralized computer systems resource that collected input material from many clients, processed the data on the service bureau's centralized system, and delivered the output reports. These computer systems' service bureaus often did not work that well for everyone. Many enterprises subscribed to these services without fully realizing what they would be getting in terms of the services, integrity, the added costs of using the service provider, and limited internal control monitoring for the enterprise's processes. These service bureau computer operations have gone away, even well before the demise of the mainframe. However, some of the same things happened then as today, with enterprises converting some of their conventional applications to a cloud environment. A major issue is that enterprises do not always ask the right questions from their service providers when converting to an SaaS cloud environment.

When making a decision to select a service provider as part of a move to cloud computing, an enterprise should ask any competing service provider vendors some hard questions about their operations and standards. Senior managers who are responsible for implementing COSO internal control processes should gain assurance in some of the following areas for selecting a cloud computing service provider:

- **Privileged user access.** Sensitive data processed outside an enterprise and in a cloud brings with it an inherent level of risk, because outsourced services in the cloud bypass conventional physical, logical, and personnel IT controls that an IT organization would exert over its in-house systems programs. The service provider should provide complete information about the people who manage an enterprise's data and systems in the cloud. Service providers should supply specific information on the hiring and oversight of privileged administrators and the controls over their access.
- **Regulatory compliance.** An enterprise is ultimately responsible for the security and integrity of its own data, even when it is held by a service provider. The cloud computing service provider should supply detailed information on its security governance policies and also provide reported results of recent external audits and security certifications. In addition, it should agree to update the enterprise on these activities on a regular basis.
- **Data location.** When an enterprise uses the cloud, it probably won't know exactly where the data is hosted—not even in which country. Because of data ownership laws, service providers should identify the specific jurisdictions where they will be storing and processing the enterprise's data. The service provider should also make a contractual commitment to obey local privacy requirements on behalf of its customers,
- **Data segregation.** Data in the cloud is typically in a shared environment, alongside data from other customers. The cloud provider should offer detailed information on what is done to segregate data at rest and also should provide evidence that its encryption programs were designed and tested by experienced specialists. Encryption accidents can make data totally unusable and even can complicate availability.
- **Recovery.** Even if an enterprise does not know the location of its cloud data, the cloud provider should document what will happen to an enterprise's data and service in case of a disaster. The service provider should provide evidence, including test results that its recovery methods will replicate the data and the application infrastructure across multiple sites. The service should assert whether it has the ability to do a complete restoration and how long it will take.
- **Investigative support.** Investigating inappropriate or illegal activity may be impossible in cloud computing. Cloud services are especially difficult to investigate, because logging and data for multiple customers may be co-located and may also be spread across an ever-changing set of hosts and data centers. A service provider should provide a contractual commitment to support specific forms of investigation, along with evidence that the vendor has already successfully supported such activities.
- **Long-term viability.** An enterprise has no guarantee that a cloud computing provider will never go broke or get acquired and swallowed up by a larger company. However, an enterprise should gain assurance that its data will remain available

even after such an event. Any service provider should provide contractual assurances that users will get their data back in a format that they could import into a replacement application.

Cloud computing and its SaaS applications are new and evolving IT systems and are important elements of the COSO internal controls framework. We can expect to see better established standards and recognized best practices here in future years. Cloud computing and SaaS are the wave of the future, and IT management will see much more of them in the years going forward.

 ## STORAGE MANAGEMENT VIRTUALIZATION

Virtualization is the concept of pooling IT physical storage from multiple network storage devices into what appears to be a single storage device that is managed from a central console. Storage virtualization helps an IT storage administrator perform the tasks of backup, archiving, and recovery more easily, and in less time, by disguising the actual complexity of the overall network of IT storage devices. This author was first introduced to storage management virtualization concepts initially in about the year 2002, when he was part of a small consulting group for EMC Corporation that was launching an ITIL consulting practice (ITIL best practices are discussed in Chapter 12). At that time, EMC was a leader in storage management devices, and its introduction of virtualization concepts was a major technology innovation. Virtualization has since become a widely used and important IT resource management process.

To understand IT virtualization, one should think back to the earlier days of computer systems—particularly, the mainframes of old. Those computers had operating systems that controlled various attached peripherals, including printers, tape drives, and what were then called mass storage devices. Although earlier mainframe computer systems initially made wide use of the relatively inexpensive magnetic tape drives to store data, technology quickly moved to storage devices based first on rotating magnetic drums and then on disk drives. Although they were much more expensive in the early days of IT, disc and drum drives quickly became more popular than tape drives. The limitation with tape drives was that to read the 100,000th record on a tape, the drive had to pass through the first 99,999 records to find it. Drum drives quickly became an almost historical anecdote, and technology moved to rotating disc drives that were much faster and had indexing schemes that located that 100,000th record almost instantaneously.

As every IT professional with a packed "C-drive" disc on her laptop, full of records and other materials, can attest, there is a strong need for mass storage space on all computers. Enterprises of all sizes need mechanisms to manage and control their stored data. With enterprises creating so much information, IT operations have been storing their data on multiple storage units or drives but have had a need to consolidate storage and get the most out of each storage unit. Schemes for managing all of those devices soon become a headache, and a solution has been storage virtualization, a technique to combine all storage drives into one centrally manageable resource.

Virtualization in general is the separation of a device's functions from its physical elements. With storage virtualization, a unit's physical drive is separated from its functions to store data, and multiple physical disks will appear to be a single unit. Virtualization is a very efficient method and internal control to manage separate physical units through specialized virtualization software. With proper controlling software, virtualization techniques can be used on a wide range of IT hardware devices beyond just storage management, including network components, servers, operating systems, or even applications. From an IT management perspective, the hardware application diagrams that had been requested as part of a review of general IT controls are no longer applicable. Virtualization software is assuming these unit by unit responsibilities.

Virtualization concepts were really the forerunner of cloud computing, discussed in the previous section. We have only mentioned virtualization here as a newer concept that senior managers will encounter as part of their understanding of evolving IT internal controls. Although IT storage management virtualization was first introduced by the storage management firm EMC, the concept was soon introduced by many hardware and storage management vendors. When a manager assessing IT internal controls encounters an environment where there is a strong use of virtualization, the manager should meet with members of the IT staff to gain an understanding of the nature of its implementation and to determine that it has been implemented in a manner that emphasizes IT internal controls, and that IT appears to be realizing benefits from the software product. Virtualization is a growing concept, and members of IT management should increase their understanding of it as an evolving trend in IT operations.

 ## COSO INTERNAL CONTROLS AND NEWER TECHNOLOGIES

This chapter has introduced three newer technologies that are changing IT operations and, to some extent, IT internal controls. We have selected areas that are significant today, but not too many years in the future, there may be new approaches that look totally different. Regarding the technology approaches, we have tried to discuss how the revised COSO internal control framework is appropriate.

The current old COSO internal control framework, despite its 1992 issue date and its failure to understand many of today's internal control processes, still had some good general guidance. No matter what the twists and turns in IT technology, the revised COSO internal control framework provides a good general approach to developing and understanding effective IT internal controls.

 ## NOTE

1. See www.salesforce.com/crm/products.jsp.

CHAPTER FIFTEEN

Another Framework: COSO ERM

T HE ORIGINAL 1992 RELEASE OF the COSO internal control framework almost immediately pointed to other related areas where consistent definitions and internal controls guidance were lacking. One of these was risk management, a concept that had been receiving multiple and sometimes inconsistent definitions and interpretations by various industry groups. This was prior to the 2002-era SOx rules, when some public accounting firms began to call themselves risk management professionals, although many did not appear to have a clear understanding of what was meant by risk management. To try to develop a consistent enterprise risk management definition, COSO contracted with the same developers of the original COSO internal control framework, PricewaterhouseCoopers, to develop a common consistent definition for risk management. The result was the COSO enterprise risk management or COSO ERM framework released in 2004.

This chapter introduces COSO ERM and explains how to use this framework as a supplement to understanding and working with the new, revised version of the COSO internal control framework, as discussed in previous chapters. On first inspection, COSO ERM almost looks and feels like the COSO internal control framework. When it was first released not that many years after the original 1992 COSO internal control framework, many professionals viewed it as almost a new version or some form of supplement to the COSO internal controls. However, it has some very different objectives and purposes as an aid to developing better management processes.

COSO ERM provides a tool or an approach to improve and manage overall risks in the total enterprise. Internal controls and enterprise risk management each take a different perspective to understanding and evaluating activities in an enterprise. While COSO internal controls tend to focus on an enterprise's daily activities, enterprise risk management focuses on activities that an enterprise and its managers may or may not do. A manager is interested, for example, in the controls necessary to accumulate accounting transactions, to summarize them in a well-controlled manner, and to publish them as the financial results of the enterprise. However, that same manager may be concerned about such enterprise risks as the financial impact on the enterprise from the launch of a new product, the reactions and actions of competitors, and overall market conditions for that new product launch. All of these do not involve the here's and now's of an internal controls framework but involve risk.

ERM DEFINITIONS AND THE ERM PORTFOLIO VIEW OF RISK

Every enterprise, whether for-profit commercial, not-for-profit, or a governmental agency, exists to provide value for its stakeholders—either the employees and the stockholders for a commercial enterprise or the voters for a governmental entity. That stakeholder value is created, is preserved, or can be eroded through management decisions at all levels of the enterprise and in all activities, ranging from day-to-day regular operations to senior management's setting strategies for some future but uncertain endeavor. All of these are subject to uncertainties or risks. Whether it is the challenge resulting from a new and aggressive competitor or the damage and loss of life caused by a major earthquake, we all face a wide range of risks. Although it is essentially impossible to estimate the probability of a totally cataclysmic event, such as the 2010 earthquake that devastated the island nation of Haiti, or the probability of many other less major events, individuals and enterprises should balance the amount of risk that they are willing to accept against the potential and adjusted returns from accepting those risks.

Using a risk-adjusted return trade-off line of thinking, an enterprise should rank a series of its identified operational and business risks by their significance and likelihood of occurring. Estimating the potential probabilities for each, the risks can be ranked for their potential significance, and such a process is a good mechanism to attract the attention of senior management. As the insurance industry has demonstrated over the years, there are numerous good practices in place to assess risks and to anticipate both their potential occurrence and the returns for accepting a given risk.

Exhibit 15.1 is an example of this risk scoring-and-ranking process. It shows ten hypothetical events, such as event A, where there is a concern that a new product line called ZZ will not be accepted by the market. Each of these items has been arbitrarily rated by their significance and probability of occurring. These probabilities can be established through fairly detailed analyses or by management's best guesses. In either case, the exhibit shows a method of ranking these risks. There are many sources to find more information on the process of estimating these probabilistic risk values, and this author's book on COSO ERM provides a good overview.[1]

While enterprises have historically assessed their more local risks reasonably well, they have not done that well on more major risks spanning overall enterprise operations and beyond. That is, management can often hedge and do an effective job in planning for the risk of a new product or revision failing in the marketplace, but it often has not done that well in planning and allowing for enterprise-wide risks, such as a major jump in interest rates or the nationalization of a plant in some country.

Enterprises historically have had problems with this risk vs. adjusted return decision model. First, there has not been a good and consistently accepted definition of risk

EXHIBIT 15.1   Risk Ranking Chart Example

Identified Risk	Significance Probability	Likelihood Probability	Risk Score (P x I)	Rank
A. New ZZ product line not accepted by the market.	0.55	0.30	0.17	8
B. Nationalization of operating unit foreign subsidiary.	0.88	0.24	0.21	7
C. New product sales miss marketing expectations.	0.79	0.66	0.52	1
D. Customer service training plan fails.	0.77	0.45	0.35	4
E. Weather disturbances in SE region.	0.35	0.88	0.31	5
F. Key competitor A gains in product sales.	0.54	0.49	0.26	6
G. Government regulations ban certain marketing practices.	0.62	0.72	0.45	2
H. Certain key technical managers resign.	0.66	0.20	0.13	9
I. New product marketing plan fails.	0.90	0.45	0.41	3
J. Product line XX misses ISO inspections.	0.12	0.88	0.11	10

across the overall enterprise, and second, we often do not think of risks in a total enterprise sense but rather only component by component. In many cases, the people who are asked to assess the risks associated with some enterprise endeavor typically do not have enough information to make any kind of credible enterprise-wide assessment. To quote John Flaherty, the first and now many years ago chair of COSO, "Although a lot of people are talking about risk, there is no commonly accepted definition of risk management and no comprehensive framework outlining how the process should work, making risk communication among board members and management difficult and frustrating." This was the same environment that faced some of the internal control failure issues in the early 1980s and was discussed in Chapter 2, when business and other professionals looked at internal control processes and related supporting definitions. The result then was the COSO internal control framework.

A second risk versus return problem is that we often take a "silo approach" to our understanding of risks, rather than considering them in terms of the total enterprise. A "silo approach" refers to the tall and narrow agricultural storage silos used on farms. Everything within a silo is secure and protected, but there is no interaction between one silo and another nearby. Although this may be appropriate when each individual silo is used to store a separate commodity, with no need for interaction, separate processes each stored in its own silo often need connections and interactions with other processes that may exist in other such silos. An enterprise may have a good risk management process for credit operations housed in the silo covering that area of operations, as well as a good risk assessment process in the silo covering IT continuity planning, but there is often a need for these two processes to communicate and to use some common approaches. Risks should be considered on a total enterprise level.

COSO ERM is a framework that will help enterprises have a consistent definition of what is meant by *risk* and to consider those risks across the entire enterprise in a consistent manner. COSO launched its ERM framework in a manner similar to the development of the COSO internal control framework. An advisory council of members from the sponsoring enterprises was formed, and PricewaterhouseCoopers was contracted to develop the draft framework description; after public comments, the COSO ERM framework was released in 2004. The following pages summarize key elements of COSO ERM and its relationship to the COSO revised internal control framework, but the reader is encouraged to read the entire description of the ERM framework from the COSO website at www.coso.org or from this author's previously referenced book on COSO ERM.

Just as the original version of the COSO internal control framework started by proposing a consistent definition of its subject, the ERM framework starts by defining *enterprise risk management* as follows:

> Enterprise risk management is a process, effected by an entity's board of directors, management and other personnel, applied in a strategy setting and across the enterprise, designed to identify potential events that may affect the entity, and manage risk to be within its risk appetite, to provide reasonable assurance regarding the achievement of entity objectives.

This is a rather academic-sounding definition, but an enterprise executive should just consider COSO ERM's key points. The main concept here is that ERM is a process, a set of actions designed to achieve a result. The idea to remember is that a process is not a static procedure, such as the use of an employee badge that is designed and built to allow only certain authorized persons to enter a locked facility. Such a badge procedure—like a key to a lock—only allows or does not allow someone entry to the facility. A process here would tend to be a more flexible arrangement. In a credit approval process, for example, acceptance rules are often established with options to alter them, given other considerations. An enterprise might bend the credit rules for an otherwise good credit customer who is experiencing a short-term problem. ERM is that type of process. An enterprise typically cannot define its risk management rules through a small, tightly organized rule book. Rather, there should be a series of documented steps to review and evaluate potential risks and to take action based on a wide range of factors across the entire enterprise.

An ERM process should be implemented by people in the enterprise. An ERM will not be effective if it is only launched through a set of rules sent in to an operating unit from a distant corporate headquarters, where those corporate people who drafted the rules may have little understanding of the various decision factors surrounding them. The risk management process must be managed by people who are close enough to that risk situation to understand the various factors surrounding that risk, including its implications.

An ERM process should be applied through the setting of strategies across the overall enterprise. Every enterprise is constantly faced with alternative strategies regarding a vast range of potential future actions. Should the entity acquire another complimentary business or just build internally? Should it adopt a new technology in its manufacturing processes or stick with the tried and true? An effective ERM should play a major role in helping to establish those alternative strategies. Because many enterprises are large, with many varied operating units, ERM should be applied across that entire enterprise using a portfolio type of approach that blends a mix of high- and low-risk activities.

The concept of risk appetite also must be considered. Risk appetite concepts are discussed in Chapter 5 for the COSO internal control framework's risk assessment component. Risk appetite is the amount of risk, on a broad level, that an enterprise and its individual managers are willing to accept in their pursuit of value. Risk appetite can be measured in a qualitative sense by looking at risks in such categories as high, medium, or low; alternatively, it can be defined in a qualitative manner. An understanding of risk appetite is an important element for implementing ERM in a variety of enterprise environments. The basic idea is that every manager and, collectively, every enterprise has some level of appetite for risk. Some will accept risky ventures that promise high returns, while others prefer more guaranteed-return low-risk ventures.

ERM provides only reasonable, not positive, assurance on objective achievements. The idea here is that an ERM, no matter how well thought out or implemented, cannot provide management or others with any assured guarantee of outcomes. A well-controlled enterprise, with people at all levels consistently working toward understood and achievable goals, may achieve those objectives period after period—even over multiple years. However, an unintentional human error, an unexpected action by another, or even a natural disaster can occur. Although it was many years ago, the December 2004 Southeast Pacific tsunami tidal wave is an example of such an unexpected event. The last recorded major tidal wave in that part of the world took place some 400 years previously. Despite an effective ERM process, an enterprise can experience such a major and totally unexpected failure. Reasonable assurance does not provide absolute assurance.

An ERM is designed to help attain the achievement of objectives. An enterprise, through its management, should work to establish high-level common objectives that can be shared by all stakeholders. Examples here, as cited in the COSO ERM documentation, are such matters as achieving and maintaining a positive reputation within an enterprise's business and consumer communities, providing reliable financial reporting to all stakeholders, and operating in compliance with laws and regulations. The overall ERM program for an enterprise should help it to achieve those objectives.

ERM-related goals and objectives are of little value unless they can be organized and modeled together in such a manner that management can look at the various aspects of the task and understand—at least, sort of—how they interact and relate in a multidimensional manner. This is the real strength of the COSO internal control framework model; it describes, for example, how an enterprise's compliance with laws and regulations affects all levels of internal controls, from monitoring processes to the control environment, and how that compliance is important for all entities or units of the enterprise. In a similar manner, COSO has developed an ERM framework model that provides some common definitions of risk management, as well as helping to achieve key risk objectives throughout the enterprise.

 ## THE COSO ERM FRAMEWORK MODEL

The revised COSO internal control framework, as discussed in previous chapters and described in Exhibit 3.2, does an effective job of describing and defining enterprise internal controls and has become a worldwide model. Perhaps because some of the same team members were involved with both internal controls and the risk management project, the COSO ERM framework—at first observation—looks very similar to the COSO internal controls. The COSO ERM framework is shown in Exhibit 15.2 as a three-dimensional cube with the components of:

- Four vertical columns that represent the strategic objectives of enterprise risk.
- Eight horizontal rows or risk components.
- Multiple levels of the enterprise, from a "headquarters" entity level to individual subsidiaries. Depending on the enterprise, there can be many "slices" of the model here.

This chapter will briefly describe the horizontal components of COSO ERM, while its other two dimensions are very similar to the COSO internal control framework. The concept behind the ERM framework is to provide a model for enterprises to consider and to understand their risk-related activities at all levels of the enterprise, as well as

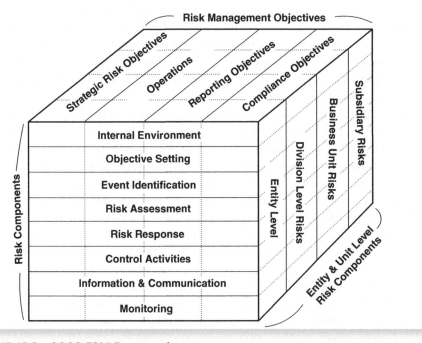

EXHIBIT 15.2   COSO ERM Framework

their impact on one another. The objective of COSO ERM is to help professionals at all levels—from board members to the professional staff—to better understand and manage the risks facing their enterprises.

Although the COSO ERM framework looks very similar to the COSO internal control framework that has been described in previous chapters, looks can be deceiving. COSO ERM has different objectives and uses, and it should not be considered as just a new and improved or revised version of the COSO internal control framework! It is much more. The following paragraphs will outline this framework and describe how it is a different but important tool for application within an enterprise.

COSO ERM Components: Internal Environment

The "Internal Environment" is placed at the top of the components in the COSO ERM framework, similar to its position in the COSO internal control framework. One should think of the ERM control environment as the basis or capstone for all other enterprise management components. It defines all other components in an enterprise's ERM model, influencing how strategies and objectives should be established, how risk-related business activities are structured, and how risks are identified and acted on. While the control environment for COSO internal controls focused on current practices in place, such as human resource policies and procedures, ERM takes these same areas and looks at them in a more future philosophy–oriented approach. The ERM internal foundation component consists of the following elements:

- **Risk management philosophy.** This is a set of shared attitudes and beliefs that will tend to characterize how the enterprise considers risk in everything it does. Although it is not often the type of message published in a code of conduct, a risk management philosophy is the kind of attitude that will allow managers and others at all levels to respond to some high-risk proposal with an answer along the lines of, "No, that's not the kind of venture our company would be interested in." Of course, an enterprise with a different philosophy might respond to this same proposal with an answer along the lines of, "Sounds interesting—What's the expected rate of return?" Neither response is really wrong, but an enterprise should try to develop a consistent philosophy and attitude for how it accepts risky ventures.
- **Risk appetite.** As discussed in previous chapters, this is a concept or an expression unfamiliar to many managers, risk appetite is the amount of risk an enterprise is willing to accept in the pursuit of its objectives. This appetite for risk can be measured in quantitative or qualitative terms, but all levels of management should have a general understanding of this concept for their business unit as well as for the overall enterprise. The term *risk appetite* represents an overall risk-taking philosophy.
- **Board of directors attitudes.** Similar to our Chapter 18 discussion on the role of the board for COSO internal controls, the board and its committees have a very important role in overseeing and guiding an enterprise's risk environment. The independent outside directors, in particular, should closely review management's actions, ask appropriate questions, and serve as a checks-and-balances control for the enterprise. If a strong senior enterprise officer has an "it can't happen here"

attitude when considering the possible risks surrounding some new endeavor, members of the board are often the best people to ask the hard questions about how the enterprise would react to a "can't happen" event that happens.

- **Integrity and ethical values.** This important ERM internal environment element requires much more than a strong published code of conduct and includes strong integrity and standards of behavior for members of the enterprise. There should be a strong corporate culture here that guides the enterprise, at all levels, in helping it make risk-based decisions. Although it was years ago now, the Johnson & Johnson Tylenol crisis of the early 1990s, discussed in Chapter 12, provides a good example of the importance of a strong set of ethical corporate values as a compass to provide direction and to help manage risks.

- **A strong corporate mission statement and written codes of conduct.** These are an important element of an enterprise's integrity and ethical values. Although most enterprises will not face a crisis on the level of Johnson & Johnson with its tainted Tylenol in the 1990s, a stronger anchor of this sort might have helped some enterprises better avoid the accounting scandals that led to the situations at Enron, WorldCom, and others, as well as the enactment of the SOx. This area should be an essential component in every ERM framework.

- **Commitment to competence.** *Competence* refers to the knowledge and skills that are necessary to perform assigned tasks. Management decides how these critical assigned tasks will be accomplished through developing appropriate strategies and assigning the proper people to perform these often strategic tasks. We have all seen enterprises that do not have this type of commitment. Senior management will make grand and loudly proclaimed plans to accomplish some goal but often will make no positive effort to achieve the goal. The stock market often punishes such activities. With a strong commitment to competence, managers at all levels will take steps to achieve their promised goals.

- **Enterprise organizational structure.** Although every enterprise should develop an organizational structure that meets its current needs and satisfies its heritage, that same structure should have clear lines of authority and responsibility, along with appropriate reporting lines. A poorly constructed enterprise structure makes it difficult to plan, execute, control, and monitor activities, and every professional has seen situations where an enterprise structure does not allow appropriate lines of communication. There will always be situations where the enterprise structure needs improvement, in order to achieve an effective ERM environment.

- **Assignment of authority and responsibility.** This concept refers to the extent or degree to which authority and responsibility are assigned or delegated in an enterprise. The trend in many enterprises today is to push levels of approval authorities down the enterprise structure, giving first-line employees greater authorization and approval authority. These enterprise structures usually encourage employee creativity, faster response times, and greater customer satisfaction. This type of customer-facing enterprise requires strong procedures that outline the "rules" for all members of the staff, as well as ongoing management monitoring of these actions so that decisions can be overruled if necessary. All individuals in the enterprise should know how their actions interrelate and contribute to the overall objectives of the enterprise.

■ **Human resource standards.** An enterprise's practices regarding hiring, training, compensating, promoting, and disciplining send messages to all members of the enterprise regarding what is favored, tolerated, or forbidden. When management winks at or ignores some "gray area" activities, rather than taking a strong stand, that message is often quickly communicated to others throughout an enterprise. A strong set of standards is needed that is both communicated to all stakeholders and enforced.

The previously referenced COSO ERM guidance materials have many other examples of the necessary components to build an effective internal environment. While many of these refer to the standards and approaches an enterprise will implement to accept and manage various levels of risk, others simply refer to good business practices that are necessary for effective operations. No matter whether an enterprise has a high or a low appetite for risk, it needs these control environment practices to manage those risks. For example, the enterprise can give its sales force a rather free rein to "do deals" without much management supervision and approval. Yet everyone on the sales team should know the legal, ethical, and management policy limits of those free-rein practices. Processes should be in place such that if anyone "steps over the line" regarding the limits of any of those practices, remedial actions will be swift and communicated to all who should know.

COSO ERM Components: Objective Setting

Ranked right below the internal environment, COSO ERM's objective setting component outlines preconditions necessary for management to establish an effective enterprise risk management processes. An enterprise should establish a series of strategic objectives covering its operations, reporting, and compliance activities. These strategic objectives are high-level goals that should be aligned with an enterprise's mission or vision.

A mission statement, as described in Chapter 4 on the COSO control environment, is also a crucial element in strategic planning for enterprise ERM processes. It creates a general, formalized statement of purpose and can be a building block for an overall strategy and the development of more specific functional strategies. It is a statement of the enterprise's purpose. Often just a simple, straightforward statement, a mission statement explains an enterprise's objectives and its overall attitude toward risks. Exhibit 15.3 lists examples of older and newer mission statements from major corporations over time. These statements say a lot about what a corporation wants to achieve and also defines its attitudes toward risk. Although very much out-of-date at present, the early Honda and PepsiCo mission statements suggest statements of purpose in which an enterprise will tolerate risks in order to achieve that objective.

Properly done, a mission statement will allow an enterprise to first develop some high-level strategic objectives to achieve the mission statement and then to select, develop, and implement a series of operations, reporting, and compliance objectives. PepsiCo's "Beat Coke" mission statement from an earlier time was made by a much

Ford Motor Company (early 1900s): "Ford will democratize the automobile."

Sony (1950s): "Become the company most known for changing the worldwide poor-quality image of Japanese products."

Boeing (1950): "Become the dominant player in commercial aircraft and bring the world into the jet age."

Honda (1960s): "We will crush, squash, and slaughter Yamaha."

3M (1970s): "To solve unsolved problems innovatively."

PepsiCo (1980): "Beat Coke."

Apple Computer (1984): "To produce high-quality, low cost, easy to use products that incorporate high technology for the individual. We are proving that high technology does not have to be intimidating for non-computer experts."

Walmart (1990): "Become a $125 billion company by the year 2000."

Walt Disney (2013): "Creativity + Innovation = Profits."

EXHIBIT 15.3 Corporate Mission Statements: Examples of Changes Over Time

---

different company. Whether or not it ever totally achieved that mission, the corporation developed some strategic objectives that turned it into a very different company. From the mission statement to strategic objectives, a next step is to develop a series of operational, reporting, and compliance objectives. While operations objectives pertain to the effectiveness and efficiency of the enterprise in its goals of achieving profitability and performance, the reporting and compliance goals cover how the enterprise will report its performance and comply with laws and regulations.

COSO ERM calls for an enterprise to formally define its goals with a direct linkage to its mission statement. Every enterprise should develop a mission statement and then have formal objectives to achieve that mission. In addition, the enterprise should develop units of measure to allow it to assess whether it is achieving those risk management objectives.

COSO ERM Components: Event Identification

Events are incidents or occurrences, internal or external to the enterprise, that affect the implementation of the ERM strategy or the achievement of its objectives. Although the tendency is to think of such events in a negative sense—determining what went wrong—they can be positive, negative, or both. There is a strong level of performance monitoring taking place in many enterprises today, but that monitoring process tends to emphasize such matters as costs, budgets, quality assurance compliance, and the like. Enterprises usually have strong processes to monitor such events as favorable and particularly unfavorable budget variances but often do not regularly monitor the following types of enterprise risk management events:

▪ **External economic events.** There are a wide range of external events that should be monitored in order to help an enterprise achieve its ERM objectives. Ongoing short- and long-term economic events may affect some elements of an enterprise's strategic objectives and thus have an impact on its overall ERM framework.

- **Natural environmental events.** Whether it is fire, flood, or earthquakes, numerous events can become identified as incidents in ERM risk identification. The types of impact here may include loss of access to some key raw material, damage to the physical facilities, or the unavailability of personnel.
- **Political events.** New laws and regulations, as well as the results of elections, can have significant risk event–related impacts on enterprises. Many larger enterprises have a government affairs function that reviews developments here and lobbies for changes. However, such functions may not always be aligned with ERM objectives.
- **Social factors.** Although an external event such as an earthquake is sudden and arrives with little warning, most social factor changes are slowly evolving events. These include demographic changes, social mores, and other events that may affect an enterprise and its customers over time. The growth of the Hispanic population in the United States is such an example. As another example of societal change, if a major corporation's CEO engaged in a consensual sexual relationship with another company employee in an earlier era, it probably would have been ignored. Changing social mores today often lead to the CEO's dismissal.
- **Internal infrastructure events.** Enterprises often make benign changes that trigger other risk-related events. For example, a change in customer service arrangements can cause major complaints and a drop in customer satisfaction. Strong customer demand for a new product may cause changes in plant capacity requirements and the need for additional personnel.

An enterprise needs to clearly define what it considers potentially significant risk events and then put processes in place to monitor those various identified risk events. The idea is to establish a series of business unit objectives and then overall enterprise-wide objectives, along with establishing measurement criteria necessary to assess those objectives as well as risk tolerance criteria to promote remedial actions.

COSO ERM: Risk Assessment Components

The risk assessment component represents the core of COSO ERM. Risk assessment allows an enterprise to consider the effect that potential risk-related events may have on an enterprise's achievement of its objectives. These risks should be assessed from two perspectives: the likelihood of the risk occurring and its potential impact. These components of COSO ERM reintroduce some of the same risk assessment fundamentals from the COSO internal controls, discussed in Chapter 5. Both emphasize management's need to consider key risk management concepts. When assessing its risk environment, management should consider two key concepts, inherent and residual risk, that are emphasized in COSO ERM:

1. **Inherent risk.** As defined by the US government's Office of Management and Budget, *inherent risk* is the "potential for waste, loss, unauthorized use, or misappropriation due to the nature of an activity itself." Major factors that affect the inherent risk of any activity within an enterprise are the size of its budget, the strength and sophistication of the group's management, and simply the very nature of its activities. Inherent risks are generally outside the control of management and usually

stem from external factors. For example, the major retailer Walmart is so large and dominant in its markets today that it faces a certain level of various inherent risks due to its sheer size.

2. **Residual risk.** This is the risk that remains after management's responses to risk threats and countermeasures have been applied. There will virtually always be some level of residual risk.

These two risk concepts imply that management and an enterprise will always face some level of risks. After they have addressed the risks that came out of the risk identification process, they will usually still have some residual risks to remedy. Following this, there will be a variety of inherent risks about which they can do little. Walmart, for example, can take some steps to reduce its market dominance–related inherent risks, but it can do essentially nothing regarding the inherent risk of a major natural earthquake in one of its main market areas.

Likelihood and impact are two other key components necessary for performing risk assessments. *Likelihood* is the probability or possibility that the risk will occur. In many instances, this can be a key management assessment stated in terms of a high, medium, or low likelihood of the risk occurring. There are some good quantitative tools here as well, but it does little good to estimate the likelihood of a risk occurring, in terms of multiple decimal points, if there is no basis for developing that precise of a number beyond a normal or regular statistical calculation.

Estimating the *impact* if a risk event occurs is a bit easier. For example, an enterprise facing the IT risk of a data server and network center catastrophic loss or failure can develop some relatively accurate estimates of such matters as the cost of replacing facilities and equipment, the cost of restoring the system, and, to some extent, the cost of lost business due to the failure. However, the whole concept behind ERM is not to develop precise, actuarial-level calculations regarding the risk but to find some way to provide for an effective risk management framework. Those detailed calculations can be delegated to insurance estimators and others.

An analysis of risk likelihoods and their potential impact can be developed through a series of fairly detailed qualitative and qualitative measures, as discussed in our previously referenced book on COSO ERM. The basic idea is to assess all of the identified risks and to rank them in terms of likelihood and impact in a consistent manner. Without going through a detailed quantitative analysis, each of the risks identified at a point in time can be ranked on an overall relative scale of high, medium, or low, with consideration given to the impact and likelihood of each. Exhibit 15.4 is an example of how these identified risks could be evaluated and then ranked by management through qualitative assessments. The example simply shows three risk areas and identified risks in what would be a much larger and more comprehensive list for any enterprise. The idea is to identify relative risks and assign some relative rankings.

An enterprise should use the best data sources available about these risks here but should view them with a level perspective. The view of potential risks can be influenced by management overconfidence or pessimism. A team approach is needed here, where the enterprise should look at all of these identified risks on a total enterprise basis and on a unit-by-unit level.

EXHIBIT 15.4   Risk Likelihood and Impact Mapping Example

Risk Name	Risk Definition	Impact	Likelihood	Risk Ranking
1. Accounting Risk	Failure to record sales activity accurately and in a timely manner may misstate financial reports.	**High**—Accounting errors may have a material impact on financial and operational information.	**Medium**—Despite strong procedures, newer personnel in various locations may make errors.	—
2. Legal Risk	Failure to understand current and changing laws and regulations may result in an inability to comply with laws in multiple operations' jurisdictions.	**Medium**—Even small technical violations of most regulations should not have a material effect on operations.	**High**—With worldwide operations in multiple jurisdictions, violations—if only technical—can occur.	—
3. Segregation of Duties	Inadequately controlled segregation of duties may allow employees to process unauthorized, fraudulent transactions.	**High**—Fraudulent operations could have a significant impact on company operations.	**Low**—Ongoing internal audits and stronger management control practices should prevent such control breakdown events.	—

Risk assessment is a very key component of the COSO ERM framework. This is where an enterprise evaluates all of the various risks that might affect its various objectives, considers the potential likelihood and impact of each of these risks, considers the interrelationship of these risks on a unit-by-unit or total enterprise basis, and then develops strategies for responses to these risks. In some respects, this COSO ERM risk assessment process is not too different from the classic risk assessment techniques that have been used over the years. What is unique is that COSO ERM suggests that an enterprise should take a total approach across all enterprise units and covering all major strategic concerns to identify its risks in a consistent and thorough manner. Having identified the appropriate risks, the next step is to develop a risk response approach that appropriately covers the various and significant inherent and residual risks identified in this risk assessment process, with consideration given to the enterprise's risk tolerances.

COSO ERM Components: Risk Response

Having assessed and identified its more significant risks, a next step in the COSO ERM process is to determine how to respond to these various identified risks. This is a management responsibility to perform a careful review of estimated risk likelihoods and potential impacts and, with consideration given to associated costs and benefits, to develop appropriate risk response strategies. As was discussed in Chapter 5, risk responses can be handled by following any of the basic approaches of risk avoidance, risk reduction, risk sharing, or risk acceptance.

Management should develop general response strategies for each of its risks, using an approach built around one of these four general strategies. In doing so, it should consider the costs versus the benefits of each potential risk response and which of these strategies best align with the enterprise's overall risk appetite. For example, an enterprise's recognition that the impact of a given risk is relatively low would be balanced against a low risk tolerance that suggests that insurance should be purchased to provide a potential risk response. For many risks, appropriate responses are obvious and almost universally understood. An IT operation, for example, spends the time and resources to back up its key data files and implement a business continuity plan. There is no question regarding this basic approach, but various levels of management may question the frequency of backup processes or how often the continuity plan needs to be tested.

An enterprise, at this point, should go back to the several risk objectives that have been established, as well as the tolerance ranges for those objectives. Then it should readdress both the likelihood and the impact associated with each of the identified risks within those risk objectives to develop an assessment of both of those risk categories and an overall assessment of the planned risk responses, as well as an idea of how those risks will align with the overall enterprise risk tolerances. At this point in the risk assessment process, an enterprise will have assessed the likelihood and potential impact of each of the risks surrounding its objectives, as well as some estimates for each. The next step is to develop a set of potential risk responses. This is perhaps the most difficult step in building an effective COSO ERM program framework. It is comparatively easy to identify a 5 percent likelihood risk that there will be a fire in the scrap materials bin and then to outline a risk response to install a nearby fire extinguisher. However, the responses to most risks are much more complex and require fairly detailed planning in the risk response plans.

The enterprise should initially go through its key high-impact and high-likelihood identified risks and develop a series of risk response plans. However, this can be a challenging management process! Although it is relatively easy—to follow our earlier example—to install a fire extinguisher to provide protection from a scrap materials bin fire, other things are usually not that simple. If there is a risk that an enterprise could lose an entire manufacturing operation, due to admittedly ancient but still working plant production equipment, potential risk responses could include:

- Acquire a set of backup production equipment to serve as spare parts for cannibalization.
- Shut down the manufacturing production line, with plans to move it elsewhere.
- Arrange for a specialized shop to rebuild/reconstruct the equipment.
- Reengineer the manufactured product, along with any necessary plans for the new product introduction.

The point here is that the processes of developing risk responses requires a significant amount of planning and strategic thinking in itself. The various risk response alternatives involve costs, time, and detailed project planning. In addition to the planning and strategic thinking, this risk response planning process requires significant management input and approval to recognize the various alternative risk responses and to have action plans in place to satisfy the appropriate responses. For example, one of the old equipment response strategies outlined above is to acquire a set of duplicate backup equipment. If that is to be the approved strategy, action must be taken to complete these various planned steps before this activity can be listed as an approved risk response strategy. Exhibit 15.5 is an example of a worksheet that management could use to analyze alternatives and develop alternative risk response strategies.

This sample document shows only one entered risk. However, the idea is to list, as well as possible, all of an enterprise's higher-concern identified risks. For each of these, the management team should attempt to estimate the probable inherent risk of occurrence. The example shown estimates the likelihood that a competitor will be first to market a product similar to the one being analyzed. This is the type of estimate that might be made through communication with development personnel and marketing. The estimate is admittedly a best guess, but it should be coupled with an estimate on the impact of the risk occurring. This example shows the impact on estimated revenue, but other factors can be used to measure the impact, such as market share. The idea is that all risks listed on such an analysis should be measured against the same impact factors.

For each risk, the appropriate response alternatives should be considered. This single example shows different strategies based on an "Accept," "Avoid," "Share," or "Reduce" type of strategy, with a brief description of each strategy. There is no need to list each of these four approaches for each identified risk. For example, another risk may have multiple possible "Avoid" strategies but none to "Reduce" risk. For each, however, the team should estimate the likelihood of that strategy occurring, given the initial risk event occurring. Again, the impact for each should be estimated, whether revenue or some other consistent measure is used throughout the analysis.

The concept behind this type of analysis is to look at all risks across a given area in a consistent manner. This can sometimes be a difficult process in a large, multi-unit, multi-product enterprise, but it provides a starting point for getting all of the various risks organized together for better identification of the more significant ones. For an enterprise, the idea is to look at these various potential risks, their probability of occurrence, and the impact of each. With a good analysis, this should highlight areas for more detailed attention.

Once a series of various risk responses has been developed, a next step is to look at multiple identified risks by objective and to consider various selected risk responses to assess whether those responses will bring the enterprise within its identified risk tolerances. Although this can be a fairly elaborate analysis if there have been multiple identified risks and alternative responses, the enterprise can use this data to develop high-level strategies for these various risk areas. If this type of analysis shows that a response does not appear to meet the enterprise's risk tolerances, it may be necessary to rethink and revise the risk response to achieve risk tolerance ranges.

EXHIBIT 15.5 Risk Response Planning Worksheet

Risks	Inherent Risk		Risk Response Alternatives	Residual Risk	
	Likelihood	Impact on Revenue		Likelihood	Impact on Revenue
1. Competitor reaches market first with new product under development.	40%	($5,000,000)	A. Accept — Provide additional resources to speed up R & D to complete new products.	30%	($25,000) less profit due to development costs.
			B. Avoid — Take no specific action. Keep current product offerings in place.	10%	Estimated 10% reduction in profits for line each year.
			C. Share — Offer incentives to current customers to encourage use of current product versions.	20%	Incentives may reduce revenues by 5% in first years, but revenues will decline more in future years.
			D. Reduce — Lower prices on current product offerings to discourage conversions to new versions.	40%	Customer acceptance of product will decline over years.
2. Identified Risk # 2	X %	$$	A. Accept		
			B. Avoid		
			C. Share		
			D. Reduce		

COSO ERM calls for risks to be considered and evaluated on an entity- or portfolio-wide basis. *Entity* refers to the total overall enterprise, but to get to that total view approach, risks should be evaluated and assessed on a business-by-business basis, by department, by function, and by any of the other approaches to look at an enterprise's risks. Risks should be summarized on a business unit, or on some other entity-level basis, into a risk portfolio. Senior management can then focus on its various risks across the enterprise to assess the overall impact on an enterprise. It is essential that each unit that is preparing its own risk portfolio perform this analysis in a consistent manner in order to measure relative risks from one group to another and across the overall enterprise. This type of risk portfolio is shown in Exhibit 15.6. This is the type of analysis and communication that should be prepared for senior management and the board of directors to help them understand the overall portfolio of risks facing an enterprise and to help them develop high-level risk response priorities.

COSO ERM Components: Control Activities

Similar to our Chapter 6 discussion of internal controls, COSO ERM defines what it calls *control activities* as the policies and procedures necessary to ensure that identified risk responses are carried out. Although some of these activities may relate only to an identified risk and an approved risk response in one area of the enterprise, they often overlap across multiple functions and units. The control activity component of COSO ERM should be tightly linked with the risk response component, as previously discussed.

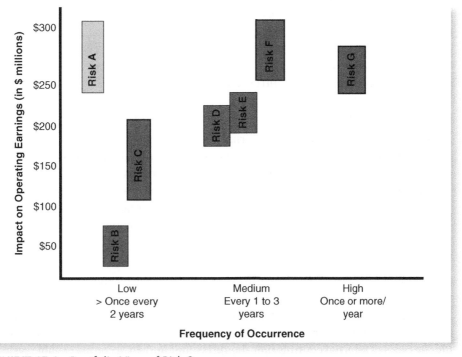

EXHIBIT 15.6   Portfolio View of Risk Summary

Having selected appropriate risk responses, enterprise management should choose the control activities necessary to ensure that those risk responses are executed in a timely and efficient manner. After enterprise management has gone through the COSO ERM risk event identification, risk assessment, and risk response processes, risk monitoring of these control activities can be executed by the following four steps:

1. Develop a strong understanding of the identified significant risks and develop control procedures to monitor or correct for these risks.
2. Create testing procedures to determine whether those risk-related control procedures are working effectively.
3. Perform tests of the control procedures to determine whether the risk monitoring process tested is working effectively and as expected.
4. Make adjustments or improvements, as necessary, to improve risk monitoring processes.

This four-step process is essentially what enterprises have been doing to review, test, and then assert that their SOx internal control processes are working adequately. A major difference between SOx internal control procedures and COSO ERM is that an enterprise *is legally required* to comply with these SOx procedures in order to assert the adequacy of its internal controls. There are no such legal requirements with COSO. An enterprise should seek to install risk monitoring control activities to monitor the various risks it has identified. Because of the critical nature of many risks to an enterprise, risk management monitoring can be essential to an enterprise's overall health, due to the nature of the various risks it may encounter.

Many control activities under COSO internal controls are fairly easy to identify and test, due to the accounting nature of many internal controls. They generally include some of the following internal control areas:

▪ **Separation of duties.** Essentially, the person who initiates a transaction should not be the same person who authorizes that transaction.
▪ **Audit trails.** Processes should be organized such that final results can be easily traced back to the transactions that created those results.
▪ **Security and integrity.** Control processes should have appropriate control procedures such that only authorized persons can review or modify them.
▪ **Documentation.** Processes should be appropriately documented.

These control procedures, and others, are fairly well-recognized and applicable to all internal control processes in place in an enterprise and also somewhat apply to many risk-related events. Many enterprise managers—whether or not they have an operations, accounting, or auditing background—can often easily define some of the key controls that are necessary in many business processes. For example, if asked to identify the types of internal controls that should be built into an accounts payable system, many professionals would identify as significant control points that checks issued from the system must be authorized by several persons, that accounting records must be in place to keep track of the checks issued, and that the check-issuing process should be such that only authorized persons can initiate such a financial transaction. These are generally well and widely understood control procedures. An enterprise often faces a more difficult task in identifying control activities to support its enterprise risk management framework.

As was discussed as part of the ERM event identification component, management needs to think of these risk categories in terms of major risk process areas, such as revenue, purchasing, capital spending, information systems, and others. Specific-risk related control activities can be defined within each of these categories, whether for the overall enterprise or covering some unit or function. Although there is no accepted or standard set of enterprise risk management control activities, the supporting COSO ERM documentation suggests several areas:

- **Top-level reviews.** While members of senior management may be somewhat oblivious to the "Do the debits equal the credits?" types of internal control procedures that are covered by their financial teams and auditors, they should be very aware of the identified risk events within enterprise organization units and should perform regular top-level reviews of the status of identified risks, as well as of the progress of risk responses. This type of regular review, coupled with appropriate top-level corrective actions, is a key ERM control activity.
- **Direct functional or activity management.** In addition to the top-level reviews outlined previously, functional and direct unit managers should have a key role in risk control activity monitoring. This is particularly important in a large, diverse enterprise, where control activities should not only take place at a local unit level and then bump up the organizational hierarchy to some central management level. Rather, risk-related control activities should take place within the separate operating units, with communications and risk resolution taking place across enterprise channels.
- **Information processing.** Whether it be information technology (IT), hard types of systems processes, or softer forms, such as paper or messages, information-processing procedures represent a key component in an enterprise's risk-related control activities. Appropriate control procedures here, with an emphasis on an enterprise's IT processes and risks, are important.
- **Physical controls.** Many risk-related events involve physical assets, such as equipment, inventories, securities, and physical plants. Whether physical inventories, inspections, or plant security procedures, an enterprise should install appropriate risk-based physical control activity procedures.
- **Performance indicators.** The typical enterprise today employs a wide range of financial and operational reporting tools. Many of these tools can be used as is or modified to support risk event–related performance reporting. In many instances, an enterprise's overall performance tools can be modified to support this important control activity component.
- **Segregation of duties.** This is a classic control activity, whether for business process internal controls or for risk management. The person who initiates

certain actions should not be the same person who approves those actions. This key controls activity is important whether it be in a smaller business unit, where an employee's supervisor would be required to inspect and approve employee actions, or with a CEO, who should obtain the oversight approval of the board of directors.

These COSO ERM control activities also can be expanded to cover other key areas. Some will be specific to individual units within the enterprise, but each of them, singly and collectively, should be an important component supporting the enterprise's ERM framework.

COSO ERM Components: Information and Communication

Although described as a separate component in the COSO ERM framework, the information and communication component is not quite a separate set of risk-related processes but instead consists of tools and processes linking other COSO ERM components. The information and communication component of COSO ERM is the process or unit of the framework that links together each of the other components. This concept is illustrated in Exhibit 15.7, showing the information flow across the COSO ERM components. For example, the risk response component received residual and inherent risk input from the risk assessment component, as well as risk tolerance support from the objective setting component. ERM risk response then provided risk response and risk portfolio data to control activities, as well as risk response feedback to the risk assessment component. Standing alone, the monitoring component does not have any direct information connections but has overall responsibility for reviewing all of the other components.

Although it is relatively easy to draw such a simple flow diagram of how information should be communicated from one COSO ERM component to another, this is often a far more complex process of linking various systems and information paths together than what is shown in this very high-level chart. These linkages become even more complex with attempts to link various ERM processes, given that many basic enterprise applications do not directly lend themselves to risk identification, assessment, and risk response–type processes.

While the information half of the information and communication COSO ERM component is normally thought of in terms of IT strategic and operational information systems, ERM communication is the second aspect of this component. COSO ERM talks about communication beyond just IT applications, and the need for an enterprise to establish strong communication mechanisms to make certain that all stakeholders receive messages regarding the enterprise's interest in managing its risks and communicating appropriate levels of information to stakeholders. The communication links discussed in Chapter 7 for COSO internal controls are very appropriate here as well.

An enterprise risk initiative will be of little value to an enterprise unless the overall message of the importance of its ERM initiative gets communicated to all enterprise stakeholders. This should be in the form of a message from the CEO.

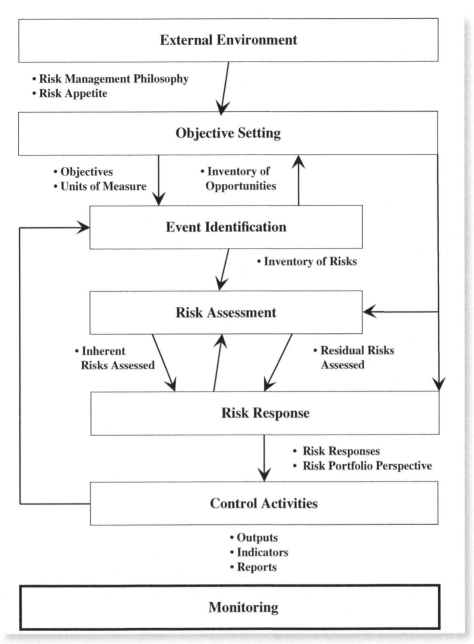

EXHIBIT 15.7 Information and Communication Flow across ERM Components

The idea is to communicate a message about the importance of ERM throughout the enterprise. These types of messages are particularly valuable when an enterprise wants to state, for example, that all stakeholders should be very cautious in regard to taking on certain potentially risky ventures. An incorrectly interpreted message can effectively open the floodgates to inappropriate risky decisions and ventures.

COSO ERM Components: Monitoring

Placed at the base of the stack of horizontal components in the ERM framework model and similar to COSO internal controls, the monitoring component is necessary to determine that all components of an installed ERM continue to work effectively. People in the enterprise change, as well as do supporting processes and both internal and external conditions. In order for all members of the enterprise to have a level of assurance that the installed ERM is working effectively on a continual basis, the ERM monitoring component should be installed and activated. This process often takes place either by installing ongoing monitoring activities or through a series of separate evaluations covering various aspects of the ERM process.

Ongoing and continual monitoring processes can be an effective method to flag exceptions or violations in some aspect of the overall ERM process. An accounts receivable billing function may provide some overall financial and operational risks if customers' bills are not paid on a timely basis. An ongoing—almost real-time—credit collections monitoring tool could provide senior management with other day-to-day and trending data on the status of collections. There are many mechanisms to provide this kind of information to management, and automated dashboard tools can often be effective here. These are automatic devices, not unlike a low oil pressure warning light on an automobile dashboard, that monitor the status of certain enterprise risk controls and send warnings when necessary. These types of monitors work on a continual basis. They are often difficult to install for the entire enterprise but can work quite well as a process or on a departmental unit basis.

Going beyond monitoring through the use of dashboard tools and the like, enterprise management at various levels should take an overall responsibility for ERM monitoring as part of their basic duties as enterprise managers at all levels. In order to establish an effective ERM framework, that monitoring should be expanded to include ongoing reviews of the overall ERM process, ranging from identified objectives to the progress of ongoing ERM control activities and including the following types of activities:

▪ Implementation of a strong and ongoing management reporting mechanism, such as cash positions, unit sales, and other key financial and operational data. A well-organized enterprise should not have to wait until fiscal month end or worse for these types of operational and financial status reports. Reporting tools should be expanded to include key ERM flash reporting at all appropriate levels of the enterprise.

▪ Installation of periodic reporting processes to specifically monitor key aspects of established risk criteria. These might include such things as acceptable error rates or items held in suspense. Rather than just periodic statistics, such reporting should emphasize trends and comparisons with prior periods, as well as with other industry sectors.

▪ Reporting of the current and the periodic status of risk-related findings and recommendations from internal and external audit reports. This periodic reporting should include the status of ERM-related, SOx-identified gaps.

▪ Updated risk-related information from sources such as government-revised rules, industry trends, and general economic news. Again, this type of economic and operational reporting should be available for managers at all levels. That same information reporting should be expanded to include enterprise risk management issues as well.

Separate or individual evaluation monitoring refers to detailed reviews of individual risk processes by a qualified reviewer, such as internal audit. Here the review can be limited to specific areas or can cover the entire ERM process for an enterprise unit. For many enterprises, a strong internal audit enterprise may be the best internal source to perform such specific ERM reviews.

The purpose of this monitoring process is to assess how well the ERM framework is functioning in an enterprise. Deficiencies should be regularly reported to the managers responsible for enterprise risks in the specific area being monitored, as well as to the ERM or risk management office. The roles and responsibilities of an enterprise management office were discussed in Chapter 8. The concept behind this monitoring is not just to find faults or deficiencies but to identify areas where the ERM framework can be improved. For example, if some event monitoring work points to areas where a function is assuming excessive levels of risk, processes need to be in place to institute corrective actions.

OTHER DIMENSIONS OF THE ERM FRAMEWORK

As discussed regarding the COSO internal control framework, COSO ERM is a three-dimensional framework, with its eight categories as one dimension, in the sections previously discussed. The other dimensions are its four objective categories, represented by its vertical columns, and its business groups and units, described in the third dimension. Although the eight ERM categories just described are very important to understanding and using COSO, those other two dimensions—its strategies and organizational units—are important as well. To understand the risks surrounding an enterprise's objectives, one must evaluate those risks in terms of, possibly, the reporting concerns associated with each risk and the specific enterprise units that become the main focus of the risk. The COSO ERM framework can be flipped about as we have done in other chapters on the COSO internal control framework.

The business executive may ask how COSO ERM fits in with the other COSO internal control processes described in other chapters of this book. Rather than thinking of COSO ERM as a subset or a related issue alongside the COSO internal controls, we should think of ERM processes and concepts as an important set of controls and concepts that is sometimes even more important than effective COSO internal controls. Exhibit 15.8 shows this relationship. COSO internal controls provide a basis and a guide for many enterprise processes, and COSO ERM is really a larger, more critical set of processes than internal controls. Both of these are then subservient to enterprise governance processes, the actions and policies of the board of directors, and CEO-level management.

COSO ERM AND THE REVISED INTERNAL CONTROL FRAMEWORK

With the current version of the COSO internal controls recently released as an update to its 1992 original, the professional may wonder whether future changes are in the works for the COSO ERM that was first released in 2004. However, there was no new version of COSO ERM released or announced with the revised internal control framework. Enterprise risk management is broader than internal control; it elaborates on internal control and focuses more directly on risk. Internal control is really an integrated part of enterprise risk management, while ERM is part of the overall governance process.

Based on our knowledge at this time of publication, there are no planned future revisions for COSO ERM. There are several major reasons for this lack of change. The first is that other professional and international organizations have done an excellent job of providing expanded risk management guidance, including

- The International Organization for Standardization (ISO) has developed excellent risk management guidance, ISO 3100, that will be summarized in Chapter 17.
- COBIT, discussed in Chapter 16, also has some excellent guidance for installing effective enterprise risk management processes.
- Another source, not included in this chapter, is the National Institute of Standards and Technology (NIST), which published its *Guide for Conducting Risk Assessment* (www.nist.gov).
- A large variety of other international standards have been established that provide guidance for enterprise risk management.

In addition to other ERM standards, the role and importance of ERM are changing in relation to COSO internal controls and the larger issue of IT governance, as was shown in Exhibit 15.8. In addition to strong COSO internal controls, effective ERM processes

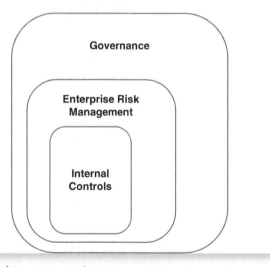

EXHIBIT 15.8   Role of Enterprise Risk Management

should operate within them and within an even bigger set of IT governance processes. Enterprise governance is perhaps a larger issue not covered in these chapters, but this author has provided an overview of effective IT governance processes in a separate publication.[2] However, given that hierarchy, effective COSO internal controls are even more important to an enterprise today.

 NOTES

1. Robert Moeller, *COSO Enterprise Risk Management: Establishing Effective Governance, Risk, and Compliance (GRC) Processes*, 2nd ed. (Hoboken, NJ: John Wiley & Sons, 2011).
2. Robert Moeller, *Executive's Guide to IT Governance: Improving Systems Processes with Service Management, COBIT, and ITIL* (Hoboken, NJ: John Wiley & Sons, 2013).

CHAPTER SIXTEEN

Understanding and Using COBIT

T HE COSO INTERNAL CONTROL FRAMEWORK is a key measure or guide
for building and measuring enterprise internal controls, but there are other
approaches or tools as well for helping senior executives and their IT managers build and implement effective internal controls in their systems and processes. In
particular, and as was discussed in Chapter 2 on earlier internal controls and the SOx
internal control requirements, there were concerns, first expressed many years ago, that
the original COSO internal control framework did not give enough attention to building and establishing effective IT-related business systems controls. As somewhat of a
substitute for COSO and other guidance materials, the Information Systems Audit Association—later renamed the IT Governance Institute—developed a more IT-oriented
internal control assessment and guidance framework called COBIT (Control **Ob**jectives
for **I**nformation and Related **T**echnology) as a tool to build and assess its IT-oriented
internal controls.

Starting with some even earlier guidance tools, COBIT—originally abbreviated
as CobiT—was first released in 1996 and has been in place long before SOx. COBIT
was initially developed for the internal and external auditors who reviewed computer systems and technology controls (often called IT auditors), but today COBIT
has become a preferred tool, in many enterprises, for complying with SOx Section
404 internal control procedures and related IT governance support. COBIT provides
guidance for evaluating and understanding internal controls, with an emphasis on
enterprise IT resources. COBIT is not a replacement for the COSO internal control
framework but is a different and sometimes preferable way to look at internal controls in today's IT-centric world to remain compliant with the revised COSO internal
control framework.

Although originally launched as guidance to help internal and external IT
auditor professionals who reviewed IT-related internal controls, COBIT today has

evolved into a helpful tool for assessing IT governance and evaluating all internal controls across an enterprise. It provides emphasis and guidance on the linkage of IT with other business resources to deliver overall values to an enterprise today. It is an important tool to help the senior enterprise executive establish effective IT governance practices.

This chapter will provide an executive-level overview of the COBIT framework and many of its key components. COBIT's current version 5.0 has just been released and at about the same time as the revised COSO internal control framework. This chapter will introduce the key elements of COBIT and how they interact. In addition, this chapter will describe the relationship between COBIT objectives and the COSO internal control framework.

Although COBIT had its origins as an IT audit guidance tool, it is much broader today. Today's executive should have high-level knowledge of the function and purposes of the COBIT framework and should be in a position to question both the enterprise's IT functions and general financial management operations about the enterprise's use of COBIT in support of IT governance activities. In addition to the COSO internal control framework, knowledge of COBIT will help a senior manager better understand the role of IT controls, governance processes, and risks in many enterprise environments.

 ## AN EXECUTIVE'S INTRODUCTION TO COBIT

An unusual or strange-sounding word for many, COBIT is an acronym describing a process that is becoming increasingly recognized by auditors, IT professionals, and some enterprise managers. COBIT is an IT governance internal control framework that is an important support tool for documenting and understanding IT, as well as COSO internal controls, SOx requirements, and recognizing the value of and risks associated with IT assets in an enterprise. While most members of an enterprise's internal audit staff today may have had at least a general or working knowledge of COBIT, senior managers throughout the enterprise also should have knowledge of its importance as an IT governance support tool.

The COBIT standards and framework are issued and regularly updated by the IT Governance Institute (ITGI) and its closely affiliated professional organization, the Information Systems Audit and Control Association (ISACA).[1] ISACA is more focused on IT auditing, while ITGI's emphasis is on research and governance processes. ISACA also manages the Certified Information Systems Auditor (CISA) examination and professional designation, as well as other similar certifications, such as the Certified Information Security Manager (CISM) and the Certified in the Governance of Enterprise IT (CGEIT) designation certification and examination. CISM certification targets IT security managers and promotes the advancement of professionals who wish to be recognized for their IT governance–related experience and knowledge.

Many IT and regular internal audit staff members in a typical enterprise are members of ISACA. For nostalgia purposes, ISACA was originally known as the EDP Auditor's Association (EDPAA), a professional group that was started in 1967 by internal auditors who felt that their then professional organization, the Institute of Internal Auditors (IIA), was not giving sufficient attention to the importance of IT systems and technology controls as part of internal audit activities. We have almost forgotten that EDP was an IT systems abbreviation that once stood for *electronic data processing*, today an almost archaic IT term. Over time, this professional enterprise broadened its focus and became ISACA.

The EDPAA, originally an upstart IT audit professional organization, began to develop IT audit professional guidance materials shortly after its formation. Just as the EDPAA evolved into the well-respected ISACA and now is part of the ITGI, its original IT audit standards became an excellent set of internal control objectives that evolved to COBIT, now in its 2013 version 5.0 edition.[2] With virtually all enterprise processes today tied to IT-related facilities, an understanding of COBIT and the overall area of IT governance is critical. The COBIT framework consists of what are called five principles, broad and interconnected areas of governance and controls, as illustrated in Exhibit 16.1. These show COBIT's five principles or five major areas of emphasis arranged as elements of COBIT's core framework concepts.

The COBIT framework has been continually enhanced and improved over the years, with the changes focused on making COBIT much more of a management and IT governance tool, rather than its earlier framework orientation being primarily an IT audit tool. Also, although its basic concepts have not changed, the framework was

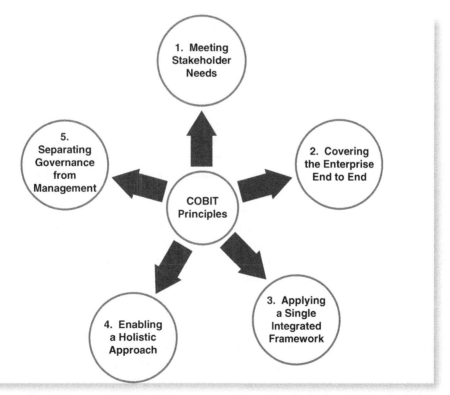

EXHIBIT 16.1   COBIT Principles

once described as CobiT, compared to today's all-caps name. COBIT today is much more integrated with frameworks such as COSO internal controls, as well as with various international standards discussed in Chapter 17. As an introduction to this framework and its importance as a tool for improving internal control processes, the following sections discuss COBIT's five basic principles in greater detail.

COBIT Principle 1: Meeting Stakeholder Needs

The COBIT framework is designed to meet all levels of stakeholder needs. Enterprises have many stakeholders, and "creating value" means different and sometimes conflicting things to each of them. A basic concept of enterprise and IT governance is about negotiating and deciding among different stakeholders' value interests. The COBIT framework calls for an enterprise governance system that considers all stakeholders when making benefit, resource, and risk assessment decisions.

These concepts are often more easily said than done, but the COBIT framework calls for these needs to be transformed into an actionable strategy. The COBIT guidance recognizes that all enterprise stakeholders have needs relating to enterprise information and related technology concerns, including enterprise, IT-related, and what COBIT calls *enabler process goals*. The term *enabler goals* may sound unfamiliar to some people. It covers actions, time lines, and other metrics relating to people, the enterprise infrastructure, and its other resources. Exhibit 16.2 illustrates this flow of goals and metrics, and we will discuss these COBIT Principle 1 concepts further in the following sections. Perhaps even going beyond COSO's three-dimensional internal control model, COBIT suggests that an enterprise consider its internal controls as an overall flow, starting with enterprise goals and establishing metrics to measure them.

COBIT Principle 2: Covering the Enterprise End to End

COBIT calls for enterprise internal controls to operate on an end-to-end basis. Rather than just an IT-related set of suggested processes, the COBIT framework calls for the alignment of IT operations and activities with all other enterprise operations. These include establishing linkages between enterprise business operations and IT plans, as well as processes for defining, maintaining, and validating quality and value relationships.

Business process owners and stakeholders of business processes, including their key IT systems, should delegate overall responsibility to appropriate governing bodies, whether IT management, enterprise financial operations, or other appropriate management authorities, who should set detailed directions as well as instruct and align matters as appropriate. Once completed, the process results should be monitored, with results reported back to the stakeholder owners. Appropriate adjustments and corrective actions can then be launched as needed.

This COBIT feedback loop described here is really a classic management process, similar to what has been described in numerous college-level introduction to management textbooks. The key point here is that COBIT is not just an IT process but is an overall management process to build and assess enterprise internal controls. Although some senior managers may have previously developed initial impressions of COBIT when its

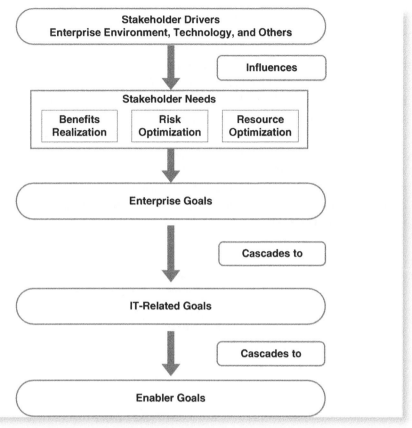

EXHIBIT 16.2   COBIT Goals and Metrics Flow

---

earlier versions were primarily IT systems oriented, COBIT today is an effective alternative approach for assessing enterprise internal controls.

COBIT Principle 3: Applying a Single Integrated Architecture Framework

Whether it is the COSO internal control framework—the main topic of this book— the ISO standards introduced in Chapter 17, or another IT-related internal control standards, COBIT has been designed as a single integrated framework or architecture that will cover all of them through ITGI published mapping processes.

Architecture has become one of those terms that once described how we build or the style of our office headquarters buildings, but today also often refers to an enterprise's IT architecture technology selections. For example, when IT functions moved away from the centralized legacy mainframe computer systems, now many years ago, to networks of smaller server systems, an enterprise IT function would state that it had adopted or implemented "client-server architecture." *Systems architecture* is a term IT functions use to refer to the main hardware or software configurations of their IT resources. COBIT has its own architecture; Exhibit 16.3 is a simplified diagram of COBIT's architecture components. This exhibit also references COBIT's enabling processes, which will be covered in a later section.

Referencing this COBIT architecture and going back to its beginnings, an important concept here is that both COBIT and the COSO internal control framework are driven by their stakeholder needs, ranging from senior management wishing to improve internal controls and IT governance processes through perhaps IT local management seeking to improve specific application processes. Stakeholders are large and differing groups who all have some common, as well as sometimes differing, interests in and concerns with an enterprise's IT governance processes. These needs are presented or delivered to established COBIT processes, with an emphasis on IT governance and value objectives. In addition, because COBIT does not simply stand alone by itself, these needs must be coordinated with other existing enterprise standards, frameworks, and processes.

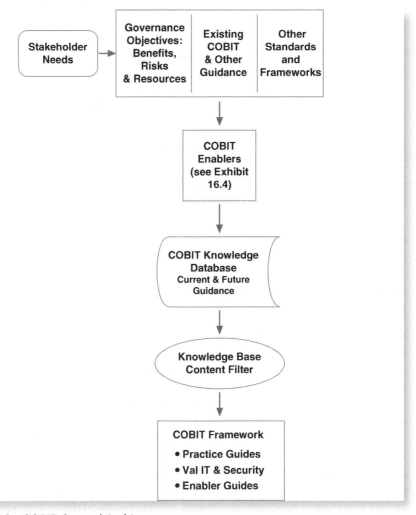

EXHIBIT 16.3   COBIT General Architecture

As illustrated in Exhibit 16.3, these needs flow through a series of what COBIT calls *enablers*, a series of separate but interconnected processes discussed later in this chapter. The purpose of these enablers is—as the name suggests—to implement and enable governance and management systems processes for enterprise internal controls and IT. Enablers are broadly defined as specific processes, mechanisms, or anything that can help achieve the enterprise's governance objectives. This includes resources, such as information and people. The COBIT framework defines seven categories of enablers:

1. Processes
2. Principles and policies
3. Organizational structures
4. Skills and competences
5. Culture and behavior
6. Service capabilities
7. Information

These enablers interact in a systemic way, meaning that a governance and management system cannot succeed unless all of these enablers are addressed and dealt with, and their major interactions are understood. We will discuss these COBIT enablers further as part of COBIT's Principle 4 in the following section.

The established enablers then provide support to a knowledge database, including both current guidance materials and structures for future activities. These then provide support for the overall implementation of COBIT processes, which also are supported by a series of ITGI-published product and reference guides. The concept or benefit behind the COBIT architecture is to support the framework's goals by providing to all stakeholders the most complete and up-to-date guidance on the governance and management of enterprise IT. To achieve this benefit, the COBIT architecture includes a wide range of automated and data-related components, such as the guidance materials discussed in other chapters.

COBIT Principle 4: Enabling a Holistic Approach

The concept of what COBIT calls a "holistic approach" means that all individual COBIT decision factors should be taken into account as a whole, interdependent of one another, for the benefit of all. For example, in enterprise operations, a holistic approach to business decisions might take into account sales operations, supply logistics, IT operations, and personnel staffing and training issues. While we cannot lump all of these together, each should be considered both separately and independently of the others.

COBIT calls these factors *enablers*, key elements in the COBIT governance and internal control process. They are the tangible and intangible elements that make something work—in this case, governance and management over enterprise IT. The COBIT simplified general architecture diagram (see Exhibit 16.3) shows a function called enablers in the center of the overall process. These enablers should be adopted by an enterprise for the governance of IT.

COBIT has defined seven different classes or types of these enablers, as separately illustrated in Exhibit 16.4. To achieve its main objectives, an enterprise must always recognize that it has and manages an interconnected set of these enablers. The general architecture diagram shows seven categories of interconnected enablers. The COBIT designated enablers are:

1. **Processes.** Organized sets of practices and activities to achieve certain objectives and produce a set of various types of output in support of achieving overall IT-related goals.
2. **Culture, ethics, and behavior.** Individual and organizational activities are very often underestimated but are important success factors in governance and management arrangements.
3. **Organizational structures.** Activities, policies, and organizational arrangements represent key decision-making vehicles in an organization or an enterprise.
4. **Information.** Critical as a pervasive element throughout any organization, information is required for keeping the organization running and well governed, but at the operational level, information is very often the key product of the enterprise itself.
5. **Principles and policies.** These enabler factors are a vehicle to translate desired behavior into practical guidance for day-to-day management.

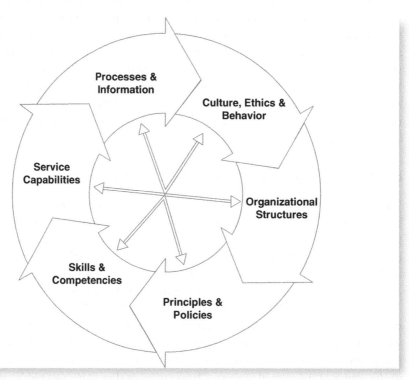

EXHIBIT 16.4 COBIT Classes of Types of Enablers

6. **Skills and competences.** These attributes are linked to people and are required for the successful completion of all activities and for making correct decisions.
7. **Service capabilities.** This enabler includes the infrastructure, the technology, and the applications that provide the enterprise with information processing and services.

Each of these enabler categories does not exist alone but needs the input of other COBIT-defined enablers to be fully effective. For example, processes need the information enabler, organizational structures need people enablers, and people need skills and behavior. The enablers deliver output to the benefit of other enablers; for example, processes deliver information, skills, and behavior. Each of these seven COBIT-defined enablers has its own five specific components:

1. **Enabler stakeholders.** Although we have discussed the importance of stakeholders as drivers of the overall COBIT process, each of the seven enablers here will also have its own internal and external stakeholders. Processes have internal and external stakeholders, each with its own role; stakeholders and their responsibility levels should be documented in ways that are attributes of the process.
2. **Goals and metrics.** Enabler goals should be defined as a statement describing the desired outcome of a process. An outcome can be an artifact, a significant change of state, or a significant capability improvement of other processes. Metrics are part of the process goals that support IT-related goals, which in turn support enterprise goals. At each level, metrics should define and measure the extent to which these goals are achieved. Metrics can be defined as a quantifiable entity and should be specific, measurable, actionable, relevant, and timely.

   Goals can be classified in various ways, ranging from economic goals, which are more efficiency-oriented, to quality goals, which are more effectiveness-oriented. Likewise, there are two types of process metrics: performance metrics, which have a predictive character, indicating the extent to which the process is performing in terms of activities; and outcome metrics, which indicate the extent to which the process really has achieved its goals and purpose.
3. **Enabler life cycles.** Each of these enablers should be supported by plans to establish them and then build, acquire, create, and implement. After their use or operation, the enabler should be periodically monitored and evaluated with an objective to update or dispose as required.
4. **Good practices.** Internal and external practices should be installed here using tools such as the COBIT framework. Good practice enablers have internal and external elements. Both of these include people skill good practices, such as the need for objective skill requirements for each role played by the various stakeholders. This can be described through defined job descriptions for different skill levels in different skill categories. The skill categories correspond with IT-related activities, such as telecommunications network management or business analysis.
5. **Enabler attributes.** Each of these will have some unique components that set them apart from other enterprise enablers.

Enablers are terms or concepts that were not that common in business operations and processes all that many years ago. The expression first became common in academic papers covering specialized IT issues. We should remember that an enabler is a tool or a process that provides measurable capabilities and competencies that enhance, rather than just automate, business processes. They are capabilities, forces, and resources that contribute to the success of an entity, an activity, or a project. They are a worthwhile concept to add to one's business vocabulary.

COBIT Principle 5: Separating Governance from Management

COBIT's last key principle focuses on the importance of separate but related concepts of management and governance in an IT-oriented enterprise. The COBIT framework makes a clear distinction between governance and management. These two disciplines include different types of activities, require different organizational structures, and serve different purposes. This distinction is a key to COBIT's view of governance and management.

A popular term in business today, we often forget that *governance* is derived from the Greek verb meaning "to steer." A governance system refers to all of the means and mechanisms that enable multiple stakeholders in an enterprise to have an organized say in evaluating conditions and options; setting direction; and monitoring compliance, performance, and progress against plans, to satisfy specific enterprise objectives. This all refers to a major set of steering activities. Means and mechanisms here include frameworks, principles, policies, sponsorship, structures, and decision mechanisms, as well as roles and responsibilities, processes, and practices to set direction and monitor compliance and performance aligned with the overall objectives. This is a rather large and extensive definition of IT governance, but we should always remember that in most enterprises, governance is the responsibility of the board of directors under the leadership of the CEO and the board of directors' chairperson.

Often differentiated from governance, management entails the judicious use of resources, people, processes, practices, and so on, to achieve an identified end. It is the means or instrument by which the governance body achieves a result or an objective. Management is responsible for execution within the direction set by the guiding body or unit. Management is about planning, building, organizing, and controlling operational activities to align with the direction set by the governance body.

COBIT emphasizes that governance and management are different types of activities, with different responsibilities. However, given the role of governance—to evaluate, direct, and monitor—a set of interactions is required between governance and management to result in an efficient and effective governance system. These interactions, using the enabler structure, are then tied to specific internal control review processes, the real strength of the COBIT framework.

USING COBIT TO ASSESS ENTERPRISE INTERNAL CONTROLS

Although COSO internal controls are built around only a single framework model and some general guidance for evaluating and assessing these internal controls, there is an extensive and detailed set of published materials supporting COBIT internal control assessments. In this section, we provide a limited summary of some of these COBIT guidance materials to give the interested enterprise executive a flavor of COBIT, but professionals may want to consult the ISACA website (www.isaca.org) for much more information and to request full copies of supporting materials. Downloaded versions are free to ISACA members or can be purchased at a nominal cost.

COBIT divides the processes necessary to evaluate IT controls and processes into what COBIT calls five domain areas:

1. Evaluate, Direct, and Monitor (EDM)
2. Align, Plan, and Organize (APO)
3. Build, Acquire, and Implement (BAI)
4. Deliver, Service, and Support (DSS)
5. Monitor, Evaluate, and Assess (MEA)

These initials, such as MEA, will be used in other COBIT materials as part of this brief introduction. These domain areas are further summarized into an overall process map for the management of enterprise IT, as shown in Exhibit 16.5. We should emphasize here that COBIT is a tool for controlling and evaluating all enterprise internal controls, even though COBIT's focus is primarily IT oriented.

For each of these process domain areas, COBIT defines what it calls specific key management practices. For example, the "Deliver, Service, and Support" (DSS) domain area, shown on the lower line of items on Exhibit 16.5, shows six process areas for that domain, from DSS 01, "Manage Operations," through DSS 06, for "Manage Process Controls." The COBIT documentation then drills down with detailed enabling process descriptions for each. For example, COBIT calls enabling process DSS 04 "Manage Continuity," then drills down to DSS 04.01, "Define the Business Continuity Policy."

The above exhibit is just a brief example of the extensive materials that make up the COBIT documentation. COBIT provides enterprise-level and IT goals throughout, as well as an extensive set of input and output for virtually every management practice. The published COBIT material may appear to be almost overwhelming for some business professionals, but it works excellently in helping to better fine-tune IT-related controls.

Similar sets of control objective process categories have been defined for each of COBIT's process categories. The purpose of the detailed but fairly specific control processes is to help make a business case for the implementation and improvement of the governance and management of IT. Their objective is to recognize both their typical pain points and their trigger events, with an overall objective of creating the right environment for IT operations and implementations.

COBIT has defined a set of 17 IT-related goals that can be mapped to each of these processes, with the goals divided into categories labeled Corporate, Customer, Internal, and one called Learning and Growth. These COBIT IT–related goals are then mapped to the factors for two COBIT processes, EDM, "Evaluate, Direct, and Monitor," and DSS, "Deliver, Service, and Support." A mapping of how each IT-related goal is supported by a COBIT-related process is illustrated in Exhibit 16.6 and is expressed using a scale, where:

▪ **P** stands for a "primary" connection between the IT-related goal and the connected COBIT-related process, when there is an important relationship in which the designated COBIT process is a primary support for the achievement of an IT-related goal.

Align, Plan, and Organize

APO 01 Manage IT Framework	APO 02 Manage Strategy	APO 03 Manage Architecture	APO 04 Manage Innovation	APO 05 Manage Portfolio	APO 06 Manage Budget & Costs	APO 07 Manage Human Resources
AP008 Manage Relationships	AP009 Manage SLAs	AP010 Manage Suppliers	AP 011 Manage Quality	AP012 Manage Risk	AP013 Manage Security	

Build, Acquire, and Implement

BAI 01 Manage Projects	BAI 02 Manage Requirements Def.	BAI 03 Manage Solutions ID	BAI 04 Manage Availability	BAI 05 Manage Org. Change Mgmt.	BAI 06 Manage Changes	BAI 07 Change Acceptance & Transitioning
BAI 08 Manage Knowledge	BAI 09 Manage Assets	BAI 10 Manage Configurations		

Deliver, Service, and Support

DSS 01 Manage Operations	DSS 02 Manage Requests & Incidents	DSS 03 Manage Problems	DSS 04 Manage Continuity	DSS 05 Manage Security Services	DSS 06 Manage Process Controls

EXHIBIT 16.5 COBIT Processes for the Management of Enterprise IT

254

Figure content — COBIT Goal and IT Objective Mapping (P = Primary, S = Secondary):

COBIT Processes		Corporate						Customer		Internal					Learning & Growth		
		1. Alignment of IT & business strategy	2. IT compliance & support for business compliance with laws & regulations	3. Commitment of executive management for making IT-related decisions	4. Managed IT-related business risks	5. Realized benefits from IT-related investments & services portfolio	6. Transparency of IT costs, benefits & task	7. Delivery of IT services in line with business requirements	8. Adequate use of applications, information & technology solutions	9. IT agility	10. Security of information, IT processing infrastructure, and applications	11. Optimization of IT assets, resources, and capabilities	12. Enablement & support of integrating applications & technology into business processes	13. Optimization of IT resources & capabilities	14. Availability of reliable & useful information	15. IT compliance with internal policies	16. Competent & motivated IT personnel	17. Knowledge, expertise & initiatives for business innovation
Evaluate, Direct & Monitor	EDM1 Set and Maintain the Governance Framework	P	S	P	S	S	S	P		S	S	S	S	S	S	S	S	S
	EDM2 Ensure Value Optimization	P		S		P	P	P	S			S	S	S	S		S	P
	EDM3 Ensure Risk Optimization	S	S	S	P		P	P	S	P	P			S	S	P	P	S
	EDM4 Ensure Resource Optimization	S		S		P	S	S	S			P		S	S		P	S
	EDM5 Ensure Stakeholder Transparency	S	S	P		S	P	P						S		S		S
Deliver, Service & Support	DSS1 Manage Operations		S		P	S		S	S	S	S	P	P	S	P	S	S	S
	DSS2 Manage Processes		S		P	S		S	S	P	S	S	S	S		S		S
	DSS3 Manage Configuration		S		S				S	S	S				S	S	S	
	DSS4 Manage Service Requests & Incidents				P			S	S						P			
	DSS5 Manage Problems				P	S			S			P	P	P	P	S		S
	DSS6 Manage Continuity	S	S		P	S		S	S	S		S			P	S	S	S
	DSS7 Manage Security	S	P		P			S	S		P			S	S			
	DSS8 Manage Business Process Controls		S		P			P	S	S	S				S	S	S	S

EXHIBIT 16.6 COBIT Goal and IT Objective Mapping Example

- **S** stands for "secondary," when there is a less important relationship, and the COBIT process is a secondary support for the IT-related goal.
- Blank says there is no strong relationship here.

For example, the DSS 05 COBIT process "Manage Security Services" has a strong or primary relationship with the IT-related goal that IT called or designated as "Compliance and support for business-related laws and regulations." That same DSS 05 process also has secondary relationships with several other IT goals, such as no. 7, "Delivery of IT services in line with business requirements."

The COBIT framework may seem almost too detailed with far too complex sets of objectives and goals. Optimal value can be realized from leveraging COBIT only if it is effectively adopted and adapted to suit each enterprise's unique environment. Each implementation approach will also need to address specific challenges, including managing changes to culture and behavior.

The COBIT guidance emphasizes that governance and management are different types of activities, each with different responsibilities. However, given governance's steering role—to evaluate, direct, and monitor—a set of interactions is required between governance and management to result in an efficient and effective governance system. These interactions, using the enabler structure, are then tied to specific internal control review processes, the real strength of the COBIT framework.

MAPPING COBIT TO COSO INTERNAL CONTROLS

The COSO internal control framework states that internal control is a process—established by an entity's board of directors, senior management, and other personnel—designed to provide reasonable assurance regarding the achievement of stated objectives. Although having similar objectives, COBIT approaches IT controls by looking at information—not just COSO's financial information—that is needed to support business requirements and the associated IT resources and processes.

COSO's control objectives cover effectiveness, efficiency of operations, reliable financial reporting, and compliance with laws and regulations. Its primary role is for fiduciary and financial internal controls. Conversely, although both the ISACA and the IT Governance Institute acknowledge and make explicit reference to COSO's financial internal controls role, they extend COBIT's role to cover quality and security requirements in the overlapping categories of effectiveness, efficiency, confidentiality, integrity, availability, compliance, and reliability of information. These categories form the foundation of COBIT's control objectives within its four domain areas.

COSO and COBIT cater to different audiences. While COSO's target audience is general and directed to senior management, COBIT is more intended for IT management, IT users, and IT auditors. Both COSO and COBIT view internal control as an entity-wide process, but COBIT specifically focuses on IT controls. This distinction in effect defines and determines to a large extent the scope of each control framework.

Because of these differences, senior management should not necessarily expect a direct one-to-one relationship between the five COSO control components and the four

COBIT objective domains. Although the use of COBIT is often concentrated in the IT function at many enterprises, and the concern with COSO internal controls is more of a senior management concern, both should realize and recognize the importance of each for assessing and implementing effective internal controls.

 NOTES

1. The IT Governance Institute (ITGI) and the Information Systems Audit and Control Association (ISACA), both at Rolling Meadows, Illinois.
2. *CobiT* 5 (Rolling Meadows, IL: IT Governance Institute, 2011).

CHAPTER SEVENTEEN

ISO Internal Control and Risk Management Standards

C HAPTER 11 DISCUSSED THE COSO internal control element that call for compliance with laws and regulations and outlined some of the many areas that need to be on enterprise management's "radar screen." Some of these laws and regulations are all but mandatory, with penalties to the enterprise operation that violates them. Others are more like standards that recommend practices that an enterprise should follow. This chapter looks at several of the ISO or International Standards Organization materials and defines preferred practices in some areas of enterprise operations.

There are some 20,000 ISO standards today, covering a wide range of areas in business operations, from the dimensions of a plastic credit card to standards for building railway bridges and much more. This chapter looks at two standards that are important for building effective COSO internal controls: the standards for enterprise risk management and the general standards for establishing enterprise internal control processes. With the exception of ISO standards covering product quality processes, many of these had been viewed as "too European" and have been all but ignored by many US business executives in the past. As we are operating today in an increasing global economy, all enterprise executives should be aware of the importance of ISO standards and how they support the internal control processes.

BACKGROUND AND IMPORTANCE OF ISO STANDARDS IN A GLOBAL COMMERCE WORLD

Based in Geneva, Switzerland, the ISO is responsible for developing and publishing a wide range of international standards in many business and process areas.[1] Some of these standards are very broad, such as ISO 14001, covering effective environmental control systems, while others are very detailed and precise, such as a standard covering the size and thickness of a plastic credit card. The broad ISO standards are important because they allow all worldwide enterprises to talk in the same language when they can claim that they have, for example, an effective ISO 14001 environmental control system, and the detailed ones are also very crucial, to allow, for example, an ATM machine anywhere in the world to expect to receive the same size and thickness of a credit card.

ISO standards are developed through the collaborative efforts of many national standards-setting organizations, such as the American National Standards Institute (ANSI) or other similar groups throughout the world. The standards-setting process gets started with a generally recognized need for a standard in some area. An example would be ISO 27001, which outlines the high-level requirements for an effective information security management system. The ISO 27001 standard was developed through the efforts of several international technical committees sponsored by ISO in cooperation with the International Electrotechnical Commission (IEC) international standards-setting group. The standard is not specific in its detailed requirements but contains many high-level statements, along the lines of "the organization shall . . ."

Because of the numerous international governmental authorities, professional groups, and individual experts involved in the ISO standard-setting process, the building and the approval of any ISO document typically is a long and slow process. An expert committee develops an initial draft standard covering some area, it is sent out for review and comment with a review response due date, and the ISO committee then goes back to review draft comments before either issuing the new standard or sending a revised draft out for yet another round of reviews and suggested changes. Typically, after many drafts and comment periods, the ISO standard will be published. Enterprises can then take the necessary steps to comply with the standard, but to certify their compliance, they must contract with a certified outside auditor, with skills in that standard, to attest to their compliance. This standard-setting process is similar to what happened with the revised COSO internal control framework, where the initial draft was first released in December 2011. A lengthy exposure draft and comment period followed, and the final revised internal control framework was released by COSO in May 2013.

Many US enterprises first got involved with these international standards through the launch of ISO 9000 quality management system standards in the 1980s. Companies were faced with the high-quality design standards found in many non-US products, such as Japanese automobiles, at that time. Japanese manufacturers then had designed many high-quality products, following what became ISO 9000 standards, and U.S. manufacturers finally began to "step up to the plate" by modifying their own processes to comply with these higher-quality product standards. Compliance with the ISO 9000 standard allowed worldwide enterprises to design their operations in accordance with a single consistent standard and then to assert that they had a quality management system in place in accordance with the international standard. ISO standards are published and controlled by the ISO organization in Geneva, following strict copyright rules. These are not the kinds of materials that can be downloaded through a casual Web search but must be purchased. Many of the actual ISO standards are simply very detailed outlines of practices to be followed.

ISO standards have much more content and are more detailed than the COSO internal controls framework or ITIL's recommended best practices. They represent performance measures for an enterprise and its peers. These are worldwide standards that will allow an enterprise to hold itself out and qualify that it is operating in accordance with a consistent international standard. Although there are many different standards to select, ISO 13485, on quality management regulatory requirements for medical devices, provides an example. This ISO standard defines the quality requirements covering human health-care devices. For example, the standard calls for an enterprise manufacturing such devices to establish appropriate calibration controls. Because of the diversity of different calibration approaches, the standard cannot specify just one approach but only states that enterprises should have appropriate mechanisms in place.

It is one thing for an enterprise to read an ISO standard and change its processes to follow it, but the enterprise must also demonstrate to others, such as customers and trading partners, that it is following the standard. In order to attest to its compliance with an ISO standard, an enterprise must contract with an authorized outside reviewer to assess its adherence to that standard. This ISO certification is a process somewhat similar to an external audit of financial records performed by certified public accountants (CPAs). Financial statement audits in the United States require a licensed CPA external auditor to assess whether an enterprise's financial reports are "fairly stated," following good internal controls and recognized accounting standards. Those good internal controls, of course, are outlined in the COSO internal control framework. When either an investor or the Securities and Exchange Commission (SEC) finds such a signed external audit report, along with the final reported results, there is a level of assurance that these financial reports are fairly stated and are based on good internal control procedures.

The ISO certification process is also similar to a CPA-led US financial audit that is currently based on compliance with generally accepted auditing standards (GAAS), performed by a major public accounting firm. Although we do not have a "Big 4" set of major ISO auditing firms here, national standards-setting organizations qualify outside reviewers to perform external audits of various ISO standards. There is no ISO GAAS, however, but a wide degree of diversity in audit objectives because a reviewer for ISO 27001 on IT security management systems will be looking for different control procedures than would an ISO auditor for ISO medical device quality management systems. In all cases, though, the qualified ISO outside auditor may identify areas for corrective actions and may publish a report to management similar to an internal audit process. Once the ISO auditor's recommendations are corrected, the outside reviewer will certify that the enterprise is in compliance with that standard.

Once certified, the enterprise can advertise to the outside world that it has an effective process in place that meets a specific ISO standard. For example, a customer for the medical diagnostic device would want to know whether a potential supplier of such a medical product is in compliance with ISO 13485. That same medical device manufacturer would also want to gain assurance that its prime component suppliers are similarly ISO qualified.

ISO STANDARDS OVERVIEW

Compliance with the appropriate ISO standards is not the same level of requirement for an enterprise as is the need for an audited financial statement. Because of SEC financial reporting rules, the lack of an audited financial report or a report with an auditor's unfavorable opinion can be very damaging for a publicly traded enterprise. While virtually all publicly traded enterprises are expected to have audited financial statements, the rules are not the same regarding compliance with ISO standards. In most instances, compliance with an ISO standard is only voluntary but still is often essential. We have cited the ISO standard covering the thickness and size of a personal credit card as an example. An enterprise that manufactured either cards or card readers that were not in compliance with such a standard would soon fail in the marketplace.

ISO standards covering quality management systems are a bit different. An enterprise can all but ignore a standard such as ISO 9000, calling for a quality management process, and can still succeed within a national marketplace. For example, in the United States some senior managers had historically looked at this ISO 9000 standard as "too much paperwork" and made only minimal efforts to achieve compliance for some of these standards. However, as we move to a more worldwide business trading environment, many senior managers request such certification today. What was once just nice to have, with the perception of too much required documentation, has become almost mandatory in the United States for manufacturing and other enterprises.

Enterprise executives should attempt to learn more about the status of ISO standards compliance within their enterprises. Some ISO standards, such as defining the thread pattern on a bolt or the thickness of a credit card, have become essentially mandatory, and an enterprise would not be in business if it did not follow them. All too often, the responsibility for ISO compliance standards is several levels down in the organization chain, in engineering or quality assurance, and may be viewed as too technically detailed by some members of management.

There is no single ISO standard that is comparable to the COSO internal controls framework, but several important standards cover areas that support the COSO framework. The following sections outline a few ISO areas where compliance with that standard will very much support adherence to the COSO framework.

ISO 9001 Quality Management Systems

ISO standards have a heritage dating back to World War II, when both sides of the conflict required strong product uniformity while operating at extremely high levels of production volume. Even if the products being manufactured were bullets and bombs, they had to work correctly, and there was a need for strict product quality control. The results on the Western Allies' side were some strong quality assurance standard procedures and the emergence of industrial engineers and production quality control specialists. After the war, ISO was established as part of the General Agreement on Trade and Tariffs (GATT), one of the international agreements to bring the world to more of a peacetime environment. ISO 9000, on quality management systems, was one of the earlier ISO standards. This international standard first received most of its attention in the newly recovering European countries.

Japan was another rebuilding and recovering postwar country that strongly embraced quality management systems. In the 1950s and the 1960s, the Japanese invited a series of US-based quality systems experts, such as Frederick Deming and others, to help at many of their plants in Japan. In many instances, these quality systems experts were all but ignored in the United States. However, their philosophies and techniques were heavily embraced by Japanese industry, and by the mid-1970s, Japanese electronic and automobile manufacturers began to make deep inroads into US markets, due to the quality and value of their products. Despite their then dominant product offerings and market advantages, many consumers in the United States began to recognize that Japanese manufactured products were superior in many respects to their own. ISO 9000 quality standards became an increasingly important factor to measure and assess the quality of products worldwide.

ISO 9000 is not only one standards document but is a family of standards for quality management systems. Maintained by ISO, these standards include requirements for such matters as

- ▓ Monitoring processes to ensure they are effective.
- ▓ Keeping adequate records.
- ▓ Checking output for defects, with appropriate corrective action where necessary.
- ▓ Regularly reviewing individual processes and the quality system for effectiveness.
- ▓ Facilitating continual improvement.

Each of the above refers to processes, not to specific actions. However, for enterprises to assert that they are in compliance with ISO 9000 (actually, 9001)—for example, that they are monitoring their key processes to be effective—the enterprises often must make significant changes to their management procedures and supporting documentation. The standards also create a required level of expectation. Any enterprise, on a worldwide scope, that holds out to such standards is stating that it has effective quality systems in place. A company or an organization that has been independently audited and certified to be in conformance with ISO 9001, for example, may publicly state that it is "ISO 9001 certified" or "ISO 9001 registered." Certification to an ISO 9000 standard does not guarantee the compliance (and therefore the quality) of end products and services; rather, it certifies that consistent business and production processes are being applied.

The actual certification is achieved through a review by a registered ISO auditor who is certified for that particular ISO standard. As discussed, this process is similar to the CPA's review and certified audit of an enterprise's financial statements except that the review here covers a specific ISO standard. Regulated by their national standards organizations, ISO auditors are authorized to register an enterprise's compliance with each unique ISO standard.

ISO 9000, as well as other ISO standards, imposes heavy documentation requirements on an enterprise and certainly more than would be expected under the COSO internal control framework. It is not sufficient for an enterprise to simply claim that some process has been once documented. There must be an ongoing process to keep that documentation current over time. In past years, many enterprises went through onetime efforts to create documentation but then never kept it current. This is the kind of situation that many internal auditors have often faced. Auditors frequently asked whether some system or process they were reviewing was documented. They were frequently met with an admission that the documentation was out-of-date or nonexistent, so this lack of documentation would often become an audit report finding that would not get much senior management attention and would result in little definitive corrective action. ISO 9000 compliance raises documentation requirements for quality processes to a whole new level. An outside reviewer must certify that the enterprise is in compliance, in order for the enterprise to state to the outside world that it is in compliance with the ISO standard.

As a clarification, ISO 9000 is not just one standard but is really a series of "certifiable" standards and guidelines:

- **ISO 9001**. Certifiable standard dealing with design.
- **ISO 9002**. Certifiable standard dealing with manufacturing.
- **ISO 9003**. Certifiable standard dealing with manufacturing and assembly.
- **ISO 9004**. Guideline defining a quality system.

These standards are periodically updated, with the current version known as ISO 9001:2008. To add to the complexity of things, an enterprise can claim that it is in compliance only with an earlier version, ISO 9000:1994, and there is also the QS 9000 series of standards that is similar but pertains only to the automotive industry. A certifiable standard means that it is subject to review by an outside ISO auditor, as discussed previously. These standards are periodically updated, with the current year appended to the standard.

ISO 9000 is a set of standards for a continual improvement-driven quality control system, no matter whether it covers a manufactured component or a service process. Exhibit 17.1 shows such a quality management system process that is driven by internal procedures for continual improvements, as well as by customer requests. This is an ongoing process in which existing processes should be monitored, actions planned for improvements, and the action items implemented for subsequent monitoring and further improvements. These are really the types of processes that should be in place when establishing and monitoring COSO internal controls and establishing an effective COSO control environment. IT systems development professionals have used essentially the same continual improvement quality processes ever since the early days of IT, in what was called the systems development life cycle (SDLC) process, to develop new IT systems. However, many SDLC-developed applications in the olden days called for a major amount of documentation, which was often ignored. Today, many IT applications are developed through more informal and iterative rapid development processes. In either case, the documentation is an important part of the COSO internal control framework.

Solid and accurate documentation is extremely important for an enterprise that is seeking to claim ISO registration. ISO is a global requirement; for example, when ISO 9001:2000, Section 4.2.3, states, among other provisions, that "A documented procedure should be established to define the controls needed," along with such subsections as "a) to approve documents for adequacy of issue," an enterprise or a process

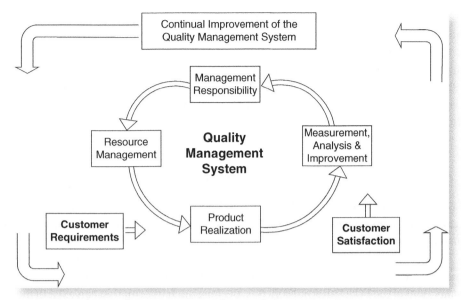

EXHIBIT 17.1   The Quality Management System Process

documentation control system is needed to demonstrate compliance with that standard. ISO best practices call for a hierarchy of documentation in any area, starting with top-level manuals to explain the *whys* and then down to instructions describing the *hows* of the practice. Exhibit 17.2 shows this documentation hierarchy with records and forms providing proof at the base of this matter. This documentation is essential to support a quality management system and certainly will be a requirement from ISO's external certification auditors.

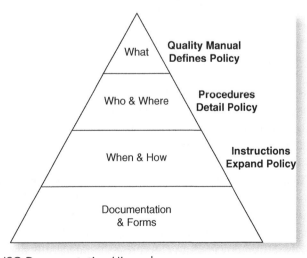

EXHIBIT 17.2   ISO Documentation Hierarchy

This section has provided only a very high-level description of the ISO 9000 quality management process. ISO standards are important for all types of enterprises to assert to their own internal management and to the outside world that they represent a quality-focused enterprise. Just to represent the breadth of ISO 9000 certification, in 1995 the American Institute of Certified Public Accountants (AICPA) became the first major worldwide professional organization to become ISO 9001 certified.[2] Compliance with ISO 9000 does not mean compliance with COSO internal controls, and vice versa. Nevertheless, enterprises at all levels should consider adopting ISO 9000 processes.

ISO IT Security Standards: ISO 27002

ISO 27002 is an IT-related security standard designed to help any enterprise that needs to establish a comprehensive information security management program or improve its current information security practices.

ISO 27002 also is a standard about both *information* and *information security* in a general and all-inclusive sense and is similar to the information and communication component of the COSO internal controls. Because such information can exist in many forms, the standard takes a very broad approach and includes a wide range of security standards covering security in regard to

- Data and software electronic files.
- All formats of paper documents, including printed materials, hand-written notes, and even photographs.
- Video and audio recordings.
- Telephone conversations, as well as e-mail, fax, video, and other forms of messages.

The concept here is that all forms of information have value and need to be protected, just as any other corporate asset does. Many enterprises today do not even consider security standards in some of these other broad areas, but the ISO standard suggests they should be covered when appropriate. In addition, the infrastructure that supports this information, including networks, systems, and functions, must also be protected from a wide range of threats including everything from human error and equipment failure to theft, fraud, vandalism, sabotage, fire, flood, and even terrorism. Similar to all other ISO standards, this published standard does not really proscribe *what* is specifically required but outlines areas where there are requirements for security-related standards.

As a first step to implementing ISO 27002, an enterprise should identify its own information security needs and requirements. This necessitates performing an information security risk assessment along the lines of the COSO enterprise risk management (COSO ERM) processes discussed in Chapter 15. Such an assessment should focus on the identification of major security threats and vulnerabilities, as well as be an assessment of how likely it is that each will cause a security incident. This process should help pinpoint an enterprise's unique information security needs and requirements.

One area that is too often missed in this "getting ready for the ISO 27002 information security standards-setting process," an enterprise should identify and understand all of the legal, statutory, regulatory, and contractual requirements that the organization and its trading partners, contractors, and service providers must meet. This requires an understanding and an identification of the enterprise's unique legal information security needs and requirements.

ISO 27002 is an international standard meant for any enterprise that uses internal or external IT systems, possesses confidential data, depends on IT to carry out its business activities, or simply wishes to adopt a higher level of security by complying with a standard. Although a relatively new standard and not in common application, at least in the United States, compliance with ISO 27002 constitutes a mark of confidence in an enterprise's overall security, in a manner just as ISO 9000 has become a guarantee of quality. Compliance should promote an increased level of mutual confidence between partners, where each can attest that it has established security standards in compliance with a recognized set of standards. ISO 27002 is a structured and internationally recognized methodology that should help an enterprise develop better management of information security on a continuing basis. It is a code of practice that supports the information security management systems requirements of the related security standard, ISO 27001.

IT Security Technique Requirements: ISO 27001

While ISO 27002 is a high-level code of practice covering security controls, ISO 27001 is what ISO defines as the "specification" for an information security management system (ISMS). That is, this standard is designed to measure, monitor, and control security management from a top-down perspective. The standard essentially explains how to apply ISO 27002 and defines the implementation of an information security management system (ISMS) as a six-part process, as follows:

1. **Define a security policy.** A fundamental component of any standard is the need for a formal, senior management–approved policy statement. All other compliance aspects of the standard will be measured against this policy statement.
2. **Define the scope of the ISMS.** ISO 270002 defines security in rather broad terms that may not be appropriate or needed for all enterprises. Having defined a high-level security policy, an enterprise needs to define the scope of the ISMS that will be implemented. For example, ISO 27002 defines an element of its security requirements as video and audio recordings. This may not be necessary for a given organization and then would be even specifically excluded from its ISMS scope.
3. **Undertake a risk assessment.** The enterprise should identify a risk assessment methodology that is suited to its ISMS environment and then both develop criteria for accepting risks and define what constitutes acceptable levels of risk.
4. **Manage the risk.** This is a major process that includes formal risk identification, risk analysis, and options for the treatment of those risks. The latter can include applying appropriate risk avoidance controls, accepting risks, taking other steps to avoid them, or transferring the risks to other parties, such as insurers or suppliers.
5. **Select control objectives and controls to be implemented.** This is the same internal control process discussed in Chapter 4 on the COSO internal control environment. For each defined control objective, the enterprise should define an appropriate control procedure.

6. **Prepare a statement of applicability.** This is the formal documentation that is necessary to wrap up the ISMS documentation process. Such documentation matches up control objectives with procedures to manage and implement the ISMS.

As can be seen from these six outlined steps, risk analysis and security policies are fundamental to this ISO standard. While setting up these practices is not an internal audit matter, an enterprise's IT auditors can provide strong help to management by offering to serve as internal consultants and help in performing adequate risk assessment procedures.

Because of strict ISO copyright rules, we have not supplied any extracts of the ISO 27001 text in this chapter. The actual ISO standards are presented in tight and unambiguous text. There is little specific detail but enough to allow an enterprise to implement its ISMS. Each formal standard concludes with an Appendix section, listing control procedures for each of the objective details in the standard. However, ISO 27001 should really not be considered a comprehensive set of control procedures that will change as technology changes; rather, it is an outline for the framework of an ISMS that should be continually implemented, monitored, and maintained.

ISO 27002 and ISO 27001 are global standards, with established compliance and certification schemes in place—particularly in the United Kingdom and the European Union. Both of these standards will continue to evolve, track technology, and will expand with even wider changes. The COBIT framework, discussed in Chapter 16, is tied closely with ISO 27002, and these ISO standards will continue to grow in their influence, and their adoption will continue to expand.

Service Quality Management: ISO 2000

Many professionals will agree that we live in a world with too many standards—many of which are similar to others with like objectives but are not connected to one another. ISO 2000, on service quality management, introduces some of this much-needed standards convergence. This is an international standard for IT service management, and it introduces many of the ITIL service management best practices that were discussed in Chapter 12. ISO 2000 consists of a Part 1, on implementing service management, and a following Part 2 section, describing best practices for service management. The Part 1 standard specifies the need for a series of service management–documented processes, such as defining requirements for implementing such a management system, new or changed service requirements, and documented relationship, control, resolution, and release processes. Quite correctly, the standard takes the best practices approach of ITIL and calls for formal documented processes to support them.

ISO 2000 asks an enterprise to adopt and certify that it has adopted the ITIL best practices discussed in Chapter 12. Formally, this standard "promotes the adoption of an integrated process approach to effectively deliver managed services to meet the business and customer requirements." ISO 2000 is the first global standard for IT service management and is fully compatible with, and supportive of, the ITIL framework. It will undoubtedly have a significant impact on the use and acceptance of ITIL best practices and the whole IT service management landscape.

In future years, enterprise management will see an increasing level of recognition of the importance of ISO service–related standards. In our increasingly global economy, no matter what national restrictions may be imposed across borders from time to time, international standards are needed to define common practices and to better facilitate communication. When an enterprise or a service organization—anywhere in the world—has achieved ISO 9000 quality management certification, customers and users can expect a certain minimum level of documentation and process standards. The ISO 27001 IT security standards should soon reach a similar level of importance and recognition. With our comments on ISO 2000 and on ITIL and ISO 9000's similarities with SOx, we should see increasing convergence trends between ISO and standards in other areas. Enterprise senior managers should have a high-level understanding of and embrace these important ISO standards.

ISO STANDARDS AND THE COSO INTERNAL CONTROL FRAMEWORK

As we become more and more of a global commerce world with many interconnections and relationships, the ISO standards become more important for all enterprises. While standards describing component dimensions—such as the thread pattern and size on a bolt—are essential for commerce, the "softer" quality system standards, such as ISO 9000, are equally important. Enterprises in one location will refuse to do business with businesses located elsewhere unless they can certify their compliance to some ISO standard.

Although many senior executives and even their internal auditors have not been that close to ISO standards in the past, we expect this to change. COBIT, introduced in Chapter 16, will almost certainly become more closely aligned with ISO 27002, and we can see internal auditors becoming increasingly involved with ISO quality standards. When appropriate, IT auditors should try to incorporate appropriate IS standards into their IT internal controls audits.

The enterprise executive might ask, however, what ISO standards have to do with the COSO internal control framework and even its newly revised version.

The concepts behind ISO quality and security standards are similar to the COSO internal control framework. A significant difference is that ISO standards outline significant expectations. That is, under ISO the enterprise should have certain internal control processes in place, such as tested documentation for some process, and external ISO auditors reviewing that area will test and assure that those ISO standards are in place and are effective. COSO only outlines some general requirements, such as the need for risk assessment processes, but there are no specific requirements beyond COSO's requirements that are necessary to achieve COSO internal control compliance.

One might argue that we are much better off with the more general framework than with the more specific ISO standards. Of course, things could be even worse if governmental authorities wrote specific rules here, which would specifically result in authorities drafting many hundreds of pages of rules covering every detailed nuance in a rules requirement.

Our objective in this chapter has been to introduce senior executives to some of the ISO standards that are similar to the COSO internal control requirements and to show some of the differences and similarities between COSO and ISO. The business executive should be aware of ISO standards and should work to implement them in certain areas, when appropriate, but should also focus an enterprise's internal controls on the COSO framework.

 NOTES

1. See www.iso.org.
2. See www.qualitydigest.com/june99/html/body_iso_9000.html.

CHAPTER EIGHTEEN

COSO Internal Controls in the Board Room

T HE BOARD OF DIRECTORS IS the ultimate manager of all stockholder- and investor-owned enterprises, as well as for most large private enterprises. Directors may be either elected as outside parties from the current stockholders, known as outside or nonemployee directors, or may be directors selected from the very senior members of management, called inside or employee directors. With their tenure in office and general responsibilities based on established corporate charter and by-law documents, boards of directors are charged with independently reviewing and approving overall internal control processes and all major decisions for the enterprises they manage. They are *the* independent managing representatives for the stockholders, with a responsibility to make major decisions for the corporation based on their assessment of the risks and potential benefits presented to them.

The board is responsible for reviewing major internal control activities throughout the corporation and for making significant and often risk-based decisions. They are key players in a corporation to make truly enterprise-wide internal control and risk-based decisions. An effective implementation of the COSO internal control framework provides an important approach and methodology for the board of directors to make better decisions for an enterprise and its shareholder owners.

This chapter will consider the importance of corporate boards of directors in understanding and subscribing to COSO internal controls, as well as good GRC principles, with an emphasis on the new revised COSO framework. The chapter discusses the importance of introducing COSO internal controls and effective GRC principles to today's boards in order to influence their corporate management and governance processes. It will suggest approaches for effectively implementing COSO internal controls both for overall enterprise decision-making guidance and as a process to help boards make decisions. While boards have a basic responsibility for the governance of their enterprises and related compliance issues, the chapter will emphasize the need for strong board-level support of the COSO internal control framework. Managers at all levels can use COSO internal controls to make better operational and various levels of strategic decisions, and the broad enterprise-wide perspective of the COSO internal control framework is also an important tool for helping board members better consider and evaluate the high-level internal controls facing their enterprises.

An enterprise's board of directors and its individual members are at a level of senior management beyond the enterprise organization charts and procedures that most employees encounter. Going well beyond an enterprise's HR function, members of the board are typically nominated by senior enterprise management, existing board members, or major investors and are only officially elected by the stockholders at an annual meeting. Although major investors and the CEO often have a role in recruiting board members, the board and a majority of the stockholders make essentially all major decisions. The board can, for example, terminate a CEO or make high-risk decisions for the enterprise. Public corporation board governance procedures and other operating procedures are essential for assessing and dealing with risks. While this chapter is not intended to be a guide on "how to be a board member," it provides some background on board member and audit and risk committee operations in light of the revised COSO internal control framework. With the exception of senior corporate officers and key members of the internal audit function, most corporation employees have little contact with their boards of directors, beyond seeing a face in the annual report. It is valuable for all employees and managers to understand how their boards operate and how they manage the operation's internal control processes and risks that affect all employees and other stakeholders.

BOARD DECISIONS AND INTERNAL CONTROL PROCESSES

Although the typical employee works a 40+ hour regular work week, board members usually are not involved in such daily, full-time work-week activities. Rather, board members usually operate on a part-time basis. A board may meet only once a month for several days. However, this is much more than the "part-time job," as we often think of such a concept. Board members will serve on multiple committees, beyond the formal full board meetings, and often will have multiple hours-long telephone committee meetings during interim periods; they are responsible for reviewing and understanding often massive amounts of financial, operational, and other reports concerning the enterprise they are managing. While this may be a "part-time job" for a given board member at a single corporation, that same individual may often serve on similar boards for several other corporations. The CEO and a limited number of other corporate officers, such as the CFO, may also sit on their enterprise's board, in addition to performing their regular job duties in the role of inside or employee directors. Although a board may officially meet formally for only a few days a month, given the long teleconferences and other interactions, their service is hardly a part-time job!

Board decisions and the directions given to the corporation they govern are based on actions taken in periodic board meetings. These decisions can have an important impact on the overall enterprise. For example, based on good financial results and a strong balance sheet, the board can declare an extra cash dividend. This type of decision is usually based on prior recommendations and agreements with senior management, who will then be responsible for communicating the decision and making changes to supporting processes to initiate the action. This is the type of regular board decision that is made in the course of the normal business cycle. As a clarification here and throughout this chapter, references to "the board" making a decision mean that a majority of board members have agreed on some action. A board of directors operates as a committee representing the stockholders.

The board can also make decisions that do not have management's full concurrence. The board may decide on a major reorganization, such as sale of a division to some other entity, or may act on a merger proposal—either friendly or hostile—from another enterprise. Sometimes, these board decisions are even made totally contrary to senior management's wishes. For example, the board may decide to shut down an unprofitable business unit. The CEO may totally disagree with such a decision, but the CEO, even if serving as an employee director and chair of the board, has only one board vote. The CEO can make a case to keep and not dispose of the unprofitable unit in an open board meeting, but if the board's majority-rule decision goes against that CEO's wishes, management will have to shut down that unit, even though senior management or outside investment advisers disagree. Of course, for many corporations, board decisions are generally collaborative, and boards are often tied very closely to the CEO and make many decisions based on that executive's recommendations. In addition, many CEOs are strong and powerful people with influence and persuasive powers that can heavily influence other board members. However, the board can overrule the CEO and can just as easily terminate the services of a CEO or some other senior officer and take action to bring in someone new. Some corporations have both a separate CEO and a chair of the board, two powerful leaders who should work closely together for the greater good of the corporation. In other cases, one leader holds the joint chair of the board and CEO titles. The trend today is perhaps for two separate leaders here.

The understanding, evaluation, and acceptance of risk should be a major consideration in almost every board decision. Because of their most senior positions in enterprises, board members are expected by many outside of the boardroom—investors, regulators, and others—to have a strong understanding of their corporation and the risks and internal control issues it faces. Just because of their very senior positions in the corporation, directors should generally have a good understanding of many of the specific internal control issues and risks that their companies face, such as risks associated with introducing a new product into a very competitive marketing environment or of internal control issues for committing capital into some new operations area. As part of good management practices, directors are expected to have a good understanding of managing a wide range of enterprise-level internal controls. While directors must comply with financial and accounting regulatory rules—such as Securities and Exchange (SEC) rules in the United States—there are no specific rules or requirements for the director-level management and understanding of internal control processes. The COSO internal control framework provides a basis for understanding these matters, but, traditionally, directors often have no specific guidance or rules covering their acceptance and understanding of dealing with the COSO framework.

Although directors have always realized that their decisions entail good internal controls practices, and that they should make their decisions in the best interests of the corporations they are governing, there has been no formal, recognized framework for establishing effective internal controls prior to COSO framework. Perhaps the most significant concept of the COSO internal control framework is its emphasis of enterprise-wide internal control management, a decision area that affects a corporate director. A manager in a product manufacturing enterprise, for example, should think of the internal controls associated with the operation of equipment on the production floor, outside vendors supplying raw materials, and risks associated with the worldwide taste for, and acceptance of, the manufactured products. COSO internal controls call for the manager to think of and deal with these internal controls on a larger, wider plane. Just as a manufacturing manager should think of enterprise internal controls on a wider horizon, a corporation director must always have this "big picture" concept in mind when making nearly all decisions. The COSO internal control framework provides an excellent model for many board-level decisions, and board members must always keep in mind that their decisions usually cover a wide spectrum. Closing a plant, for example, can present logistics risks in adjusting and moving people and equipment to sustain operations, legal risks associated with various plant-closing notification risks, and public relations needs in appropriately communicating the closure plans. The COSO internal control framework is a very important board of director–level concept.

An overall objective here should also be to promote good corporate GRC principles on a board of directors' level. The first of those three concepts—*governance*—deals with understanding and communicating the rules. This is and has been an ongoing board requirement. Similarly, *compliance* is a board requirement that deals with following both internal and external rules and procedures. Board members have a personal and professional legal responsibility here. The R, or *risk*, portion of GRC can cause greater challenges at the board level.

Although directors are expected to have a good understanding of their corporations and its issues, it operations management problems, and many other surrounding rules, directors of major corporations today may not always seem to have a good understanding of the overall COSO internal control framework beyond their external auditors advising them that they are in compliance with the COSO framework, as part of their SOx year-end internal control assessment. The revised framework, described in these chapters, is another area for greater understanding.

Previous chapters have discussed the importance of recognizing and managing internal controls and the COSO framework at all levels, but this understanding is particularly important for the most senior managers of an enterprise—its board of directors. Persons within an enterprise who have the most direct contact with board members, such as the CEO, the CFO, legal counsel, and the chief audit officer (CAE) should work with their board members to assure that there will be a consistent management and understanding of the COSO internal control framework. An understanding of the board committee enterprise structure, governance responsibilities, and its key committees is essential for comprehending board decision-making processes and how COSO internal controls might be better incorporated in board decisions.

BOARD ORGANIZATION AND GOVERNANCE RULES

Employees working for a corporation are accustomed to following a fairly structured set of enterprise rules and procedures, no matter what their employment level or position in an enterprise. All are expected to follow their corporate code of conduct guidelines, to generally tailor their work hours to normal operating procedures, and to follow enterprise policies and procedures. These are corporate and legal rules. Other employee practice guidelines are also defined through various professional standards or labor-related, bargaining-unit agreements. An accountant, for example, should be following generally accepted accounting principles (GAAP) today as part of his or her work, and internal auditors are expected to follow the standards published by their professional organization, the Institute of Internal Auditors (IIA). However, an employee or even a supervisor on the shop floor will probably not be aware of these specific GAAP accounting or IIA auditing guidance procedures. Some of these rules or standards may apply to all employees, while others are very specific to certain work positions. Beyond legal and corporate policy rules, enterprise stakeholders are expected to follow a wide range of good practice general guidelines.

Just as an employee has many rules and published procedures to consider as part of day-to-day work activities, an elected board member also must follow a wide range of legal, ethical, and good business practice rules and procedures. In addition, because the board of directors is responsible for the overall governance of its corporation, the collective board and its individual members are responsible for ensuring compliance with virtually all of the rules and regulations that may affect the corporation and all of its employees. However, an individual board member and particularly an independent or nonemployee director are not subject to the same types of detailed rules that govern a typical employee. There often are no "employee handbooks" for a board member to provide guidance for ongoing decision-related activities. A board will have established a high-level corporate charter and bylaws that sets broad rules for all governance activities. In addition, past board resolutions and policies establish governance practices, but a board is an independent high-level committee that can set many of its own rules. It can rely on key employees, such as help from the CFO on finance question issues, and the board will often bring in other inside or outside experts and other published guidance materials to provide help in many areas. Yet as the senior or ultimate decision makers in an enterprise, the board can really set many of its own rules beyond legal restrictions. Although many, if not most, boards and their members exercise prudent care over the corporations they govern, there will always be boards of directors that make high risk, bad, or even criminal decisions. When this occurs, they can be subject to criticism or even legal action by stockholders or actions by regulatory authorities, such as the SEC.

While the newly revised COSO internal control framework and a strong overall set of GRC principles will not prevent a board from making high-risk or bad decisions, they can provide some help and guidance for making better decisions on a board or board committee level. Because a board of directors is structured on a different level than a typical hierarchical business enterprise, we often forget that a board operates in a majority-rule committee structure. The board chair—usually, but not always, the

CEO—may want the board to take some action for the corporation, but a majority of board members may vote to take a different action. The following paragraphs discuss this typical board of director committee structure and how individual board members should manage and understand enterprise-level risks.

CORPORATE CHARTERS AND THE BOARD COMMITTEE STRUCTURE

A corporate charter is the authorizing document that sets the corporation's high-level rules and procedures. In the United States, corporations are registered through state-by-state registration authorities, with various governance and taxing rules being different for each state. Based on this registration, every legal corporation will have a corporate charter, as well as detailed bylaws. These documents establish the basic governance rules for a corporation, such as the size and the terms of service of board members and board meeting voting arrangements. The purpose of this chapter is not to discuss basic corporate board enterprise concepts or rules but to highlight the importance of the COSO internal controls and GRC principles in a board of directors framework and to discuss how board committees support these initiatives. A basic book on corporate organization will provide this information. A corporation's charter and its bylaws are similar to a constitution for a country or a political unit. They provide the high-level rules that are used to govern the corporation. Just as a political unit in a democracy is empowered and governed by its franchised voters, who established that constitution and have the power to vote to amend it, a corporate charter and its bylaws set the high-level and broad rules of corporate governance and can be changed only by amendments through a majority vote of the stockholders. Among many other matters, the corporate charter and bylaws define the size and the general organization of the board, any special board voting rules, and the terms in office for individual directors. For publicly held corporations, governmental securities regulators set another very important level of rules. In the United States, the SEC has released a large set of other corporate and board governance rules that are above the charter and bylaws rules. For example, the SEC has an extensive set of rules covering board audit committees—rules that became even more significant after SOx. The importance of the audit committee and other committees in the effective management of risks is discussed further on.

Boards operate very much in a majority-rule type of committee structure, where the board chair conducts meetings but must abide by committee majority votes. As in any committee enterprise structure, many decisions and actions depend on the strengths, opinions, and persuasive powers of individual board members. The board chair may exercise a powerful influence over other board members but can be outvoted through a board member majority vote decision. For many corporate employees, whether on staff or even fairly senior management, the board of directors' structure often seems remote and difficult to understand. Following their established meeting schedules, nonemployee director board members typically arrive at corporate headquarters or at an off-site location for their scheduled—often, monthly—board meetings. Inside or employee directors, such as the CEO and the CFO, will join these meetings, as will other invited persons, such as the general counsel, the CAE, and the external audit partner. Under the leadership of the board chair, they will meet in what is usually an almost closed-door meeting. The point here is that regular board meetings are not open to the public sessions, and the nonemployee directors may even ask the CEO to leave the room for certain critical decision matters. Internal minutes are taken, and decisions are documented through formal board resolutions. Although some board activities, such as the release of financial results or plans to launch an acquisition, are communicated through press releases or other announcements, much of the board activity takes place in private in a confidential, closed-door environment. The exception here is the annual stockholders meeting, where stockholders are invited to attend an open session and to vote on nominated directors, changes to charter-based corporate rules, and shareholder proposals. At the annual meeting, stockholder attendees can ask members of the board direct questions in an open forum. Otherwise, most board meeting activities are relatively confidential.

Much of a board's activities take place through a series of specialized committees, such as the compensation and the audit committees. Board members typically will sit on one or more of these board committees, which will meet concurrently with regular board meetings or at other times. Although many corporate functions have large support staffs, board members operate essentially as individuals. For example, a corporation may have a large finance and accounting staff, while only a small numbers of directors make many high-level decisions here, with the help and support of the CFO, external and internal auditors, and other consultants. The committees have their own enterprise charter documents, meet multiple times as necessary, keep minutes of their decisions, and report any recommendations for change to the full board for action.

As discussed earlier, a board of directors and its committees often seem rather remote to most enterprise employees. However, those same employees might find the activities of an enterprise board similar to the committee operations of many professional and civic enterprises. Many business executives are involved with their church, professional organizations, or local government bodies that are managed by a board of directors, and the executive may be asked to serve on one or another of these boards. Although the direct comparison to a corporate board falls down for many reasons, these volunteer organization boards of directors have sets of bylaws to describe or limit the boards' activities. While this analogy between a charitable or professional organization board and a corporate board can easily be stretched too far, those professional organization board members must consider certain organizational internal controls as well.

The failure of a volunteer board in some activity can be embarrassing to its organizing members and may put a dent in the organization's finances. However, the risks are often not that much greater. Activities and risks are very different for a corporate board and its individual board members. Board actions can be viewed as contrary to state securities regulations and, much more significantly, SEC reporting and governance rules. Violations can result in fines and legal or even criminal actions. Individual corporate board members can also be subject to legal actions, but corporations generally acquire what is called directors & officers (D&O) insurance to protect board members from civil legal actions.

A board of directors has many responsibilities in managing the overall operation of an enterprise. Risk oversight and the management of internal controls are major components of those activities and board responsibilities. This was stated quite appropriately by the National Association of Corporate Directors in a 2009 report on a board's risk oversight responsibilities:

> The board's role, quite simply, is to provide risk oversight. This means making sure that management has instituted processes to identify, and bring to the boards attention, the major risks the enterprise faces. It also means the continual reevaluation of these monitoring processes and the risks with the help of the board and its committees.[1]

These are strong words, but they place a challenge on the individual members and the total board. Members must try to identify the potential internal control risks facing the enterprise and then understand their potential implications and the consequences of significant internal control violations. This can be a daunting task for the board member who only receives supporting data about an upcoming potential risk-based decision, has an opportunity to ask further questions about the matter only during a tight agenda and a limited-time board meeting, and then must vote to take appropriate actions regarding that internal control–related action. This type of activity is coupled with all of the other matters that may be of concern before the board.

Because board members and particularly the nonemployee independent members operate as part-time participants with typically many other professional responsibilities, they usually face a huge number of items of concern that require more time to review and resolve. This is a particular challenge because board members operate as individuals, without a supporting staff. To add some efficiency to board operations, committees are established to help with their decision-making processes. Some of these committees are required under SEC rules, while others will be established due to a board decision. Major board committees include:

- **Audit committee.** This SEC-mandated board committee is responsible for supervising the internal audit function, hiring and managing external auditors, approving periodic financial reports, and performing many other activities. Audit committees and their role in the risk management process will be discussed in an upcoming section.
- **Nominating committee.** This committee is responsible for helping to recruit new director candidates, when a need arises, and to place them on voting ballots at subsequent annual meetings.
- **Compensation committee.** Another SEC-required committee, the compensation committee makes officer- and bonus-related decisions for the corporation. Working closely with the corporation's human resources function, the compensation committee also reviews and approves stock option and other deferred benefit programs.

Corporate boards may establish a wide range of other committees, depending on the type of issues surrounding the corporation. For example, a corporation involved in developing new technology-related products and acquiring other smaller companies to develop these lines of business may establish a board technology committee to review items of interest and make recommendations for action to the overall board. With ongoing interests in the area, many corporations today have established ethics and governance committees. The following paragraphs discuss the roles and responsibilities of two important risk management–related board committees, audit committees and a newer, evolving corporate board risk committee.

THE AUDIT COMMITTEE AND MANAGING INTERNAL CONTROLS

With their tasks of supervising the internal and external audit functions and approving periodic financial reports, audit committees have had a high level of responsibility in corporate governance for an extended period of time. However, until the late 1980s, many audit committees were little more than "paper tigers" because many often did not really exercise that much independent audit authority. In those earlier years, there were no restrictions on which directors could serve on their audit committees. This sometimes resulted in employee directors—even CFOs—serving on their boards of audit committees and approving their own corporate financial results. A classic "fox guarding the chicken coop" situation and hardly a separation of duties! The rules for corporate audit committees began to change in the 1980s with, first, the New York Stock Exchange and then other security exchanges requiring that all members of an audit committee be independent, nonemployee directors. Then, in December 1999, the SEC issued audit committee rules covering such matters as director independence, qualifications, charters, and outside auditor involvement.

Although suggested improved standards for board audit committee members were a frequent topic in corporate governance literature, things really changed after the fall of Enron and the passage of SOx in 2002. Legislative hearings at that time found out that—yes—the Enron Audit Committee was composed of nonemployee directors. However, testimony and hearings revealed that many members of that Enron Audit Committee could demonstrate no strong understanding of the complex financial transactions that caused, or at least helped, Enron to fail as fast as it did. In addition, that Enron Audit Committee spent only the most limited amounts of time reviewing and approving some very complex financial transactions. It did not help that the Enron Audit Committee relied on the advice of its then external auditor, Arthur Andersen, who turned out to be very close to many of these complex financial transactions.

The world has changed, and today the audit committee has become perhaps the most high-attention and visible of board of director committees. Beyond decisions made by the overall board and its chair, audit committees receive attention because of their financial and internal control review responsibilities. These audit committee board members review and act on often confidential audit findings, as well as review and approve the enterprise's audited financial statements; this committee has long since been required to be a committee of nonemployee directors.

One of the requirements that came out of SOx was that subscribing corporations must publish their audit committee charters in their 10K reports and elsewhere. Although there are no requirements for the content of these audit committee charters, the idea is perhaps to allow the investing public to see that a corporation has established a charter for its audit committee that follows some solid internal control management principles.

There are many examples of corporate audit committee charters, and a Web search will yield the audit committee charters of many. For example, the 2009 proxy statement of the major and very well-respected semiconductor manufacturer Intel Corporation has a lengthy and otherwise excellent audit committee charter that outlines the major functions of the Intel Audit Committee in a fairly lengthy list, including

- Directly responsible for the appointment, replacement, compensation, and oversight of the work of the independent auditor, who reports directly to the Audit Committee.
- Reviews and discusses with management, the independent auditor, and the company's chief audit executive (CAE):
  - The adequacy and effectiveness of the company's internal controls (including any significant deficiencies and changes in internal controls reported to the Committee by the independent auditor or management);
  - The company's internal audit procedures; and
  - The adequacy and effectiveness of the company's disclosures, controls, and procedures, and management reports thereon.
- Reviews annually with the CAE the scope of the internal audit program, and reviews annually the performance of both the internal audit group and the independent auditor in executing their plans and meeting their objectives.[2]

The previous items are extracted from a lengthy list of Intel Audit Committee responsibilities. Another item on that list is, "Reviews and discusses with management the company's major financial risk exposures and the steps management has taken to monitor and control such exposures." This statement contains the only reference to *risk* in the entire audit committee charter, and the emphasis here is on financial risk and not on overall enterprise risk.

An audit committee has a major involvement with COSO internal controls. As part of the year-end closing process, enterprise internal auditors or others review and assess whether an enterprise's internal controls are in compliance with the COSO internal control framework. The external auditors then review this internal control review and testing work in order to render their opinions. The board audit committee reviews and approves this work. In order to understand this process and ask appropriate questions, an audit committee member should have some understanding of the COSO internal control framework, with an emphasis on its current version.

Prior to SOx, a board seat on an audit committee was not a heavy time responsibility type of role. Although they also had a responsibility to supervise their internal audit functions, pre-SOx audit committees were heavily weighted and tied to their external auditors. They provided regular updates of their audit activity progress, often made strong suggestions that the external audit firm engage in needed consulting activities, and managed many aspects of the financial audit process. SOx requirements have really changed all of that, and corporate management and the audit committee now have a much more important role in managing and overseeing their audit, internal control, and financial reporting processes. For many audit committees, what were once only limited, perfunctory meetings held each quarter before the regular board meeting have now turned into monthly face-to-face sessions, along with numerous telephone conferences during the interim. Audit committee members today are busy!

 ## BOARD MEMBER INTERNAL CONTROL KNOWLEDGE REQUIREMENTS

In the years prior to SOx, there were no background or experience qualifications for audit committee members. They were expected to review and understand some often complex financial and accounting issues, even though they may not have had the necessary experience or qualifications. This matter really was highlighted during the hearings after the fall of Enron. Audit committee members there, often with impressive other job titles, were asked to testify on why they passed judgment on what were sometimes very complex financial transactions. When asked why, it turned out that some people did not really understand or have the qualifications to understand. For readers here who have had some accounting training or experience, several of those Enron Audit Committee members did not even appear to understand the concept of an accounting accrual transaction—basic accounting and auditing language!

The finding that nonqualified audit committee members were part of the Enron board and that they could not have really been monitoring things and understanding audit issues as they should led to a requirement in the initial SOx rules stating that at least one member of any corporate audit committee must be an accounting and auditing "expert." Those rules, first issued in a draft format, however, were so tight that existing major corporations' audit committee members would not have been qualified to remain in their positions. The rules were subsequently softened to make them more reasonable. However, at least one member of any corporate audit committee today must have a demonstrated level of skills or experience to be able to review and understand some of the financial and accounting internal control issues surrounding a public corporation.

Just as at least one of the nonemployee director members of a corporate audit committee must have some specialized accounting and auditing experience, today's corporate directors should have at least some knowledge of the COSO internal control framework. Although there certainly is no SEC requirement here or even an accepted standard, Exhibit 18.1 outlines some of the skill requirements that might be expected of a board member who could claim a demonstrated knowledge of internal control assessment and analysis skills.

EXHIBIT 18.1 Board of Directors Internal Control Knowledge Requirements

In addition to SEC rules requiring that at least one member of an audit committee must be a designated "financial expert" with designated and demonstrated attributes, all members of corporate boards also should have a good general understanding of internal control principles, as demonstrated by the COSO internal control framework.

A board member's knowledge of internal controls should have the following attributes:

- A good understanding of the COSO internal control framework, with an emphasis on techniques for building an effective control environment, risk identification and quantitative risk assessment approaches, and internal control monitoring.
- An understanding of analyzing and developing appropriate internal control plans for a broad range of financial and operational areas in active organization environments or experience in actively managing one or more persons engaged in internal control management activities.
- An understanding of the COSO internal control framework, as well as its financial and general internal controls and procedures, with an emphasis on financial reporting requirements.
- A general understanding of information system risks, including security and telecommunications.

COSO INTERNAL CONTROLS AND CORPORATE GOVERNANCE

The board of directors plays a critical role in overseeing an enterprise-wide approach to internal control management. Because management is accountable to the board of directors, the board's focus on effective internal control oversight is critical to setting the tone and culture toward effective management through strategy setting, formulating high-level objectives, and approving broad-based resource allocations.

Members of a board should have a broader understanding of an enterprise, including its potential multiple operating units, international business locations, financial arrangements, and regulatory pressures, than the knowledge base of all but the most senior enterprise executives. Board members should strive to use this broad knowledge of the enterprise and its various potential internal control risks and issues with the dimensional nature of the COSO internal control framework and always remember its various interconnections.

Boards of directors use their board committees in carrying out certain of their risk oversight duties. The use and focus of committees vary; each should focus attention on elements of enterprise risk management. While risk oversight, like strategy, is a full board responsibility, some companies may choose to start the process by asking the relevant committees to address risk oversight in their areas, while focusing on strategic risk issues in the full board discussion.

The original COSO internal control framework has been with us for a long while, and it now appears to be an appropriate time for board members to revisit the newly revised COSO framework. Robust engagement by the board in enterprise internal control oversight strengthens an enterprise's resilience to significant internal control and risk exposures. The newly issued COSO internal control framework can help provide a path of greater awareness of the potential internal control vulnerabilities an enterprise faces. The interrelated nature of these internal controls, more proactive management of the control issues, and more transparent decision making around risk/reward trade-offs can contribute to a greater likelihood of an enterprise achieving its internal control objectives.

With the worldwide financial turmoil of recent years, the importance of effective internal controls has entered the board rooms of corporate management today. In any event, the audit committee in today's corporation should give more time and attention to assessing and managing its internal controls. The interested board member should become more acquainted with the concepts of the newly revised COSO internal control framework and how it will help a board better understand and manage enterprise-level risks. For the senior executives who are not members of boards but are close to board operations, such as the CAE or the CFO, the concept here should be presented to key and interested board members. It is a soon-to-happen future development in corporate governance.

NOTES

1. National Association of Corporate Directors, December 2009, www.nacdonline.org.
2. See Intel Corporation, 2009 Proxy Statement, Audit Committee, www.intc.com/intelProxy2009/governance/audit.

CHAPTER NINETEEN

Service Organization Control Reports and COSO Internal Controls

T HERE WAS ONCE A TIME when enterprises built, implemented, and relied on their own internal control processes and systems. The original COSO internal control framework was largely built with that model in mind, where enterprise personnel were totally responsible for building and creating their own internal control systems and processes. The world has very much changed today; we now use outside service providers to manage many outside processes through a wide variety of contractual arrangements, and we need to rely on the internal controls that those outside providers administer, even though we do not have direct authority and responsibility for those internal controls.

When some other service provider has been chosen to perform contracted procedures, the contractor enterprise does not have direct control over those systems and processes. When some other nonenterprise entity or service may be operating certain systems and processes, enterprise management cannot say that any internal control or other problems are not its responsibility because someone else is doing the work. No matter whether an enterprise is doing the work itself or is contracting with another party to perform procedures, the enterprise is still responsible for the quality and management of its own internal processes.

Unless there has been a formal right-to-audit agreement or certain court-ordered legal actions, an enterprise cannot just go over to another entity and ask to review its internal control processes or even detailed supporting records. Similarly, one's external auditors also cannot just cross over, but procedures have been established over time such that an external auditor can assess the internal control processes of another entity.

An enterprise can gain assurance that the internal controls offered by outside providers are adequate through the use of service organization control (SOC) reports, an AICPA-initiated set of processes to review and assess internal control services provided by outside parties. This chapter will provide a management-level understanding of the SOC report procedures that an enterprise's external auditors might use and will discuss why they are important to senior management for reviewing and assessing COSO internal controls provided by outside, nonenterprise resources.

These matters are the responsibility of one's external auditors, but an enterprise executive should be aware of these service organization reports and processes and why they are important for establishing effective internal controls. This chapter discusses the background and introduces service organization control reports, not from an external auditor's perspective but with the information that enterprise management should know and understand to use these reports to better understand its internal control processes. Although it is often a difficult-to-use procedure, the chapter also discusses right-to-audit clauses in service provider agreements.

IMPORTANCE OF SERVICE ORGANIZATION INTERNAL CONTROLS

There was once a time—many years ago—when business enterprises and their employees were almost totally responsible for virtually all of their overall administrative and production processes. Although long ago, an example of such a totally self-sufficient facility might be found in the Ford Motors, River Rouge Dearborn, Michigan, plant that got started around 1911 to build Ford's extremely popular Model T cars. Ford constructed a plant facility to build these cars, starting from many raw materials to the completed vehicle. For example, Ford leased forest land to cut down trees that went into Ford-owned sawmills. The lumber then went to River Rouge, where it was cut up and finished for use as the floorboards and other wood trim that were part of those early cars.

Similarly, Ford owned mines and quarries from which raw materials were brought into River Rouge, where glass for windshields was made and iron and steel were smelted to produce the rolled steel sheets and castings for car parts. Ford employees did essentially everything to produce their then highly popular automobiles. Whether it was handling accounting tasks, producing glass for windshields, or casting and assembling engines, Ford and its employees did essentially everything.

The world has certainly changed today. Enterprises make arrangements to bring in other resources under contract to perform a wide range of specialized services. For example, rather than hiring their own cooks and kitchen personnel, enterprises today typically contract with food service firms to run and manage their company cafeterias. Everyone typically benefits from these arrangements. Running a cafeteria and its kitchens is not a core competency for an accounting firm, for example, and the food service workers there have better job opportunities than within that accounting firm.

Over the years, enterprises have made extensive use of contracted services for various IT activities, ranging from developing new IT applications to managing the total data center, doing data input in the old batch-processing systems, and more. For example, back in the earlier IT mainframe and batch-processing days, some enterprises contracted with what were called service bureaus, specialized IT data centers with computer hardware to accept input and run key applications. Enterprises used these service bureaus because some firms did not have sufficient expertise or resources to run and manage their own IT applications. Today, the classic IT service bureau have largely gone away, because IT resources are now cheap and plentiful, and there is no more need for batch-processing system processes. However, we still use outside IT service providers today through our reliance on cloud computing resources and other specialized online services.

The use of outside service providers—particularly, for IT services—has always caused internal control concerns for senior management and its external auditors. As part of its contractual negotiations, the outside provider could typically say, "Yes, our internal controls are excellent," but the external auditors in particular needed an accepted audit procedure to verify those internal controls. Because the external IT resources were directly controlled by another provider, sometimes at a different or even more remote location, the primary enterprise's external auditors, enterprise management, or internal auditors could not go over to the remote service provider to perform an internal control review or audit. They needed some means of gaining assurance that the internal controls at that external service facility were adequate.

EARLY STEPS TO GAIN ASSURANCE: SAS 70

IT service bureaus have been with us for a long time, perhaps dating back to the mid-1970s. Some of them were well managed, with adequate internal controls, while a few others were horror stories in the making. Yet no matter what the results, the management of those service providers typically gave assurances to the companies contracting with them to use their services that all of the internal controls at the service bureaus were good. An external audit firm, reviewing the IT internal controls of any applications that an audit client had arranged to run at such a service organization, did not have any means of obtaining external audit satisfaction. There were no external audit standards covering these concerns, but what came to be known as SAS 70 eventually became a recommended solution.

Prior to SOx, the AICPA's Auditing Standards Board was responsible for establishing guidance for external auditing standards. These were issued in the form of numbered Statements of Auditing Standards (SAS) documents. For example, and highlighted in Chapter 1, SAS 55 was released several years after the original COSO internal control framework, and it required that external auditors use that COSO internal control framework as a basis for evaluating an audit client's internal controls.

SAS 70, titled "Service Organizations," was originally released in 1988, and it provided guidance for external audits of the financial statements of entities that outsourced work to service organizations. SAS 70 defines the standards an external auditor must employ in order to assess the contracted internal controls of a service organization. Service organizations, such as hosted data centers, insurance claims processors, and credit-processing companies, provide outsourcing services that affect the operation of the contracting enterprise. However, this "Service Organization" SAS presented problems for external auditors and management almost immediately after its release. Intended for use by the customer's auditor, SAS 70 required either what was defined as a Type I attestation report, stating that the service organization's processes as documented are sufficient to meet specific internal control objectives, or a Type II attestation report, which additionally includes an on-site evaluation to determine whether the processes and controls actually function as anticipated.

In a Type I report, the external auditor evaluates the efforts of a service organization at the time of audit to prevent accounting inconsistencies, errors, and misrepresentation. The auditor also evaluates the likelihood that those efforts will produce the desired future results. A Type II report includes the same information as that contained in a Type I report; in addition, here the auditor attempts to determine the effectiveness of agreed-on controls since their implementation. Type II reports also incorporate data compiled during a specific time period, usually a minimum of six months.

SAS 70 turned out to be an expensive audit process to support compliance with financial reporting rules, and it was often avoided by some external auditors. However, it was frequently treated by vendors and their customers as a certification "proving" security and compliance with privacy or other regulations that require enterprises to monitor their exposure to vendor internal control risks. Yet from a management and external audit perspective, these assertions were not really proved that strongly. Seemingly, no one was happy with this process. The attestation report requirement was subsequently replaced with an AICPA attestation standard.

SERVICE ORGANIZATION CONTROL (SOC) REPORTS

Without going into auditing theory and implementation details, SAS 70 reports were just not working for external auditors who were attempting to assess their audit clients' internal control processes in our current era, where enterprises use service organizations for more and more IT and other business services. Enterprise executives today can easily forget the number of services provided within their enterprise by service organizations, including employee travel expense management, customer returns, special marketing promotions, and annual report proxy solicitations, as well as many IT processes. The adequacy of the internal controls for some of these services does not have a direct impact on the adequacy of an enterprise's financial reporting controls, but they still affect all aspects of enterprise internal controls, as defined in the COSO internal control framework.

During the 25+ year period that SAS 70 has been in place, service organizations have begun to use more technology in their service lines, and their clients—enterprise users— usually wanted more information about not only a service provider's internal controls over financial reporting but also its security and IT controls. Although the SAS 70 report was always intended to be an auditor-to-auditor communication, over time service organizations realized that these SAS 70 reports were also useful to user organization management, stakeholders, and regulators, and even though SAS 70 reports were designed only to report on financial reporting controls, they were being used to report on other IT controls as well.

In response to the past misuse of the SAS 70 report and the need for service organizations to be able to report on their IT control systems, the AICPA in 2011 released a new service organization control reporting structure consisting of three alternative service auditor internal control reports, called SOC 1, 2, and 3, with each type of these SOC reports designed to help service organizations meet specific user needs. These SOC reports are issued by CPA external auditors on a service organization's internal controls. SOC reports enable CPA external auditors to better protect the public by assuring user enterprises of a service organization's controls and help user entities obtain an objective evaluation of the effectiveness of internal controls that address the compliance, operations, and financial reporting of a service organization.

■ **SOC 1 reports.** These retain the original purpose of SAS 70 reports and provide a vehicle for reporting on a service organization's system of internal controls that is relevant to a user organization's internal controls over financial reporting. SOC 1 reports are intended to be auditor-to-auditor communications, just as the SAS 70 report had been.

Their specific content will depend on the service auditor and the service organization's system. Their basic elements include the independent service auditor's opinion report, management's description of the service organization's system of internal controls, and the independent service auditor's tests of controls, as well as the results of these tests. Additional information provided by the service organization but not covered by the service auditor's opinion may also be included within the SOC 1 report.

■ **SOC 2 reports.** These offer service auditors and service organizations a reporting option when the subject matter is not relevant to controls over financial reporting. The SOC 2 report addresses controls at a service organization that are pertinent to security, availability, processing integrity, confidentiality, and privacy internal control issues. In an SOC 2 report, management should identify one or more major internal control principles that it believes it has achieved and the criteria on which it will base its assertion of achievement.

SOC 2 reports are intended for user organization management and other stakeholders, such as business partners and customers, along with regulators who are knowledgeable about the subject matter and who may also benefit from the information contained within an SOC 2 report. The report includes many of the same elements as an SOC 1 report, including the independent service auditor's report, a description of the system, and a section containing the service auditor's tests of the operating effectiveness of controls and the related test results.

■ **SOC 3 reports.** These allow service organizations to provide user organizations and other stakeholders with a report on controls that is relevant to security, availability, processing integrity, confidentiality, and privacy. Unlike SOC 1 and SOC 2 reports, SOC 3 reports do not include a description of the system or a detailed description of tests of controls and related test results. Moreover, SOC 3 reports are short-form, publicly available documents that state whether the service organization's system for providing its services to user entities is suitable.

A senior executive should meet with the enterprise's external auditors to assess which of these three types of SOC reports will best meet the varying needs of different audiences and cover different subject matter. This process can be puzzling, but Exhibit 19.1 is a simple diagram outlining this decision-making process. An enterprise should work with its external auditors, as well as directly with its service providers, to obtain reports giving it assessments of the internal controls provided by its service organizations.

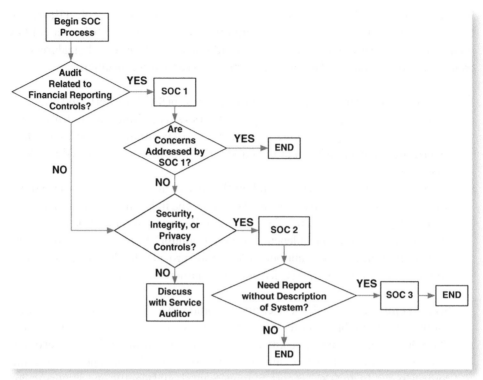

EXHIBIT 19.1 SOC Reporting Decision Process

A key point here for enterprise management is to insist that any assertions regarding good internal controls that are made by service providers should reference the COSO internal control framework. We mentioned how, in the early days before SAS 70, the service providers often claimed their internal controls were "good," whatever that meant. While there should be no problems with one's external auditors, enterprise management should insist that any references to its internal controls refer to the newly revised COSO internal control framework, as we have described in previous chapters.

 RIGHT-TO-AUDIT CLAUSES

We have discussed the difficulties in obtaining sufficient information from external service providers to determine that their internal controls were adequate. In the old days, it was common for an enterprise to place "right-to-audit" words in its contracts with service provider clients, but that was often little more than a meaningless phrase that was never really enforced or only for massive fraud situations. There were no real rules or specific conditions when any audits were to be performed, and typically there was no one—such as internal auditors—available to perform these audits. We explained how SAS 70 rules provided a method for external audits to review financial internal controls, but, as we have noted, those rules and procedures were difficult and often expensive to enforce.

Large U.S. government contracts, involving significant amounts of resources and time, also have the same right-to-audit rules, but there are government contract agencies with large staffs and supporting detailed procedures available to audit their service providers. However, that is really a different world, compared to business enterprises. With the exception of major corporations, the typical enterprise does not have the resources to regularly audit its service providers. The relatively new SOC rules will help, but an enterprise should retain provisions to audit the internal controls of its service providers.

Exhibit 19.2 shows a sample right-to-audit contract provision that an enterprise could use to review the internal controls and other processes in place at its service providers. In this sample clause, the term [Contractor] is used to describe the service provider in contracts, grants, and agreements with the [Company]. The sample language here, however, is not intended to represent legal advice. An enterprise should consult with appropriate legal counsel before using this information.

EXHIBIT 19.2 Sample Right-to-Audit Clause

[Contractor] shall establish and maintain a reasonable internal control system that enables [Company] to readily identify [Contractor]'s assets, expenses, costs of goods, and use of funds. [Company] and its authorized representatives shall have the right-to-audit, to examine, and to make copies of or extracts from all financial and related records (in whatever form they may be kept, whether written, electronic, or other) relating to or pertaining to this [Contract or Agreement] kept by or under the control of the [Contractor], including, but not limited to those kept by the [Contractor], its employees, agents, assigns, successors, and subcontractors. Such records shall include, but not be limited to, accounting records, written policies and procedures, and other systems and documentation records covering processes managed and performed by the [Contractor] for the [Company].

[Contractor] shall, at all times during the term of this contract and for a period of seven years after its completion, maintain such records, together with such supporting or underlying documents and materials. The [Contractor] shall at any time requested by [Company], whether during or after completion of this [Contract or Agreement], and at [Contractor]'s own expense make such records available for inspection and audit (including copies and extracts of records as required) by [Company]. Such records shall be made available to [Company] during normal business hours at the [Contractor]'s office or place of business and subject to a three-day written notice/without prior notice. In the event that no such location is available, then the financial records, together with the supporting or underlying documents and records, shall be made available for audit at a time and location that is convenient for [Company].

[Company] may request an audit of [Contractor]'s internal control systems and processes as provided for the [Company]. Audits may include reviews of online systems records or a physical visit. Audits will be requested at least five days in advance of the work and the [Contractor] shall ensure [Company] has access to appropriate systems and files, appropriate working space, and access to [Contractor]'s employees, agents, assigns, successors, and subcontractors.

Audits will be performed by [Company] internal auditors, external auditors, or other people identified at the time of the audit request. Costs of any audits conducted under the authority of this right-to-audit and not addressed elsewhere will be borne by [Company] unless arrangements are made at the time of the audit. If the audit discovers substantive findings related to fraud, misrepresentation, or non-performance, [Company] may recoup the costs of the audit work from the [Contractor].

An enterprise should put this type of right-to-audit provision in all of its contracts with service organizations. Even more appropriately, it should be prepared to send members of its internal audit staff to visit service providers on site to investigate and recommend corrective actions if any service provider appears to be having internal control problems. At the extreme, the result of unfavorable findings in any such service organization audit may result in the termination of a contract and the search for a new service provider. However, merely the threat of an audit visit will encourage any type of service organization to establish strong internal control processes.

 ## INTERNAL CONTROL LIMITATIONS

The COSO internal control framework is complex, but there is no such thing as a perfect internal control system for an enterprise, despite its size, business operations, and senior management objectives. For example, staff size limitations may obstruct efforts to properly segregate duties, which require the implementation of compensating controls to ensure that internal control objectives are achieved. Limited inherent risks in any system are the elements of human error, misunderstandings, fatigue, and stress. Employees, for example, should be encouraged to take earned vacation time in order to improve operations through cross-training, while enabling employees to overcome or avoid stress and fatigue.

The cost of implementing a specific internal control should not exceed the expected benefit of the control. Sometimes there are no out-of-pocket costs to establish adequate internal controls. A realignment of duty assignments may be all that is necessary to accomplish some internal control objective. In analyzing the pertinent costs and benefits, managers also need to consider their possible ramifications for the enterprise at large and attempt to identify and weigh the intangible, as well as the tangible, consequences.

An effective internal control system should provide reasonable assurance that an enterprise's operating systems, financial controls, IT systems, reporting, and other processes are working effectively. No matter how well designed and managed, internal control systems cannot provide absolute assurance that all enterprise internal control objectives have been, and will continue to be, met.

Designing and implementing effective systems of internal control require senior management to clearly understand an enterprise's objectives and its operating environment. Management always needs to recognize the inherent limitations in the design and application of systems that may have an impact on the ultimate delivery of agency objectives and services.

The original COSO internal control framework provided an excellent method for establishing effective enterprise internal controls. Revised and updated to reflect changes in enterprise organizational relationships and the predominance of IT technologies and the Internet, the newly revised COSO internal control framework that we have been describing in these chapters should help members of senior management and their enterprises to establish better, more effective internal control processes.

CHAPTER TWENTY

Implementing the Revised COSO Internal Control Framework

A S WE HAVE STATED IN previous chapters, the COSO internal control framework is not a standard or firm set of rules requiring compliance but represents best practices guidance. In that context, COSO's May 2013 revisions have introduced some changes to allow enterprises to better implement and understand their internal control processes. However, as part of an enterprise's Sarbanes-Oxley Act (SOx) Section 404 internal control requirements, it is required to attest that its internal controls are in compliance with the COSO internal control framework. Yet with the new revisions to the framework, a manager might ask, "Which COSO framework should I use—the 1992 or the new version?"

To help in this process, COSO has outlined transition rules for converting to the revised internal control framework. In the final chapter in this book, we outline COSO's proscribed transition rules for converting to the revised framework and attesting to their SOx Section 404 compliance. The revised standards do not require major changes to enterprise operating procedures, but enterprise executives should be aware of changes that need to be put in place.

UNDERSTANDING WHAT IS NEW IN THE 2013 FRAMEWORK

Perhaps the most significant changes to the revised COSO framework are the 17 principles highlighted in Chapter 3 and discussed further in subsequent chapters. Each of these principles is assigned to one of the five components of internal control, such as the control environment, and each must be present and functioning if an enterprise is to have effective internal controls. The 1992 framework did not contain such principles or requirements beyond just the five components of internal control to be considered. Each of these 17 2013 internal control principles is further explained by the points of focus, also introduced in prior chapters. Though not specific requirements, these should assist enterprise managers and their auditors in evaluating whether an internal control principle is present and functioning.

The 1992 guidance was not at all detailed, but these new COSO principles are far more specific and subject to questions. For example, the fifth control environment principle states, "The organization holds individuals accountable for their internal control responsibilities, in the pursuit of objectives." Now, beyond it simply being a good-sounding topic, an enterprise and its executives should take a hard look at what they mean by *internal control responsibilities*. For example,

- Are internal control processes adequately documented, and are responsible personnel trained in the use and administration of those control processes?
- Is there evidence that control responsibilities have been formally assigned to individuals, as well as documentation indicating that assigned persons know and understand their responsibilities regarding that specific internal control process?
- Through plans and published audit finding results, is there evidence that internal audit has been reviewing internal controls in the specific area of interest?
- Have appropriate corrective actions been taken, in light of any internal control violations?

These are just examples of questions, but management should work with its internal auditors to determine that appropriate review procedures have been installed. We would expect to see more detailed guidance, published by the major public accounting firms and others, going forward to help an enterprise attain compliance with these new, more specific internal control principles.

Some of the other guidance in the revised COSO internal control framework and discussed in these chapters includes

- More guidance that ties control objectives to the risks related to specific areas.
- Much more relevant guidance on IT issues that relate to specific areas, processes, and reporting.
- Greatly enhanced expansion of enterprise and IT governance concepts.
- An increased emphasis on the globalization of markets and operations, as well as changes in business models and organization structures.
- Much more use and reliance on evolving technologies such as wireless and Internet-based processes.
- A substantially increased discussion of fraud as it relates to internal control.

In the days going forward, the new COSO framework will no doubt be featured and summarized in many business and professional publications. Senior managers should work with their management team and internal audit leadership to ascertain that all parties understand this new internal control framework and those actions that can be taken to achieve compliance with its principles.

 ## TRANSITIONING TO THE NEW COSO GUIDANCE

The COSO board has stated that users should transition to the new 2013 framework in their applications and related documentation as soon as possible, given their particular circumstances. The COSO board believes that the key concepts and principles embedded in the original 1992 framework are fundamentally sound and broadly accepted in the marketplace, and it will continue to make the 1992 version available through December 15, 2014, after which it will be considered superseded.

Although only the Securities and Exchange Commission (SEC) can provide specific guidance regarding the application of the new COSO framework to SOx Section 404 requirements, COSO believes that users should transition their applications and related documentation to their updated framework as soon as is feasible under their particular circumstances. COSO further believes that entities reporting externally on internal controls should clearly disclose whether the original 1997 or the new revised framework was used when reporting on the status of their internal controls.

An enterprise needs to fully understand the status and any potential weak points in its current internal control structure. It may have been given a pass on one or another potential weak point in a past SOx review, but it should reexamine those and make corrections where necessary. This is also a time to review any past internal audit report findings that may have been identified as internal control weaknesses, even if these do not have external financial reporting significance, and the enterprise should take action to strengthen its controls and take corrective actions.

This task of transitioning to the new COSO framework will not be unique to each enterprise, and, in general, smaller and newly public enterprises face greater challenges. Larger enterprises usually have more sophisticated systems and controls in place that continuously track and adapt to changes in their business environment, such as those resulting from technology and globalization initiatives. Enterprises that have been consistently updating and improving their internal control processes to meet SOx requirements, due to changes in their business environment, may find that conforming to the new COSO framework requires little adjustment. Smaller enterprises with fewer resources may have more work to do in filling any gaps identified through the COSO principles.

Whether large or small, the new COSO framework will mean at least some additional work for many members of an enterprise, and audit committee members will also have an important role to play in helping their enterprises integrate the new guidance into existing internal control processes.

STEPS TO BEGIN IMPLEMENTING THE NEW COSO INTERNAL CONTROL FRAMEWORK

In prior chapters, we have tried to present an overview of all aspects of the newly revised COSO internal control framework and why it is and will continue to be important. Although implementation may not be easy, an enterprise and its executive leaders should concentrate on the following:

▪ Fully understand the new COS guidance, with an emphasis on its 17 principles and the related points of focus.
▪ Determine where an enterprise is strong or where it has weaknesses, based on these 17 COSO principles.
▪ Actively implement enterprise changes in areas of weakness.

With the prior original COSO framework having an important role in enterprise internal control standards and concepts since its 1992 initiation until the present, we can all but assume the revised framework is going to be with us for a while. Management should focus on these 17 principles and build appropriate and strong internal controls as needed.

Index

Printed and bound by CPI Group (UK) Ltd, Croydon, CR0 4YY

23/04/2025

14661011-0002